IRISH PASSENGER STEAMSHIP SERVICES

VOLUME 2 SOUTH OF IRELAND

The arrival of the mail boat at Dun Laoghaire, c 1897. The *Ulster* (left) and one of her sisters are at Carlisle Pier. The large paddle steamer is one of the City of Dublin mail steamers built in 186[illegible]

Irish Passenger Steamship Services

VOLUME 2 SOUTH OF IRELAND

D. B. McNEILL

DAVID & CHARLES: NEWTON ABBOT

ISBN 0 7153 5248 2

Printed in Great Britain by
Latimer Trend & Co Ltd Plymouth
for David & Charles (Publishers) Limited
South Devon House Railway Station
Newton Abbot Devon

CONTENTS

LIST OF ILLUSTRATIONS

PLATES

MAPS

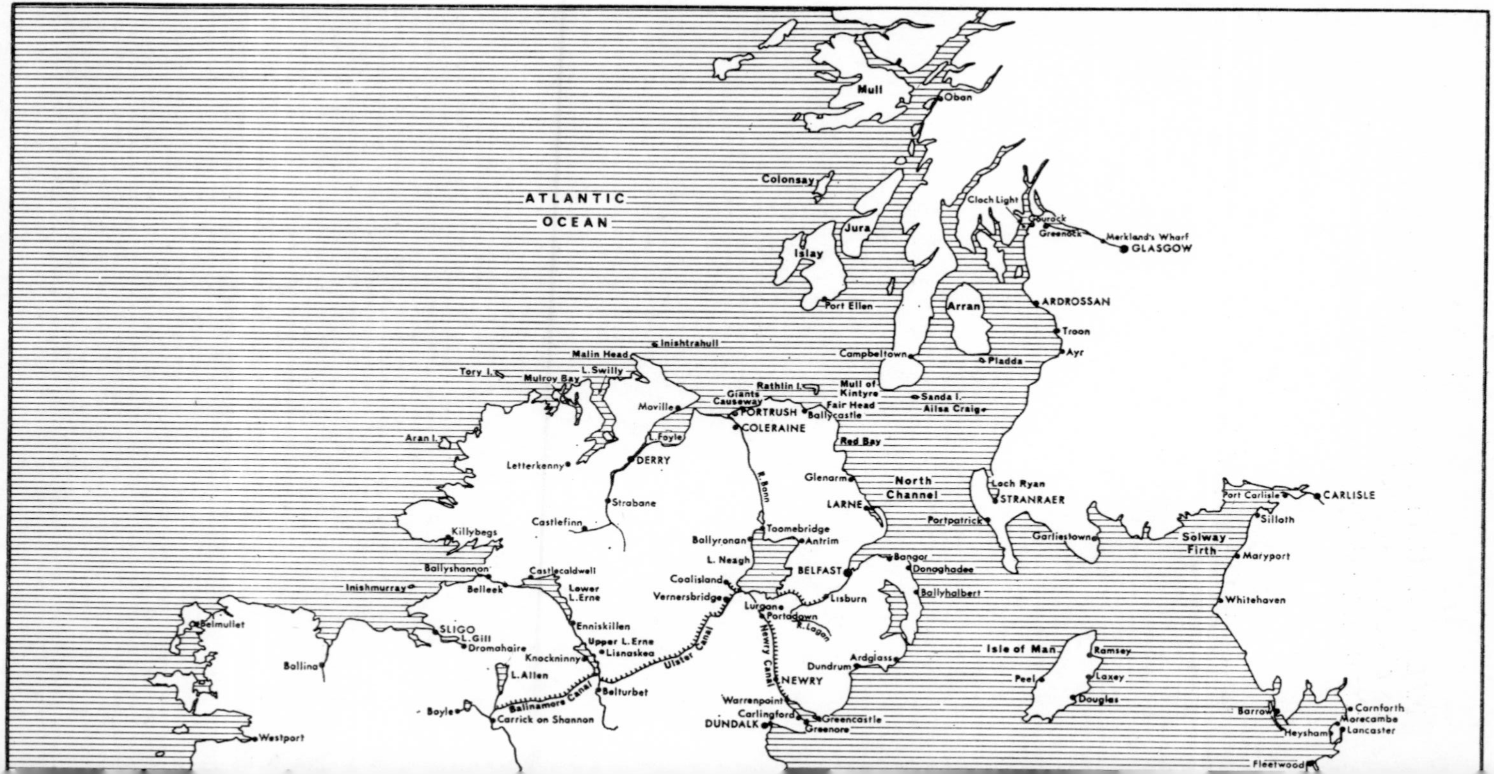
ATLANTIC
OCEAN
Mull
Oban
Colonsay
Jura
Islay
Port Ellen
Cloch Light
Gourock
Greenock
Merkland's Wharf
GLASGOW
ARDROSSAN
Arran
Troon
Ayr
Pladda
Campbeltown
Mull of Kintyre
Sanda I.
Ailsa Craig
Inishtrahull
Malin Head
L. Swilly
Tory I.
Mulroy Bay
Rathlin I.
Giants Causeway
PORTRUSH
Ballycastle
Fair Head
COLERAINE
Moville
Aran I.
L. Foyle
DERRY
Letterkenny
Red Bay
Glenarm
North Channel
Loch Ryan
STRANRAER
LARNE
Portpatrick
Port Carlisle
CARLISLE
Silloth
Strabane
Castlefinn
Killybegs
R. Bann
Toomebridge
Antrim
Ballyronan
L. Neagh
BELFAST
Bangor
Donaghadee
Ballyhalbert
Garliestown
Solway Firth
Maryport
Whitehaven
Ballyshannon
Castlecaldwell
Coalisland
Vernersbridge
Lisburn
Inishmurray
Belleek
Lower L. Erne
Lurgan
Portadown
R. Lagan
Belmullet
SLIGO
L. Gill
Dromahaire
Enniskillen
Upper L. Erne
Lisnaskea
Knockninny
Ulster Canal
Newry Canal
Isle of Man
Ramsey
Laxey
Douglas
Peel
Ardglass
Dundrum
NEWRY
Ballina
L. Allen
Belturbet
Ballinamore Canal
Boyle
Carrick on Shannon
Warrenpoint
Carlingford
Greencastle
Greenore
DUNDALK
Westport
Barrow
Heysham
Cornforth
Morecambe
Lancaster
Fleetwood

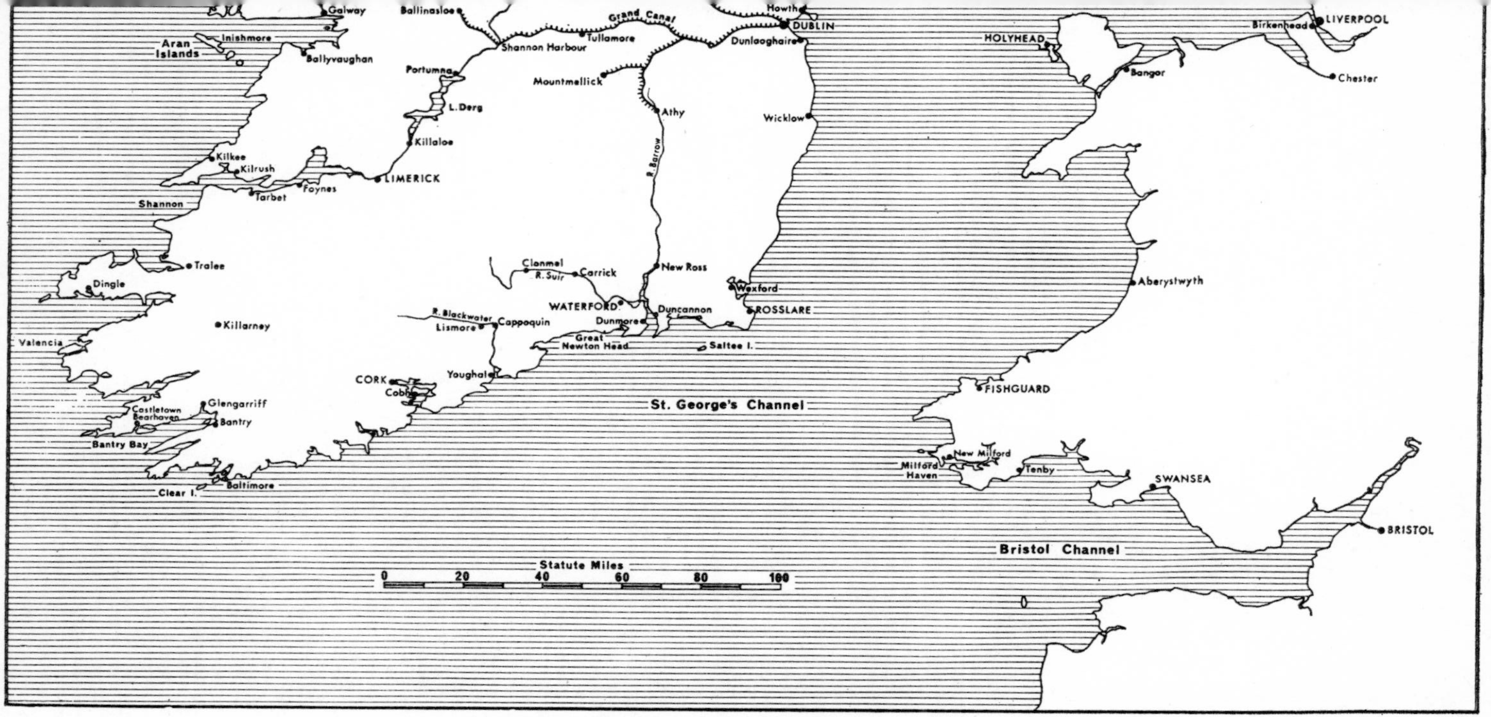

Ireland, the Irish Sea and the west coast of Great Britain

INTRODUCTION

IN this volume the passenger steamers which worked between the South of Ireland and Great Britain are described, along with the small vessels which plied on the estuaries and rivers in this part of Ireland. Steamers have been employed on some of the more prosperous cross-channel routes for 150 years whilst on the not so prosperous, such as those from Dublin to Barrow, the vessels made only a few crossings. The majority of the passenger cross-channel services depended on the cattle trade as their major source of income. Indeed, until the coming of the car-ferry, the only well established route on which facilities for the carrying of cattle had never been provided was on the 'mail' between Dun Laoghaire and Holyhead. The Holyhead route, however, has always received a mail subsidy, and rail connections with the steamers have always been so good on both sides of the Irish Sea that, even in the present era of the motor-car holiday, over half of the people travelling by sea to the Republic patronise the mail steamers.

The changes brought about when steam replaced sail on the Irish Sea in the 1820s have had their counterpart in the arrival of car-ferries and unit-load cargoes in the late 1960s. In the era before car-ferries, passengers and goods had to 'break bulk' in transferring from rail to ship, an irritating and, for cargo, costly procedure. In the car-ferry age private motorists and their passengers can drive straight on board; lorries and their trailers can travel from any part of Great Britain or Europe to the most remote part of Ireland with their loads intact. The summer tourist with his car and the demand for 'door-to-door' freight service has so stimulated the car-ferries trade that by 1970 the only non-car ferry passenger service to Ireland was the one worked by the Dun Loaghaire–Holyhead mail steamers.

The number of routes, ships and shipowners engaged in the Irish trade have been rationalised and reduced over the years. In 1970 there were eleven routes operated by four separate owners, compared with about thirty routes maintained by a dozen owners at the turn of the century. At the beginning of the twentieth century steamers plied on all the principal inlets of the sea and on the larger rivers and lakes; in 1970 the only remaining river service in the Republic was worked by CIE on the Shannon and the only in-shore steamer services were those maintained by the *Noamh Eanna* between Galway and the Aran

Islands and the summer excursions worked by the *Tara* at Dublin and the *Cill Airne* at Cork.

In the early days of steam little thought was given either about safety or the basic needs of deck passengers. The presence of a steam engine seemed to be regarded as a charm for warding off accidents in much the same way that untried troops believed an ungarnished camouflage net provided a cloak of invisibility in the 1939–45 war. In 1839 Capt H. M. Denham, a consultant marine surveyor at Liverpool, stated in evidence to a Parliamentary committee 'I have known instances of steam vessels leaving the docks and foundering within a few hours . . . so long as the engines can go, they go to sea.' This same committee reported in favour of steamers carrying lifeboats, fire buckets, an anchor, an *engineer* and a steam trumpet for use in fog. No recommendations were made about navigation lights but the published proceedings of the committee recorded there were eleven different systems of displaying navigation lights on the Mersey, these varied from a solitary bright light at the mast head to five assorted coloured lights placed at different parts of the vessel. Indeed, the present custom of having a clear light on the fore mast with red and green lights to port and starboard respectively, did not become a general practice until the early 1850s. The comfort and well being of deck passengers on cross-channel steamers did not receive much attention until the late 1840s. In 1849 a government committee of inquiry, with Capt Denham as chairman, produced a harrowing report. This revealed that deck passengers ranked after livestock for humane consideration when afloat. Livestock were generally loaded first, after which 'deckers' were permitted to go on board to find what room they could. Once on board many of these went straight to the cattle pens where they spent the night huddled close to the cows and sheep for warmth. If no horses were on board, the more privileged were permitted to travel in the stables. Capt Denham recommended the maximum number of deck passengers carried should not be numerically larger than 50 per cent of the gross tonnage of the vessel, that covered accommodation should be available for a third of those on board, and that a gallon of water should be carried for each passenger. Today, the 'quality' and the 'deckers' often cross over together in 'one class' car-ferries. On the *Leinster*, which works between Dublin and Liverpool, it is customary for those who patronise saloon bars ashore to find themselves forward in the Shamrock Lounge, whereas those who prefer their Guinness in quantity congregate amidships in the bar named Tara where the motion of the ship and the price/volume ratio of liquid refreshment are considered to be at a minimum.

1: SERVICES FROM HOLYHEAD

In the opening years of the twentieth century Holyhead was an exceedingly busy port. There were two sailings a day to Dun Laoghaire worked by the City of Dublin SP Co and one to the same place operated by the London & North Western Railway. The railway steamers also ran three or four times a day direct to Dublin (North Wall) and provided a daily service to Greenore. At 'off peak' periods in 1970 the service from Holyhead consisted of one mail sailing each day to Dun Laoghaire, a daily car ferry to the same port and cargo workings to North Wall, Dublin.

The Royal Mail Route

Holyhead has been used as a port for the Irish mail since the time of Elizabeth I. At first the mail was carried over the Irish Sea in privately owned sailing vessels but toward the end of the eighteenth century the Post Office set up its own sailing packets which ran between Holyhead and the Pigeon House Quay in Dublin. In August 1818 the Irish terminal was changed to the new harbour at Howth but this was difficult to enter, especially when the wind was in the east. On the completion of the deep water jetty on the East Pier at Dun Laoghaire in 1827 some of the mail steamers started to use this port thereby inaugurating a practice which ultimately led to the close down of Howth as a mail packet station in January 1834. In December 1859 the mail steamers moved their terminal at Dun Laoghaire to Carlisle Pier, which had been opened earlier in that year, and it is from this pier that the mail steamers sail today.

Before the coming of steam the average crossing took about fifteen hours and could, at times, be quite exciting. On 8 March 1780 the sailing packets *Bessborough* and *Hillsborough* were captured by the American privateer *Black Prince*, a misadventure which cost the Post Office over a thousand pounds in ransom money. In the early days of steam the average passage took about seven or eight hours, but the time for the journey by mail coach from Holyhead to London remained at about thirty hours. By the mid-nineteenth century the time for the sea crossing had come down to four hours and the advent of the railway enabled the land journey from Holyhead to London to be completed in nine hours. The service reached its zenith immediately before the 1914–18 and 1939–45 wars when the overall times to get from Dublin to London were reduced to nine hours.

The good reputation of the Holyhead route may be claimed as one of the better products of the union between Ireland and Great Britain in 1800. After the Union the seat of Irish political and financial power moved to London. The result was that those in authority had to make frequent journeys between the two capitals and so gained first hand experience of the troubles and inconveniences of nineteenth century travel which they passed on to those in 'high places'. This continuous informed scrutiny led not only to numerous government inquiries but also to the provision of a top class service worked by the fastest cross-channel steamers of their era, supported by the best trains the railways could provide on either side of the Irish Sea. In the days when all letter mail went by this route there was a real sense of urgency about the service. En route to Ireland it was essential that the steamer reached Dun Laoghaire on time, otherwise the English mail in every town in Ireland would be late. On the return journey the vessel had to leave Dun Laoghaire punctually, a late departure meant that Irish letters missed the first delivery in London next day. The evening train was scheduled to leave Euston at 8.45 pm, a departure time it was given for its first run on 1 August 1848, and which it was using in August 1939. The corresponding up train left Holyhead at about midnight. The train included a travelling post office in its formation, and on board ship there was a postal room so that the sorting of mail could continue, with little interruption, all the way from London to Dun Laoghaire. The 'Irish Mail' also brought the 'correct time' to Ireland. This was conveyed in a registered packet, containing a chronometer showing Greenwich Mean Time, which was sent to the GPO at Dublin every evening. The practice started in the days of the mail coach and continued until the 1939–45 War.

On the Irish side of the channel the departure of the 'Evening Mail Boat' was the event of the day. As each train arrived at the pier hordes of porters descended upon the vans and within a short time mountains of mail bags would be transferred to the ship. The last train was due alongside ten minutes before sailing time but this was sufficient for the passengers and mail to be got on board. The same urgency infected the Irish railways, for the fastest trains between Dublin, Cork, Galway and Belfast were the *Limited Mails*. Each train had a travelling post office so that mail could be collected, sorted and exchanged en route. At every stopping place on the up journey people were at the station to post their last-minute letters in the late-fee boxes in the mail vans, for everyone knew that letters posted in the train would make the first delivery in London next day. Indeed, at some stations a stampede of message boys carrying their masters' letters would arrive on bicycles just as the train was coming in. In the outward direction, letters posted in the late-fee box at Euston before 8.30 pm were delivered at breakfast time next morning in Dublin and were in their recipients hands at Cork, Derry and Galway by noon.

In 1819 the first steamer started to work regularly from Holyhead and shortly afterwards her owner petitioned the Post Office for permission to carry the mail. The Post Office at first hesitated but later relented and in 1820 entered into a contract with the owner of the *Talbot*, and her consort the *Ivanhoe*, for the carriage of mail between Holyhead and Ireland. In the same year the Post Office placed an order for two steamers of its own and, in the course of the next few years, it acquired more vessels, so that by 1830 there were six Post Office steamers stationed at Holyhead. In April 1837 the Admiralty took over the mail steamers and operated them until 1850 when the mail contract reverted to privately owned vessels. From 1 May 1850 until 27 November 1920 the mail from Holyhead was brought over by the City of Dublin SP Co. The steamers provided by the company for the mail were always among the fastest of their generation. This tradition was set by its *Connaught* of 1860 which was the first steamer in the world to exceed 18 knots, and maintained by the 1897 *Ulster* and her sisters which were the first cross-channel steamers to attain a speed of 24 knots. Four vessels were required for the mail. One worked the morning service, a second took the evening crossing, a third was at stand-by with fires made up, ready to come into service at short notice, and the fourth was either in for survey or refit, after which she would be laid up until required to take her place in the active list. The City of Dublin Company obtained, and held, the contract in the face of intense competition from the Chester & Holyhead Railway (later LNWR). The railway always maintained it was entitled to the contract but the combination of the Dublin company and the Irish members of Parliament was a stronger lobby than the LNWR and its supporters, as a result of which the railway did not get the contract until 1920. This was at a time when the Dublin company was at a low ebb having lost two of its mail steamers during the 1914–18 war. Furthermore, after the war Ireland was unsettled and many of the Irish members of Parliament had ceased going to Westminster.

Today the glory has departed from the Irish Mail. The mail service for the greater part of the year consists of a daily sailing in each direction worked by a 21 knot vessel, whereas in its heyday there were two sailings on weekdays worked by 25 knot steamers. The change is not really surprising when it is realised that people in a hurry now fly and most first-class mail is sent by air. The route however is still exceedingly busy and is patronised by over 55 per cent of those who cross over by sea to the Republic each year. In summer there are generally two sailings a day and at weekends the vessels are crowded with tourists and Irish exiles. Under these conditions the crossing can be unpleasant but in normal times there is ample room on board. The route is convenient, provided one does not mind a 2 am transfer from train to steamer at Holyhead, for there are excellent rail connections on either side of the Irish Sea. The vessels are comfortable, they have stabilisers and, for the bad sailor, there is the added attraction that the crossing is a short one!

In 1970 rail communication between Holyhead and the mainland was severed when the Menai Bridge was badly damaged by a fire on the night of 23–4 May. As a result of this the mail terminal was temporarily moved to Heysham and the following schedule brought into use for the 'evening mail'.

2055	dep	London	arr	0830
0315	dep	Heysham	arr	0415
1045	arr	Dun Laoghaire	dep	2045

The late arrival in Dublin meant that passengers for Cork and other places in Ireland missed the early trains from Dublin.

PS *Talbot*, PS *Ivanhoe*

The *Talbot* was the first steamer to work regularly between Holyhead and Howth. She was launched at Port Glasgow in April 1819, and went into service later in the year. She generally took about seven and a half hours for the crossing. In 1820 she was chartered as a mail packet but was displaced by the arrival of the Post Office steamers in May 1821. After this she was stationed at Bristol, and then worked for a time between London and Calais. She was then sold to the General SN Co who used her for trading between London and the Continent until her wreck near Ostend in 1833.

The *Ivanhoe* ran as a consort to the *Talbot* for a few months in 1820 after which she worked between Bristol and Cork and later between Liverpool and Dublin. In 1823 she was purchased by the Post Office

Page 17 (above): PS *Cambria* (1848)
(left): TSS *Anglia* (1920) at Holyhead, c 1930
(below): TSMV *Cambria* (1949) at Holyhead, c 1969

Page 18 (above): PS *Munster* leaving Dun Laoghaire, c 1875
(below): TSS *Holyhead Ferry I* at Holyhead, 1968

who used her on the Milford–Waterford mail service until her return to Holyhead in 1825. Like all the other Post Office steamers she was transferred to the Admiralty in 1837 and was subsequently renamed *Boxer*. She ended her days as a naval tug at Sheerness. The *Ivanhoe* was a little larger than the *Talbot* with a length of about 100ft. She was powered by a side lever engine which developed 60hp. Thomas Moore, the Irish poet, once had an abominable seven-hour passage from Holyhead on board this vessel. He states in his memoirs, 'sailed on the *Ivanhoe*, took my berth and peppermint lozenges but felt deadly sick all the way'.

The arrival of the *Ivanhoe* enabled a daily steamship service to be started between Holyhead and Ireland. This began early in May 1820. The vessels were advertised to sail from Howth at 8.30 am, immediately after the arrival of a special coach which had departed from the Royal Hibernian Hotel in Dublin about an hour and a half earlier. After working for two months from Howth the steamers moved their Irish terminal to Sir John Rogerson's Quay on the south bank of the Liffey at Dublin.

PS *Lightning*, PS *Meteor*

These Post Office packets went into service in the 1820s. In 1824 the *Meteor* was sent to Milford and four years later she was transferred to the Weymouth–Channel Island service, a route on which she met her end in February 1830 by running ashore near Portland. The *Lightning* was commanded by Capt Skinner, a friend of George IV, who used this steamer when he crossed to Ireland in August 1821. In honour of the occasion the *Lightning* was renamed *Royal Sovereign* and Dun Laoghaire, where His Majesty landed, became Kingstown, a name it retained for over a hundred years. The vessel had a long career in the government service. She worked between Holyhead, Howth and Dun Laoghaire from 1821 to 1824 and then moved to the Milford–Waterford run where she remained until 1836. After this she was employed for a time on the Liverpool mail service. At her transfer to the Admiralty in 1837 she was renamed *Monkey*.

PS *Aladdin*, PS *Cinderella*, PS *Dragon*, PS *Escape*, PS *Fire Queen*, PS *Flamer*, PS *George*, PS *Gulnare*, PS *Harlequin*, PS *Tartar*, PS *Trident*, PS *Urgent*, PS *Vivid*, PS *Vixen*, PS *Watersprite*, PS *Wizard*

These government-owned steamers were employed on the mail service from Holyhead at different times from the mid-1820s to 1849. They were very unpopular and there were numerous complaints about the way in which they were run. They were badly maintained, their management was incompetent, fares were high, passenger accommodation on board had not improved from the days of sail and the cabin staff was surly. All the Post Office steamers were transferred to the Admiralty in 1837, who continued to run them in a similar way until the close-down of the government mail service, by which time the vessels had become museum pieces. The only apparent change made by the Admiralty was to give the steamers new names; these are given in the Fleet List on page 180.

When the Admiralty ceased operating the mail those vessels which were still relatively seaworthy were employed on different naval duties. Thus the *Flamer* was armed as a three-gun gunboat and was sent to Africa where she was wrecked on 22 November 1850.

PS *Banshee*, PS *Caradoc*, PS *Llewellyn*, PS *St Columba*

These were the last mail packets to be ordered for the Admiralty. They were built in 1847 at a cost of £39,000 each. The *Banshee* was the fastest of the four with an average time of just over four hours for the crossing. The *Llewellyn* and *St Columba* were purchased by the City of Dublin SP Co when they took over the mail contract in May 1850. The *Llewellyn* remained with the company for over thirty years and, after being displaced by the new mail steamers in 1860, was employed for some time on the Dublin–Liverpool crossing. In her latter days she was renamed *St Patrick*. The City of Dublin SP Co also chartered the *Banshee* and *Caradoc* for a few runs in the early 1850s.

PS *Eblana*, PS *Prince Arthur*

These vessels, together with the former government mail packets *Llewellyn* and *St Columba*, were used by the City of Dublin SP Co to work the mail in the 1850s. The *Eblana*, which was called after the classical name for Dublin, went into service in 1849. In the 1860s she was relegated to the Dublin–Liverpool trade and was also chartered on occasions to work between Dublin and Glasgow. The *Prince Arthur* was completed in 1851. After the arrival of the new mail steamers in 1860 she was transferred to the Liverpool–North Wales run, a service in which she remained until 1887.

PS *Ulster*, PS *Munster*, PS *Connaught*, PS *Leinster*

In October 1860 the overall time for the journey from London to Dun Laoghaire was reduced to eleven hours. The revised times allowed 6hr 40min for the rail journey from Euston, 35min for the transfer of the mail to the steamer at Holyhead and 3hr 45min for the crossing. In practice the time for transhipment was often reduced to ten minutes and the mail generally got to Dun Laoghaire ahead of schedule, for a late arrival meant the City of Dublin SP Co had to pay a fine of 34s for every minute the vessel was behind schedule.

The steamers built for working the speeded-up service were named after the four provinces of Ireland. They were outstanding in every way and were capable of 18 knots. The *Connaught* was the fastest of the quartet with a time of 3hr 14min for the crossing to her credit. All four vessels had turtle-backed forecastles, clipper bows and a length of about 340ft. When first built several of the new steamers had four funnels but the number was reduced to two when the vessels were given extensive refits in the 1880s. Passenger accommodation for those travelling first class was good. W. S. Lindsay in *History of Merchant Shipping* states that 'saloon and cabins are large, lofty and well ventilated, the principal one being 60ft in length, 17ft in breadth and 9ft 6in high . . .'

In 1896 the *Munster* and *Leinster* were sold to the Liverpool & Douglas Steamers Co who intended to use them on a new Liverpool–Isle of Man run. The service did not materialise and next year they were sold to the Isle of Man SP Co who disposed of them for breaking up shortly afterwards. The other two steamers were broken up at about the same time.

PS *Ireland*

In 1885 the company obtained the *Ireland*, the largest paddle steamer ever built for the Irish cross-channel trade. At the time of her launch she was considered to be the fastest steamer in the world. After twelve years on the mail run she was displaced by twin screw steamers and sold to the Liverpool & Douglas Steamers Co who used her on its Liverpool–Isle of Man service. By this time she had become somewhat dated and was disposed of in 1900 for breaking up.

The *Ireland* was a good looking steamer with a clipper bow and two well-proportioned funnels. Superficially she was a success but in practice she was a 'white elephant'. Her engines were cumbersome and antiquated. Steam was provided at 30psi and, to develop the necessary power to drive her at 20 knots, she had to have enormous cylinders (102in × 102in). The technical press of her day commented unfavourably on the great size and mass of the moving parts of her engines and suggested that high pressure steam and compounding would have produced the same power more efficiently.

TSS *Ulster*, TSS *Munster*, TSS *Leinster*, TSS *Connaught*

Like their namesakes of 1860 the 1897 'provinces' were outstanding vessels. When they went into service they were the largest (2,600 gross tons) and fastest (24 knots) cross-channel steamers in the world. They had neat, business-like lines with a turtle-back forecastle and two well-raked funnels, Their twin screws were driven by four-cylinder, triple-expansion engines which took steam pressed to 175psi from four double-ended boilers.

All four were excellent timekeepers and could get across in 2hr 45min in comparatively rough seas. At the outbreak of the 1914–18 war the *Connaught* went trooping and when so engaged was lost in the English Channel in 1917. The other three steamers remained on the Holyhead mail service, which was maintained in spite of persistent attacks by German submarines. The *Ulster* was struck by a torpedo which did not explode in 1918, and on 10 October of the same year the *Leinster* was torpedoed and sank with the loss of over 500 lives.

In 1920 the mail contract went to the LNWR and on 27 November of that year the *Munster* sailed for the last time with the mail from Holyhead, and the *Ulster* from Dun Laoghaire. After this both steamers were laid up at Holyhead and four years later they were towed to Germany for breaking up. A. C. Yeates gives a very complete account of the City of Dublin mail steamers in an article published in *Sea Breezes* for July 1961.

TSS *Anglia*, TSS *Hibernia*, TSS *Cambria*, TSS *Scotia*

When the LNWR took over the mail contract in 1920 it had on order from William Denny & Bros of Dumbarton four turbine twin-screw steamers. Each of the new vessels had a gross tonnage of 3,400 tons and was capable of 25 knots, a speed which put them among the fastest cross-channel steamers in the world. The *Scotia*, which returned 25·12 knots at her trials, was the fastest commercial steamer ever built by the Denny Brothers.

In the mid-1920s it was realised the service could be worked with only three steamers, so the *Anglia*, which had been the first of the quartet to go into service, was laid up at Barrow where she remained for the greater part of her career. She was finally broken up at Troon in 1935. The other three steamers were given extensive refits in the 1930s, in the course of which the cowls were removed from their funnels and the forward end of their promenade decks enclosed by glass panels. Like all vessels built for speed they could roll. One Dublin doctor always claimed he was seasick as soon as his feet touched the gangway on boarding the *Scotia*. The last time he sailed on her was from Dunkirk in 1940; this time he was not ill but it was the steamer's last trip to Great Britain for she became a war casualty on her next visit to the beaches. The *Cambria* and *Hibernia* survived the war and were replaced by vessels of the same names in 1949.

TSS *Princess Maud*

The all-year twice-daily service between Holyhead and Dun Laoghaire was not revived after the 1939–45 war. In winter the outgoing mail steamer left Dun Laoghaire at 8.45 pm and the incoming vessel was due in just before 7 am, thus only two steamers were required for the service with a third in reserve. In 1947 the *Princess Maud* was moved from the Larne–Stranraer crossing to Holyhead to be the 'third' or 'reserve' steamer, a task on which she was employed until her sale to Cypriot owners in 1965 (see Vol 1).

TSMV *Hibernia*, TSMV *Cambria*

These motor vessels came into service in April and May 1949 respectively. They are the largest cross-channel packets to have been employed in the Irish trade. They have a gross tonnage of 5,000 tons and a speed of 21 knots, four knots less than the steamers they replaced. Accommodation on board is excellent; steerage, now called second, compares favourably with the saloon in the 1920 steamers. Furthermore, they were the first cross-channel steamers in the Irish trade to be fitted with stabilisers. Both vessels had extensive refits during the winter of 1964–5 when their second-class accommodation was enlarged by taking in some of the space previously occupied by saloon passengers. The alterations reflect the change in cross-channel clientele for today many of those who previously travelled saloon go by air, while many who could not afford to travel in the 'pre-holidays-with-pay' era can now afford a second-class passage across the Irish Sea. A technical account of the *Hibernia* was published in *Shipping World* on 23 March 1949.

Holyhead–Dublin (North Wall)

The Holyhead–Dublin (North Wall) crossing can trace its origin to the Chester & Holyhead Railway steamers which went into service in 1848 in anticipation of the railway getting the contract for the mail between Holyhead and Dublin. The contract, however, went to the

City of Dublin SP Co who carried the mail until 1920. In October 1861 the railway changed its Irish port from Dun Laoghaire to Dublin, which today is still the terminal for its cargo boats running to Holyhead.

The LNWR, who absorbed the CHR in 1859, did much to improve Holyhead and North Wall. At the former it built the present Inner Harbour, and the adjoining passenger station through which passengers can pass under cover all the way between the trains and the steamers. The work was completed in 1880, from which time the railway steamers have used the Inner Harbour whereas those of the City of Dublin Co continued to work from the Admiralty Pier which is about half a mile further out to sea. The latter was reached by a branch line which was not of a sufficiently high standard to take an express locomotive. Consequently all the mail trains had to change engines before going on to the pier, whereas the trains working to the harbour station in connection with the railway steamers could proceed non-stop from Chester or Crewe. In March 1925 the mail steamers, which by this time were owned by the railway, moved to the Inner Harbour which has been used ever since by all steamers making regular connections with passenger trains at Holyhead.

At Dublin the LNWR built an hotel on the quay at North Wall and in September 1877 opened a passenger station at the same place, to which trains ran from the other Dublin termini in connection with the steamer sailings. After this the LNWR advertised that passengers using its vessels could get to any station in Ireland without the inconvenience of crossing Dublin. This was aimed at the City of Dublin SP Co for, until the opening of the City of Dublin Junction Railway between Amiens Street and Westland Row in May 1891, passengers travelling via Dun Laoghaire had to go by road from Westland Row to the other railway termini in Dublin. The LNWR also pointed out the advantage of shipping cattle via North Wall and Holyhead by stating that the company's livestock specials ran from the latter to Edgehill, which was adjacent to the Liverpool cattle markets, whereas animals sent to Liverpool by direct steamer had to be driven through the streets to reach the sales. The Mersey livestock trade was, and still is, an exceedingly important factor in the Irish economy and today the National Bank and the Royal Bank of Ireland have branches in Liverpool and Birkenhead respectively.

In 1909 the LNWR moved the terminal of its principal daylight service back to Dun Laoghaire, an action which gave this packet station three workings each day to Holyhead. In November 1920 the railway steamers began to carry the Irish mail, the first mail workings for the company being taken by the *Anglia* and *Curraghmore*. Today the railway passenger services are based on Dun Laoghaire and its cargo and livestock steamers work from North Wall. The latter vessels do not now carry passengers but in the inter-war years steerage passengers were accommodated on some of the cargo/livestock sailings from North Wall.

In the early days of the railway service its 'express' steamers carried passengers only but, after the move to North Wall, the railway boats worked as dual purpose vessels carrying passengers, livestock and goods. The service was well patronised for fares were cheaper than via Dun Laoghaire and third-class passengers could travel in the boat expresses from Holyhead, whereas the mail trains working to the City of Dublin steamers conveyed first- and second-class passengers who, at one time, had to pay supplementary fares. In 1876 the railway introduced an express daylight crossing on which it used the 20 knot paddle steamers *Rose* and *Shamrock*. Four years later it began a corresponding night service with the *Lily* and *Violet*.

Examples of the services provided by the LNWR and City of Dublin SP Co are given in the timetables shown in Table 1.

TABLE 1

Dublin–London via Holyhead

1855

↓	↓	↓		↑	↑	↑
0915	1700	*2045*	London (Euston)	2255	*0450*	*1106*
1715	1235	*0549*	Holyhead	1430	*1900*	*0200*
2200	0600	*1100*	Dun Laoghaire	0900	*1300*	*1930*

1881

↓	↓	↓	↓		↑	↑	↑	↑
0715	0900	1800	*2025*	London (Euston)	*1825*	2035	*0645*	0835
1350	1700	0200	*0305*	Holyhead	*1140*	1500	*2355*	0100
1400	1730	0215	*0315*	Holyhead	*1115*	1430	*2330*	0030
1750	↓	↓	*0705*	Dun Laoghaire	*0700*	↑	*1915*	↑
1820			*0735*	Dublin (Westland Row)	*0640*		*1845*	
	2000	0700		Dublin (North Wall)		0930		1930

Additional steamers sailed from North Wall at 1100 and 1930 and from Holyhead at 0230 and 1830. These carried cargo and steerage passengers.

1914

↓	↓	↓	↓		↑	↑	↑	↑
0083	1330	*2045*	2215	London (Euston)	*1740*	2300	*0600*	0730
1405	1855	*0217*	0330	Holyhead	*1200*	1730	*0022*	0200
1415	1915	*0225*	0355	Holyhead				↑
1700	2150	*0530*	↓	Dun Laoghaire	*0815*	1340	*2015*	↑
1730	2220	*0600*	0700 (N)	Dublin (Westland Row)	*0800*	1310	*1930*	2120 (N)

Additional railway steamers sailed from North Wall at 0730 and 1245 and from Holyhead at 0200 and 1815. These carried cargo and steerage passengers, all other steamers, whether railway or City of Dublin SP Co carried saloon and steerage passengers; (N) indicates steamer runs to Dublin (North Wall).

1939

↓	↓		↑	↑
0845	2045	London (Euston)	1750	0530
1405	0225	Holyhead	1240	0013
1430	0255	Holyhead	1210	2345
1725	0550	Dun Laoghaire	0915	2050
1740	0610	Dun Laoghaire	0905	2040
1800	0630	Dublin (Westland Row)	0845	2010

City of Dublin SP Co's services in italics
Railway steamer services in roman type
(Until October 1916 Irish Time was 25 minutes behind Greenwich Mean Time)

PS *Anglia*, PS *Hibernia*, PS *Cambria*, PS *Scotia*

These four steamers were built for the Chester & Holyhead Railway in anticipation of the company getting the contract for carrying the mail between Holyhead and Dun Laoghaire. The contract did not materialise, nevertheless the four vessels were used to open a passenger service between Holyhead and Dun Laoghaire on 1 August 1848.

The steamers had clipper bows and two funnels and their speed, when new, was 15 knots. The *Cambria* and *Hibernia* spent all their active lives at Holyhead. In the late 1870s the *Hibernia* was sold to the Waterford & Limerick Railway for use as a coal hulk at Waterford, where she remained until her disposal for breaking up in 1897. The *Anglia* and *Scotia* crossed the Atlantic to become blockade runners in the American Civil War, a service in which both were captured. This ended the recorded career of the *Scotia* but was the beginning of a new life for her consort. The *Anglia* was sold at a prize court in New York but after several changes of ownership returned to be a Confederate blockade runner once more. This time she was called the *Fanny and Jane*, but her change of name did not change her ill luck for she was sunk. After the war she was salvaged and went into the West Indian trade where she remained until about 1914.

PS *Hercules*, PS *Ocean*, PS *Queen*, PS *Sea Nymph*, PS *Telegraph*

These were second-hand steamers which the LNWR acquired in the 1850s. The *Ocean* and *Hercules* were originally owned by the St George SP Co and the *Sea Nymph* and *Telegraph* belonged at one time to the Belfast Steamship Co (see Vol 1).

PS *Admiral Moorsom*, PS *Alexandra*, PS *Stanley*

These vessels were used on the passenger/cargo services to North Wall from the 1860s until the mid-1880s. In 1888 the *Stanley* was sold to the Irish Traders Cooperative SS Co at Derry; her subsequent career is described in Vol 1.

PS *Countess of Erne*

In her prime the *Countess of Erne* plied between Dublin and Holyhead. She was built for the LNWR by Walpole & Webb of Dublin in 1868. She had a gross tonnage of 800 tons and was capable of 13 knots. In 1873 she was transferred to Greenore where she was employed intermittently until her sale to the Bristol SN Co in 1889. A year later she was 'gutted' and became a coal hulk at Weymouth. Here she remained until wrecked on Portland breakwater during a gale in September 1935.

PS *Duke of Sutherland*, PS *Duchess of Sutherland*

These two 15 knot vessels were built at Hebburn in 1868 and 1869 respectively. Both were stationed at Holyhead for their entire working careers. In 1888 the *Duchess of Sutherland* was converted into a twin-screw cattle boat and her two-cylinder simple engine replaced by two triple-expansion ones.

PS *Edith*

The *Edith* was built as a paddle steamer in 1870 and converted to twin screws in 1885. The greater part of her career was spent working from North Wall (Dublin) but for a short time in 1873–4 she was employed on the Greenore–Holyhead route. On the afternoon of the official opening of this service, she cruised on Carlingford Lough with the Viceroy of Ireland and other distinguished guests on board. Next day—1 May—at 7.15 pm she took the first commercial sailing from Greenore to Holyhead while her temporary consort, the *Countess of Erne*, sailed from Holyhead in the early hours of 2 May on the first westbound crossing. After her change to screw propulsion she was used exclusively as a cattle boat until withdrawn for breaking up in March 1912.

PS *Eleanor*, PS *Earl Spencer*

The career of the *Eleanor* lasted for eight years. She was built for the Greenore service in 1873 and on 21 January 1881 got so badly off course in thick fog that she was wrecked at Lee Stone Point near Kilkeel. Fortunately, all on board got away safely. The *Earl Spencer* was a notoriously bad sea boat.

PS *Rose*, PS *Shamrock*

These vessels were used for the opening of the express daylight service between Holyhead and North Wall which began in July 1876. They had a gross tonnage of about 1,300 tons and a speed of 20 knots; their whole working life was spent on the Irish crossing from Holyhead.

PS *Isabella*, PS *Eleanor*

The *Isabella* was built by Laird of Birkenhead in 1877 and the *Eleanor* came from the same shipyard four years later. Both vessels were similar in that they had a gross tonnage of about 900 tons and a service speed of 15 knots. Here their similarity ended, for the *Isabella* had a single-expansion engine with oscillating cylinders whereas the engine of the *Eleanor* was compound. The *Isabella* spent her entire career on the Greenore–Holyhead crossing and was withdrawn in 1898. At about the same time the *Eleanor* was moved from Greenore to the North Wall cargo service and was sold for breaking up four years later.

PS *Lily*, PS *Violet*

These vessels inaugurated the night express service from North Wall which began in 1880. When first built they were not as fast as the dayboats *Rose* and *Shamrock*. In 1891 they were sent to Laird Bros of Birkenhead for an extensive refit. This included replacing their simple low-pressure oscillating cylinder engines by high-pressure triple-expansion ones using steam at 150psi. This increased their speed to 19·5 knots, with no increase in the space required for engine rooms and boilers. After leaving the railway fleet at the turn of the century they were employed by the Liverpool & Douglas Steamers Co on a short-lived service between Liverpool and the Isle of Man. The venture was not a success and both vessels were sold for breaking up.

PS *Banshee*

The *Banshee* was the last paddle cross-channel steamer built for the LNWR. She went into service in 1884 and spent her whole time with the railway working on the Holyhead–North Wall run. In 1906 she went to the Mediterranean.

She was a handsome vessel with two well-proportioned funnels placed fore and aft of her paddle boxes. When new she had a single-expansion engine which gave her a speed of 19 knots; this was replaced by a triple-expansion one in 1894, which gave her the same speed at a greatly reduced operating cost. She was one of the first steamers working to Dublin to have electric light.

TSS *Rosstrevor*, TSS *Connemara*, TSS *Galtee More*

These twin screw steamers were built for the Greenore service by Denny of Dumbarton between 1895 and 1898. They were virtually sister ships with a gross tonnage of about 1,100 tons and a speed of 18 knots. The *Rosstrevor* and *Galtee More* remained on the crossing until the close down in 1926 after which they were sold for breaking up. The *Connemara* was sunk on 3 November 1916 after a collision with a collier some three miles from Greenore. At the time there was a furious south-westerly gale blowing and the collier was proceeding without lights, as these had been blown out by the wind and it was impossible to relight them. There were no survivors among the eighty-six people on board the *Connemara* and only one of the crew of the other vessel got ashore.

After the arrival of the *Rosstrevor* and her consorts the service was accelerated and the time for transfer from train to steamer was cut to about a quarter of an hour. Sometimes this was exceeded, one such occasion being on 20 June 1904. On that evening a special train, packed with harvesters en route from Sligo and Leitrim to work in Great Britain, ran into the buffer stops at Greenore. They all got a shaking but no one was seriously injured. The station master organised suitable refreshment for all involved and gave each man five pounds as compensation. When the steamer eventually sailed she was filled with happy, well-fed and thoroughly lubricated harvesters all armed with a 'fiver' to see them through the rigours of the journey. There were no subsequent claims for damages against the company!

TSS *Cambria*, TSS *Hibernia*, TSS *Anglia*, TSS *Scotia*

These vessels, which came into service over the period December 1897 to April 1902, were the LNWR reply to the challenge of the City of Dublin Company's *Ulster* and her consorts on the Dun Laoghaire crossing. They were typical railway cross-channel steamers of their time with two cowl-topped funnels and elliptical sterns. They had twin screws which were driven by four-cylinder triple-expansion engines which gave them a speed of 21 knots.

During the 1914–18 war the *Anglia* became a hospital ship when she ferried wounded across the Straits of Dover. She was torpedoed on 18 November 1915 but shortly before this she had the distinction of bringing His Majesty George V back from France after he had been injured by falling off his horse. The *Hibernia* became the armoured merchant cruiser HMS *Tara* and, while so employed, was sunk in the Mediterranean on 5 November 1915.

In 1920 the *Cambria* was renamed *Arvonia* and the *Scotia* became the *Menevia*, thereby releasing their names for the new turbine steamers which came out later in the same year. Under their new names the two vessels were employed as required on the other railway cross-channel services to Ireland and the Isle of Man. The *Arvonia* was withdrawn from service and sold for breaking up in 1925, and was followed by the *Menevia* three years later.

TSS *Rathmore*, TrSS *Greenore*

The *Rathmore* was the last cross-channel steamer with reciprocating engines to be built for the LNWR. During the 1914–18 war she was sunk but was ultimately salvaged and returned to her place on the Greenore–Holyhead crossing. At the close-down of the passenger service in 1926 she was transferred to the Tilbury–Dunkirk service, and renamed *Lorraine*. In 1932 she was sold for breaking up.

The *Greenore* was the first turbine steamer to be built for the LNWR. She was about the same size as the *Rathmore* (1,500 gross tons) and had the characteristic thick funnels with cowl tops which were the fashion for cross-channel steamers at that time.

TSS *Curraghmore/Duke of Abercorn*

This was the last steamer built for the Greenore route. She was ordered from Denny of Dumbarton in 1914 as a replacement for the *Galtee More*, but the outbreak of the war delayed her completion until 1919. For her first two seasons she was used on the Dublin–Holyhead crossing as at that time the railway company was short of fast cross-channel vessels. She then went to Greenore where she remained until the passenger sailings ended in 1926. For the next three years she acted as a relief vessel on many of the LMS routes to Ireland and the Isle of Man. In 1930 she was moved permanently to the Belfast–Heysham service and was renamed *Duke of Abercorn* (see vol I). She was replaced by the *Duke of York* in 1935 and broken up later in the same year.

The *Curraghmore* was the first LNWR steamer to have a cruiser stern and turbines with single-reduction gear. An illustrated article describing her was published in vol 129 (1920) of the *Engineer*.

TSS *Holyhead Ferry I*, TSS *Normannia*, TSS *Dover*, TSS *St David*

In July 1965 British Railways began a drive on/drive off car ferry service between Holyhead and Dun Laoghaire which is now worked by *Holyhead Ferry I*. This vessel has a gross tonnage of 3,900 tons and is fitted with stabilisers. To assist in docking she has twin rudders and a bow thrust unit. She is the first one-class passenger steamer to be regularly employed in the Irish Sea trade. Accommodation is provided for 150 cars and there are sleeping berths for fifty passengers, which is ample as her crossings are generally made in daylight. She is normally scheduled to make one round trip daily in winter and two in summer. The ferry service has proved so popular that the Dover–Boulogne car-ferry *Dover* was sent to Holyhead in the summer seasons of 1969 and 1970 to help in the transport of cars to Ireland.

The *Normannia*, which was normally employed on the English Channel services, spent a few days at Holyhead early in July 1965 to 'fill in' pending the arrival of the *Holyhead Ferry I*.

The Rosslare–Fishguard car-ferry *St David* spent the summer of 1970 acting as relief steamer at Holyhead and Heysham.

TSS *Anglesey*, TSS *Colleen Bawn*, TSS *Holyhead*, TSS *Irene*, TSS *North Wall*, TSS *Olga*, TSS *Slieve Brown*, TSS *Slieve Bloom*, TSS *Slieve Donard*, TSS *Slieve Gallion*, TSS *Slievemore*, TSS *Snowdon*, TSS *South Stack*

These vessels were employed on the North Wall passenger/cargo/cattle service at different times between 1863 and 1939.

Holyhead–Greenore

The LNWR opened this route in May 1873. The original plan was for a railway, known as the Dundalk & Greenore Railway, to be built between Dundalk and Greenore where a harbour was to be constructed. The LNWR and the Irish North Western Railway supported the proposal, and it was agreed that the former should own the steamers and that the railway should be operated by an independent company in which the LNWR and the INWR had substantial interests. The railway, which in the meantime had changed its name to the Dundalk, Newry & Greenore Railway, was extended from Greenore to Newry in 1876.

The Greenore route was not a financial success. The railway was generally run at a loss and the steamship service did not make a working profit until 1912. This was due to the remoteness of Greenore from the industrial parts of Ireland and the general inconvenience of the route for passengers. Businessmen in a hurry could get as quickly from Belfast or Derry to London by using one of the short sea-routes—Larne/Stranraer or Dun Laoghaire/Holyhead—while those who preferred their beds could patronise one of the overnight steamers to Fleetwood or Liverpool. Furthermore, when the route was opened the INWR, which went from Dundalk to Derry via Enniskillen, was an independent company and it was hoped that most of the cattle from Fermanagh and Monaghan would be shipped through Greenore. In 1878 the INWR became one of the constituent companies of the Great Northern Railway (Ireland). This meant that cattle dealers at such places as Enniskillen and Clones could send their livestock to Great Britain via Belfast on as good terms as via Greenore. Cattle was always one of the principal exports through Greenore but the trade, although good, was never sufficient to make either the DNGR or the steamers moderately prosperous.

In normal times between 1873 and 1926 a steamer sailed from Greenore on weekdays in the early evening and the return working was scheduled to leave Holyhead at about one in the morning. The service was curtailed during the 1914–18 war, and restored in 1920. After the suspension of sailings during the General Strike in May 1926 the passenger service was not revived. The railway to Greenore remained open and the railway steamers continued to work cattle and cargo from the port until the close down of the route in 1951. In recent years Greenore has come to life again as a port for 'unit load' cargoes which are brought to the quayside by motor lorries from every part of Ireland.

Greenore was the first railway port in Ireland. The town is a LNWR creation with only two streets, which are named Euston Street and Anglesey Terrace. Its only prominent building is the former Railway Hotel which used to house part of the station. Indeed, the entrance to the passenger station was through a doorway at the side of the hotel. The station consisted of one platform from which passengers could get to the steamers under cover by going through a subway which passed under the goods shed. The whole place had a LNWR atmosphere, an atmosphere augmented by the 0–6–0 Crewe saddle tanks which worked trains painted in LNWR livery and by such minor details as LNWR lettering on notices and pink second-class tickets.

When the service opened it took fifteen hours to get from Greenore to London, but forty minutes of this were spent at a breakfast stop at Chester. The return journey took an hour less! The boat train from Greenore took through carriages for Armagh, Belfast and Derry.

The service was much improved at the end of the nineteenth century by the acceleration of the boat trains and the introduction of twin-screw steamers. A restaurant car express was put on from Belfast which was worked through to Greenore by a GNR (I) 4–4–0 express locomotive, but the through carriages to Armagh and Derry were withdrawn. The following extract from the 1907 timetable shows the working of the improved service. The additional fifteen minutes required for the outgoing journey from Belfast to London is not due to faster running on the way back, but to the fact that until October 1916 Irish time was twenty-five minutes later than Greenwich Mean Time.

↓		↑
7.00pm	Belfast	7.45pm
8.30pm	Greenore	6.15am
2.00am	Holyhead	1.40am
7.30am	London	7.30pm

In the 1920s, when the clocks in England and Ireland kept the same time the journey from Belfast to London (Euston) via Greenore took about fourteen hours.

2: DUBLIN AND LIVERPOOL

THE passenger service between Dublin and Liverpool evolved in a somewhat similar way to that between Belfast and the Clyde. It commenced with individually owned steamers working either alone or in groups against one another. From this general 'free for all' one group began to emerge as the strongest. At Belfast this was G. & J. Burns and at Dublin it was the City of Dublin SP Co which became the established company. The similarity ended in 1920, for today the vessels working between Dublin and Liverpool are owned by the British & Irish SP Co, who bought out the City of Dublin SP Co at the end of the 1914–18 war, whereas those plying between Belfast and the Clyde are operated by Burns & Laird, the direct descendents of G. & J. Burns.

The service was opened by George Langtry's *Waterloo* in 1820. Shortly afterwards she was joined by his *Belfast*. In 1822 the *St Patrick*, *St George* and *Emerald Isle* went into service. They were owned by the St George SP Co, a company which sired the Cork SS Co in 1843 and survives today as the City of Cork SP Co, a subsidiary of the British & Irish SP Co. The City of Dublin SP Co entered the fray on 20 March 1824 when its *City of Dublin* made her maiden voyage. By the middle of the next year the City of Dublin company had four steamers in service and by 1826 it owned fourteen vessels. By mid-century its commitments included the Dun Laoghaire–Holyhead mail service, two sailings a day between Dublin and Liverpool, two sailings a week between Dublin and Belfast, and bi-weekly sailings between Belfast and Liverpool. In addition its steamers plied regularly between Dublin and the Continent and provided services on the Shannon. The driving force behind all this was Charles Wye Williams. His company favoured iron hulls for steamers and introduced the modern practice of having these subdivided into watertight compartments by iron bulkheads. As the century progressed the company kept well ahead of its competitors and it continued to hold the Dun Laoghaire mail contract in the face of severe opposition from the London & North Western Railway until the end of the 1914–18 war. The company, at the time, was in financial difficulties and the contract passed into the railway's hands. After this the City of Dublin SP Co went into liquidation and its assets on the Dublin–Liverpool route were transferred to the British & Irish SP Co.

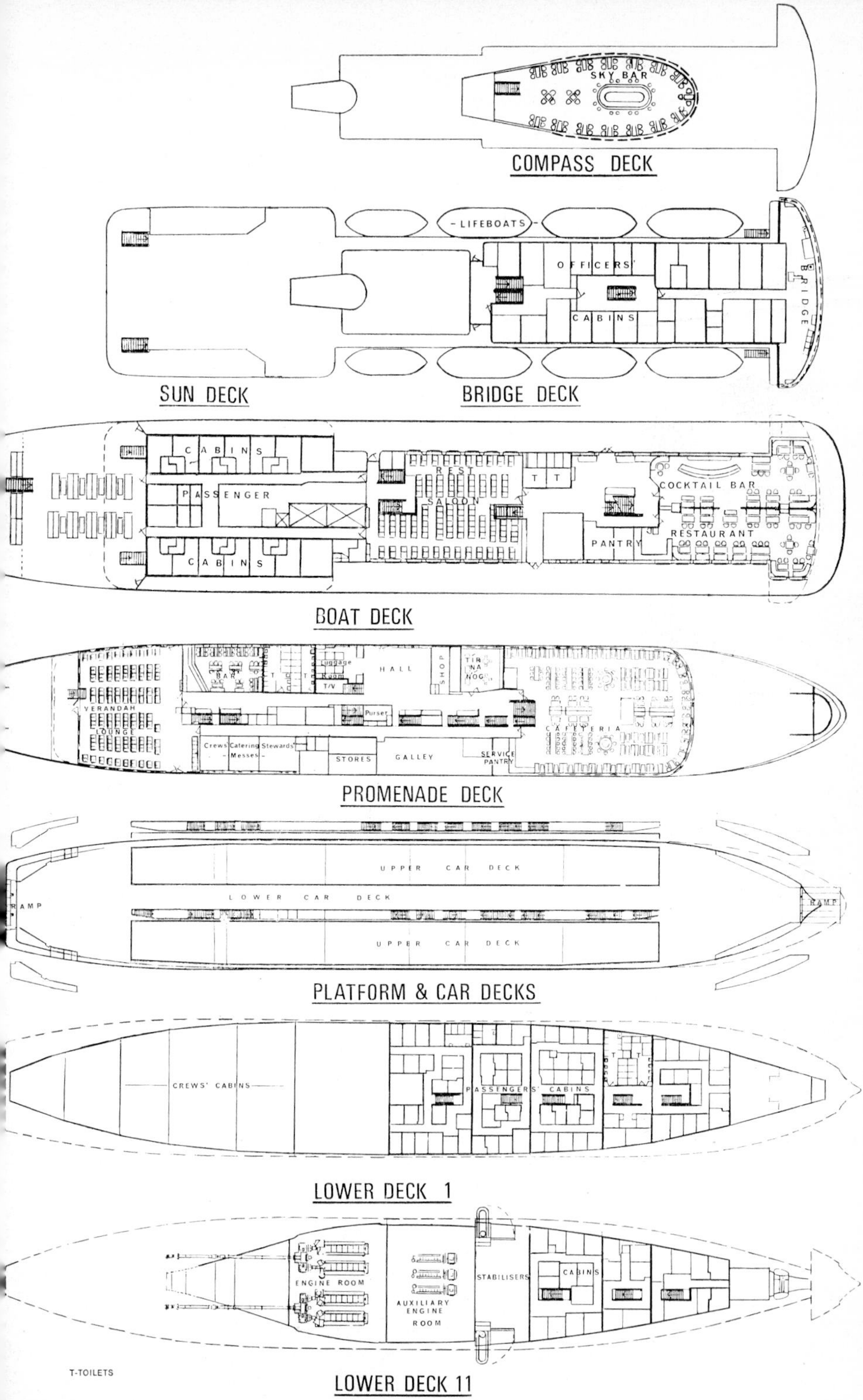
SKY BAR
COMPASS DECK
LIFEBOATS
OFFICERS' CABINS
BRIDGE
SUN DECK
BRIDGE DECK
CABINS
PASSENGER
CABINS
REST SALOON
T T
COCKTAIL BAR
RESTAURANT
PANTRY
BOAT DECK
BAR
T T
Luggage Room
T/V
HALL
SHOP
TIR NA NOG
VERANDAH LOUNGE
Purser
Crews Catering Stewards - Messes -
STORES
GALLEY
SERVICE PANTRY
CAFETERIA
PROMENADE DECK
UPPER CAR DECK
RAMP
LOWER CAR DECK
RAMP
UPPER CAR DECK
PLATFORM & CAR DECKS
CREWS' CABINS
PASSENGERS' CABINS
T T
LOWER DECK 1
ENGINE ROOM
AUXILIARY ENGINE ROOM
STABILISERS
CABINS
T-TOILETS
LOWER DECK 11

Page 35: TSMV *Leinster* (1969), passenger accommodation

Page 36 (above): TSS *Scotia* (1902), second-class lounge
(below): TSMV *Hibernia* (1949), second-class lounge after refit in 1964–5

The City of Dublin SP Co never enjoyed a monopoly for long. At first competition came from the St George SP Co and the Dublin & Liverpool SN Co. The next competitor was the Government, which began to operate its own mail steamers between Dun Laoghaire and Liverpool in August 1826. After twelve years of bitter competition, the company and the Post Office came to an understanding whereby the morning sailings were taken by the government packet and the evening ones by private enterprise. This continued until the close down of the mail workings from Liverpool in 1848.

The next threat took place in the late 1840s, at a time when thousands of Irishmen were pouring across the channel to escape from the Famine and its aftermath. The Dublin & Liverpool Screw SP Co, which had previously carried cargo and livestock in auxiliary schooners, began to convey deck passengers at 1s per head. The City of Dublin SP Co retaliated by admitting shilling passengers to its cargo steamers, which were also auxiliary screw schooners. The auxiliary vessels of both companies had no shelter on deck, indeed conditions were so deplorable that the government set up a committee of enquiry under Capt Denham to investigate them, see page 12. In the early 1850s the Dublin & Liverpool Screw SP Co was reorganised and entered the better class passenger business with its chartered steamers *Mail* and *Times*. These carried saloon passengers as well as steerage, cargo and livestock. In the 1880s its vessels were acquired by the City of Dublin SP Co, but they continued to run under the Dublin & Liverpool name between the 'two capitals of Ireland' until well into the twentieth century.

Minor competitors also appeared from time to time. In 1836 the Waterford-owned *Mermaid* ran for a few months; in 1851 the *St Kiaran* and *St Columb* worked for a short time between the two cities and in 1872 a steamer called the *Defence* plied for a few weeks on the crossing. In the same year the coal importers, Robert Tedcastle & Co, went into the Dublin–Liverpool passenger trade, a business in which they remained until the 1914–18 war. In 1880 the vessels of the Sligo SN Co (see Vol 1) began to call at Dublin and, for the next few years, provided a weekly service between the capital and Liverpool.

The 'opposition' generally competed by offering cheap fares. Thus, in 1880, when the single fares by the City of Dublin steamers were 13s 6d saloon and 5s steerage, corresponding fares by the Sligo steamers were 6s and 2s 6d and passengers on the Tedcastle vessels paid 5s and 3s. By 1914, however, the Tedcastle fares had increased to 8s and 3s whereas the City of Dublin steamers still charged the 1880 rates for a passage. In 1967 the single fares on the two-class *Leinster* and *Munster* were 65s and 40s whilst in 1970 the cost of a passage on the one-class car-ferries of the same name was 60s, a rate which was reduced to 47s 6d if one was travelling with a car. The car-ferries could make the crossing in seven hours and operated as day or night boats whereas their immediate predecessors were built for the night service and were scheduled to take nine hours to get from Dublin to Liverpool.

PS *Waterloo*, PS *Belfast*

Accounts of these vessels, which opened the Dublin–Liverpool service in 1820 are given on page 74 and in Vol 1. In their Dublin days they provided a twice-weekly service and landed their passengers 'opposite Mr Rosborough's' on Sir John Rogerson's Quay. The advertisements announcing their sailings gave the following advice to patrons, 'Passengers have no occasion to provide themselves with sea stores as necessary refreshments can be supplied by the steward on board.'

PS *Britannia*, PS *Mountaineer*

These vessels made some crossings in the early 1820s; the owners of the *Britannia* claimed she could make the crossing in under fourteen hours. This vessel at one time worked between Derry and Glasgow and may have been one of the steamers which visited Howth in 1816 (see page 140).

PS *St Patrick*, PS *St George*, PS *Emerald Isle*, PS *William Huskisson*

These steamers were used by the St George SP Co in the Dublin–Liverpool trade in the mid-1820s. They are described in Chapter 6.

PS *City of Dublin*, PS *Town of Liverpool*

The first steamer owned by the City of Dublin SP Co was the wooden paddle steamer *City of Dublin*. She was built in Liverpool and made her first crossing to Dublin on 20 March 1824. Later in the same year she was joined by the *Town of Liverpool*. They differed from their predecessors by continuing their sailings throughout the winter months. Hitherto steamers had not been considered to be sufficiently robust to face the Irish Sea in winter and people did not go to sea at this time of year unless driven by dire necessity.

PS *Liffey*, PS *Mersey*, PS *Commerce*

These vessels went into service for the Dublin & Liverpool SN Co over the period September 1824 to July 1825. In February 1826 their owners were bought out by the City of Dublin SP Co. Later in the same year the *Liffey* was put on the Belfast–Liverpool run, where she remained until 1828. In 1829 she and the *Mersey* were chartered to run with the *Town of Drogheda* on the Drogheda–Liverpool crossing.

PS *Britannia*, PS *Hibernia*

The arrival of these City of Dublin SP steamers in 1824 intensified the trade war with the St George SP Co, and reduced fares until it cost only 6d to get a deck passage to Liverpool. The public seems to have appreciated the low fares, for on occasions the steamers are reputed to have crossed with over 700 passengers on board. The *Hibernia* remained nearly twenty-five years with the company, during which time she was occasionally employed on the Belfast–Liverpool crossings. In the winter of 1827–8 she was chartered to the St George SP Co, for use in the latter's Dublin–Bristol trade. The *Britannia* was wrecked in 1829.

PS *Comet*, PS *Dolphin*, PS *Etna*, PS *Thetis*

The Government mail service between Liverpool and Dun Laoghaire was worked by these steamers from 29 August 1826 until the end of the 1830s. During the first few months of the service calls were made at Holyhead. This practice was abandoned in November 1826 and the overall time for the crossing was reduced to fifteen hours.

The vessels were built to the same design and carried only cabin passengers and their servants. The former paid 27s 6d for a passage, which was 6s 6d less than that charged on the Holyhead–Dun Laoghaire packets. Passengers' carriages could be brought over for 63s and the freight on a horse was 31s 6d.

When the service began the captains received an annual salary of £400 but this was supplemented by a bonus of 2s 6d for each passenger carried and by a share in the profits made from victualling those on board; indeed the additional emoluments were valued at about £450 per annum. Neither the captain nor the chief engineer were rationed on board but the rest of the crew were given two pounds of meat and a pound of bread daily, a necessary supplement as the wages of firemen and sailors in those days were 70s per month.

PS *Athlone*, PS *Ballinasloe*, PS *Birmingham*, PS *City of Londonderry*, PS *Gipsy*, PS *Leeds*, PS *Manchester*, PS *Mona*, PS *Nottingham*, PS *Shamrock*, PS *Sheffield*

These City of Dublin SP Co passenger/cargo steamers went into service between Dublin and Liverpool in the 1820s and 1830s.

The *Athlone* spent a considerable part of her career on the company's

Belfast–Liverpool service. She is remembered in the north as the vessel in which the Revs James Glasgow and Alexander Kerr set off from Belfast on 25 August 1840 on their way to India to establish the first Irish Presbyterian mission in that country.

The *Ballinasloe* was built mainly for the Dublin–Liverpool cattle trade. She was one of the first steamers in the world to have had forced ventilation in her holds. This was worked by a steam pump which expelled the foul air from her cattle decks up a hollow iron pipe which also served as one of her masts.

The *City of Londonderry* was purchased in October 1829. Previous to this she had worked between Derry and Liverpool, (see Vol 1.) The *Nottingham*, *Shamrock* and *Sheffield* spent a fair amount of time on the Belfast–Liverpool crossing and the first mentioned steamer also worked on occasions between Liverpool and Derry. The *Shamrock* was built for the Belfast SP Co in 1824 for its Belfast–Liverpool service. Two years later she was acquired by the City of Dublin SP Co who used her to open its Dublin–Belfast service in October 1826.

PS *Duchess of Kent*, PS *Iron Duke*, PS *Princess*, PS *Queen Victoria*, PS *Royal Adelaide*, PS *Royal William*, PS *Windsor*

In the late 1830s the City of Dublin SP Co always allocated four of the above steamers to the Liverpool mail, an arrangement which ensured that there was always a spare vessel at each terminal ready to take over in the event of a mishap.

The *Royal William* was the first of the eight vessels to be completed. She did not go at once into the cross-channel trade but was chartered to the Trans-Atlantic SS Co, a subsidiary of the City of Dublin SP Co. She sailed from Liverpool at 6.30 pm on 5 July 1838, and arrived at New York nineteen days later, thereby becoming the first steamer to make a transatlantic crossing from Liverpool. She set off from New York on her return voyage on 4 August carrying passengers and mail. The former paid $140 (inclusive of wine!) for a passage, whilst mail was charged 25 cents per sheet. After two more round trips she was transferred to the cross-channel trade and ran on the Liverpool–Dublin mail; she also took turns working between Liverpool and Belfast and was used occasionally in the deep-sea services of her owners. She ended her days as a coal hulk, having been purchased for this humble duty for £11. A detailed description of this cross-channel packet, which is claimed to be the smallest vessel to have steamed all the way from Europe to America, is given in H. P. Spratt's monograph, *Transatlantic Paddle Steamers*.

The *Queen Victoria* went into service in 1837 and was wrecked near Howth Head during a snowstorm on 15 February 1853. There were about 120 people on board at the time, 80 of whom lost their lives.

The *Duchess of Kent* brought back the body of Daniel O'Connell to Ireland on 2 August 1847.

After the close down of the mail terminal at Liverpool in 1848 the company still continued the evening passenger service between Dun Laoghaire and Liverpool, but as time went on the number of sailings decreased until in the early 1860s there were only two sailings per week.

PS *Medina*, PS *Medusa*, PS *Merlin*, PS *Urgent*, PS *Richmond*

The *Medina*, *Medusa* and *Merlin* were built in Pembroke Dockyard for the Dun Laoghaire–Liverpool mail service in 1838–40. When the Admiralty ceased working this crossing in August 1848 the three vessels were transferred to the Mediterranean, where they were employed for a few months in carrying mail between Marseilles, Malta and Alexandria. After this they were given other naval duties; thus the *Merlin* and *Medina* spent some time as survey ships in the Baltic and Mediterranean respectively.

The *Urgent* was obtained second-hand for £37,000 in 1837. In addition to working the Liverpool mail she was employed from time to time on the Holyhead–Dun Laoghaire service. The *Richmond* was a small mail tender which was generally stationed at Liverpool.

When the City of Dublin SP Co obtained its share of the mail contract in 1838 its shareholders automatically acquired the privilege of free travel on board the government steamers, a perquisite which they had previously enjoyed on their own vessels (see Vol 1).

SS *Dublin*, SS *Liverpool*, SS *Waterwitch*, SS *Diamond*, SS *Emerald*, SS *Pearl*

These were the notorious auxiliary screw schooners of 1848–9 which figure so prominently in the Denham Report, see page 37. The first three vessels were owned by the Dublin & Liverpool Screw SP Co, a company closely associated with the Grand Canal Co. They had three masts and their engines developed 30hp which gave them a speed of 8 knots. They generally took about fourteen hours for the crossing but in winter the passage sometimes required over twenty-four. At peak periods over 300 people would be packed on board in addition to a full complement of cargo and livestock. The *Diamond*, *Emerald* and *Pearl* were owned by the City of Dublin SP Co.

PS *Albert*, PS *Duke of Cambridge*, PS *Eblana*, PS *Liverpool*, PS *Mona*, PS *Roscommon*, PS *St Columba*, PS *St Patrick*, PS *Trafalgar*

These City of Dublin steamers were employed on the Dublin–Liverpool trade in the mid-nineteenth century. The *Eblana*, *St Columba* and *St Patrick* (formerly *Llewellyn*) began their careers on the Holyhead Mail (see Chapter 1) and were relegated to the Liverpool route in the 1860s. The *Albert* spent forty years with the company. The *Mona* was a small paddler which was built for the Isle of Man SP Co in 1832. She was acquired by the City of Dublin SP Co in 1841 but after a short time she was taken off cross-channel work and used as a tug at Dublin.

PS *Kildare*, PS *Mullingar*, PS *Longford*, PS *Leitrim*, PS *Cavan*, PS *Mayo*, PS *Meath*, PS *Galway*

These vessels were the backbone of the Dublin–Liverpool service from the late 1860s until the arrival of the screw steamers some thirty years later.

SS *Louth*, SS *Wicklow*, SS *Carlow*, SS *Kerry*, SS *Cork*, SS *Kilkenny*

These were virtually sister ships with a length of 262ft and a beam of 34ft. The first five were built in the 1890s and the *Kilkenny* was launched in 1903. The City of Dublin SP Co used them on the Dublin–Liverpool crossing on which they were advertised to make the sea passage in eight hours and to maintain a twice-daily service leaving Liverpool at 10 am and in the late evening. Saloon passengers patronising the latter could obtain dinner for 2s 6d and were permitted to remain in their cabins until 9 am after the crossing. It was during the lifetime of these steamers that the company acquired a bus to provide free transport for passengers and their luggage between Central and Exchange Stations and its steamers at Liverpool. The bus service, which began early in 1897, did not run to Lime Street, as at that time relationships between the City of Dublin Co and the LNWR were somewhat strained.

The first four vessels were taken over by the British & Irish SP Co in 1919 and a year later received the prefix *Lady* to their names. The *Louth* was transferred to the City of Cork SP Co late in 1920 and was renamed *Bandon*. The *Cork* was sunk during the 1914–18 war and the *Kilkenny*, which was the last steamer to be built for the City of Dublin SP Co, was sold to the Great Eastern Railway in 1917. The Railway changed her name to *Frinton* and stationed her at Harwich as a cargo steamer until 1926.

SS *Lady Louth*, SS *Lady Limerick*, SS *Lady Longford*

The arrival of these steamers in 1923 and 1924 established the popularity of the overnight service between Dublin and Liverpool. The vessels connected at Liverpool with the same trains as did the overnight steamers from Belfast. This enabled travellers to leave Dublin at 8.30 pm and be in London by noon next day, having had a full night's sleep on board. On the return journey passengers left London at about 6 pm and reached Dublin at breakfast time next morning. The through fares from Dublin to London by this route were 62s 3d first and 43s 6d saloon on the steamer and third rail, whereas by the Holyhead Mail the corresponding fares were 64s 9d and 46s 3d.

The *Lady Louth* and *Lady Limerick* were built for the company, whilst the *Lady Longford* was built as the *Ardmore* for the City of Cork SP Co in 1921. In 1923 she was transferred to the British & Irish SP Co who renamed her *Lady Longford*.

The three steamers were displaced by the arrival of the *Graphic* and her sisters in 1929 and were then transferred to Burns & Laird Lines Ltd. The *Lady Louth* and *Lady Limerick* were used on the Belfast–Glasgow overnight service where they ran under the names of *Lairdsburn* and *Lairdscastle*; they are described in Vol 1. The *Lady Longford* became the *Lairdshill* and was employed mainly on the company's Dublin–Glasgow thrice-weekly run.

TSS *Lady Connaught/Longford*, TSS *Lady Leinster/Lady Connaught*, TSS *Lady Munster/Louth*

The Belfast SS Co's *Heroic*, *Patriotic* and *Graphic* were given these names when they were transferred to the Dublin–Liverpool service in the early 1930s. The careers of these vessels are described in Vol 1.

TSMV *Leinster*, TSMV *Munster*

These vessels were the most comfortable of the thirteen cross-channel ships built by Harland & Wolff for Coast Lines over the years 1929–48. Their passenger accommodation was roomy, light and airy. Sleeping berths were provided amidships, in single- and two-berth cabins, for over 400 saloon passengers and aft there were berths for over a 100 in the steerage. The *Leinster* was a hospital ship during the 1939–45 war. She was transferred to the Belfast SS Co in 1945 and renamed *Ulster Prince*. A description of this vessel is given in Vol 1. The *Munster* was sunk after hitting a mine off the Mersey Bar in February 1940; there was no loss of life.

TSMV *Munster*, TSMV *Leinster*

These motor vessels went into service in 1948. The *Munster* was completed early in the year and then spent her first few months working on the City of Cork SP Co's Cork–Fishguard service until the arrival of the *Leinster*. The two vessels then commenced their regular overnight runs between Prince's Dock, Liverpool, and North Wall which lasted until the withdrawal of the *Munster* in October 1967. The service was then reduced to three sailings a week, which were taken by the *Leinster*. The *Munster* was subsequently sold to the Epirotiki Lines who changed her name to *Theseus*. In 1969 she became the *Orpheus* and under this name now cruises in the Aegean. The *Leinster* became the *Aphrodite* in 1968, and in 1969 plied between Piraeus, Brindisi and Ancona.

The 1948 vessels were very similar in appearance to the 1938 ships of the same name, their main difference to a casual observer was that the 1938 ships had square ports on A deck whereas the ports in the 1948 vessels were round. The accommodation followed the 1938 pattern with the saloon smoke room being built around the main stairway on the promenade deck. This gave an air of spaciousness more in keeping with a transatlantic liner than with an overnight steamer. The safety devices on board included sprinkler fire-fighting points throughout the whole ship.

TSMV *Munster*, TSMV *Leinster*

These one-class vessels now operate the twice-daily ferry service between Carrier's Dock, Liverpool, and the New Ferry Terminal at Dublin. The daylight crossing is scheduled to be completed in seven hours. The night crossing takes two hours longer and gives an arrival time of 7 am at each port.

The *Munster* went into service in the spring of 1968 and was followed by the *Leinster* a year later. The former was designed in Denmark and built in Hamburg for the Baltic trade. During construction she was purchased by the British & Irish SP Co. She was designed for working through ice in winter and has an ice strengthened hull, a feature which makes her the only 'ice worthy' cross-channel steamer to be regularly employed on the Irish Sea. She can be turned round in an hour, during which time she can disembark and take on board 1,000 passengers and 220 cars, a feat made possible by the careful design of her bow- and stern-loading doors. She is fitted with a bow thrust unit and stabilisers.

Her four diesel engines can drive her at 22 knots, a speed which enables her to maintain the tight schedule demanded for the daylight crossing. Her passenger amenities include a children's playroom, the first time this facility has been provided on an Irish cross-channel steamer.

The *Leinster* was launched at Passage, Co Cork, in November 1968. She is somewhat similar in appearance to her consort but has a multi-window deck house on her upper deck which contains an observation lounge and cocktail bar.

SS *Mail*, SS *Times*, SS *Despatch*

Shortly after the publication of the Denham report in 1849 the Dublin & Liverpool Screw SP Co moved into the better class passenger trade. It chartered the *Mail* and the *Times* for a service between Dublin (North Wall) and Liverpool (Trafalgar Dock). The *Despatch*, which was advertised as a new steamer, made a few trips for the company in 1856.

SS *Standard*, SS *Star*, SS *Torch*

The *Standard* was the first passenger steamer owned by the Dublin & Liverpool Screw SP Co. She was acquired in 1854 and gave her owners over thirty years' service on the Dublin–Liverpool crossing. In 1860 she was joined by the *Star* and shortly afterwards the *Torch* came into the company's fleet. These vessels provided a thrice-weekly service and were allowed eleven hours for the crossing, whereas the City of Dublin steamers got over in nine hours. The fares charged by either company were the same.

SS *Express*, SS *Belfast*

These vessels were built for the Dublin & Liverpool Screw SP Co in 1874 and 1884 respectively. In the latter year the two steamers were acquired by the City of Dublin SP Co who kept them on an independent passenger/cargo service to the Mersey which continued to be advertised under the name of Dublin & Liverpool SP Co until about 1910.

PS *Defence*

In 1872 a company known as the Dublin Traders SP Co ran the 'new and powerful steamer' *Defence* twice a week between Custom House Quay, Dublin, and Victoria Dock at Liverpool. The vessel was a 'cut rate' steamer for her passengers were charged 9s and 3s for a single passage.

The *Defence* was built as the blockade runner *Rosetta* but, by the time she was completed, the American Civil War had ended. She was then acquired by the Bristol SN Co who found that her shallow draught and light construction did not make her particularly suitable for crossing the Irish Sea in winter. In 1870 she was sold to Liverpool owners who changed her name to *Defence*. After three more changes of ownership she went to Brazil in 1878.

SS *Dublin*, SS *Magnet*, SS *Adela*, SS *Eblana*, SS *Cumbria*, SS *Blackrock*

In 1872 Robert Tedcastle & Co went into the Dublin–Liverpool passenger business. At the time the company owned a fleet of sailing ships and steamers which brought coal to Dublin. In 1885 Tedcastle absorbed the Whitehaven SN Co and in 1897 amalgamated with J. McCormick to form Tedcastle & McCormick who, themselves, were taken over by the British & Irish SP Co in September 1919.

The *Dublin* and the *Magnet* were the first Tedcastle steamers to carry passengers; they remained with the company until about 1890. The *Adela* was also a passenger/cargo steamer, she spent all her working life with the company, from 1878 to 17 February 1917, when she was torpedoed with serious loss of life.

The *Eblana* and *Cumbria* were built for Tedcastle in 1892 and 1896 respectively. The latter was sent to Cork in 1919 to reopen the Cork–Fishguard service after the 1914–18 war.

The *Blackrock* was the only passenger/cargo steamer owned by Mr McCormick. She was a three-masted vessel with her engines aft and limited accommodation for passengers of both classes, who were charged 7s and 3s for a single passage. She survived the 1914–18 war and was taken over by the British & Irish SP Co in 1919. In her McCormick days her advertisements were headed 'Dublin & Mersey SS Co'.

At the turn of the century the *Eblana*, *Cumbria*, *Blackrock* and *Adela* provided four sailings each way per week between Dublin and Liverpool.

3: OTHER SERVICES FROM DUBLIN

ABOUT a dozen passenger cross-channel services have worked from Dublin. The most important of these were the crossings to Holyhead and Liverpool which are described in Chapters 1 and 2. The third in importance was that to Glasgow which operated from 1826 to 1968. The Dublin–Cumberland coast service (1830–1939) may be considered as fourth. The other two long-lived routes were those to Bristol (1822–1908) and Morecambe (later Heysham), the latter began in 1889 and survived the 1914–18 war. None of the remaining services lasted for more than a couple of years.

There are now only four passenger services working regularly from the Dublin area. One is provided by the car-ferries of the British & Irish SP Co which ply twice daily between Dublin and Liverpool and the others operate from Dun Laoghaire. One of the latter is the summer only bi-weekly car-ferry service from Dun Laoghaire to Heysham. This commenced in June 1970, since which date it has been worked by the Dun Laoghaire–Holyhead ferries *Dover* and *Holyhead Ferry I*.

Dublin–Ardrossan

In the late 1850s a steamer was advertised to run between Dublin and Ardrossan with a call at Newry en route. Dublin–Newry bookings were accepted.

Dublin–Barrow

In 1877 the Sligo steamers *Glasgow* and *Liverpool* (see Vol 1) were chartered to work between Dublin and Barrow. The notices advertising the crossing were headed 'New Short Sea Route' and ended with the name of the agent—James Little & Co, who at the time managed the Barrow–Belfast steamers jointly with the Midland Railway. The service lasted for about a year.

Dublin–Bristol

The Bristol–Dublin service opened in May 1822 and ended in 1908. The first steamer to make the passage was the *St Patrick* which, at that time, was working between Liverpool and Dublin and took the Bristol call by extending her run from Dublin. In July of the same year she was joined by her Dublin–Liverpool consort, *St George*, and between them the two steamers maintained a weekly service between Dublin and Bristol. Both vessels are described on page 106. In May 1823 a Bristol company, known as the War Office SP Co, put a steamer on the route, and for the next sixteen years there was intense rivalry between the two companies. The 'war' ended in 1839 when the St George SP Co withdrew, thereby leaving the War Office SP Co, and its direct descendant, the Bristol SN Co, with a monopoly which was maintained until the close down of the service.

In the 1830s and early 1840s two or three sailings each week were made between Dublin and Bristol. Some of the steamers ran from North Wall at Dublin, others worked to the new pier at Dun Laoghaire. Calls en route were made at times at Tenby, Swansea and Ilfracombe. By the late 1840s the frequency had been reduced to one sailing each week and this was maintained until the close down of the service sixty years later. The fares charged in the last decade of operation were 15s saloon and 7s 6d steerage. There was a reduction of fares for a short time in 1851 when the company was competing for a share in the through Dublin–London passenger traffic. One could then get by this route from Dublin to London for 14s 10d: 5s for a steerage passage to Bristol and 9s 10d third class rail Bristol to London. In the latter part of the nineteenth century saloon return tickets issued between Dublin and Bristol could be used to return on the Waterford SS Co's steamers to Waterford and on the City of Cork steamers from Bristol to Cork.

The St George SP Co employed no less than twelve different steamers during the seventeen years it was interested in the crossing, but only two of these—*Emerald Isle* and *Express*—spent more than three years in the Dublin–Bristol trade. The company's steamers are described in Chapter 6 and their dimensions are given in the fleet list associated with that chapter. Full accounts of the careers of the War Office SP Co's vessels and the bitter war between this company and the St George SP Co are given in Grahame Farr's book *West Country Passenger Steamers*. The names and dimensions of the vessels employed by the War Office SP Co and the Bristol SN Co are given in the Fleet List on page 190. Three of the company's steamers, *Albion*, *City of Bristol* and *Killarney*, were lost when trading between Bristol and Ireland and two of its vessels, *Flora* and *Juno*, became blockade runners in the American Civil War. The *Duke of Lancaster*, which was the first steamer to ply between Waterford and Bristol, is described on page 87.

In the summer of 1837 the Dublin & Glasgow Sailing & SP Co ran its wooden steamer *Mercury* on a short-lived triangular service between Dublin, Bristol and Glasgow. The career of this vessel is described on page 56.

PS *City of Bristol*

This steamer was built in Bristol for the War Office SP Co in 1827. At the time she was rigged as a two-masted schooner and was fitted with a 170hp engine. She was a fast vessel and in 1833 made a passage from Dublin to Bristol in twenty-two hours. In 1834 she was transferred from the Dublin–Bristol to the Waterford–Bristol route. When employed in the latter she was driven ashore on Worms Head, near Swansea, in a gale in 1840. At the time there were twenty-seven people on board but only two survived. The *City of Bristol* was also employed by her owners on the short-lived New Ross–Bristol service of 1832.

SS *Calypso*

The *Calypso* was the first iron vessel owned by the Bristol SN Co. On her first passage from Dublin to Bristol, made in May 1855, she got over in 18hr 25min. Shortly after this she went 'trooping' for the French in the Crimean War and survived to ply again between Dublin and Bristol. On the outbreak of the American Civil War she became a blockade runner and set off for Nassau in December 1862. She was ultimately captured and then changed sides to become the Union warship USS *Calypso*. At the end of the war she once again reverted to the merchant service, and was registered at New York as the *Winchester*. After this she traded peacefully in the New World until 1886.

SS *Argo*

The *Argo* was owned by the Bristol SN Co. She had an iron hull with engines aft and accommodation for about sixty saloon passengers. She spent all her working career, which extended from 1871 to 1908, plying between Dublin and Bristol, she sailed from the former on Tuesdays, and returned from the Cumberland Basin, Bristol, on Fridays. She generally took about twenty hours for her passage and often called at Tenby. In her old age she ran into bad luck—she lost her rudder in 1902, she collided with the steamer *City of Malaga* in 1905 and in 1907 was out of commission for a time when her place was taken by the Dublin–Glasgow steamer *Duke of Gordon*. Finally, on 29 June 1908, she was so badly damaged after striking some submerged wreckage off the mouth of the Liffey that she was sold for breaking up.

Dublin–Cumberland

Passenger services ran between Dublin and the Cumberland coast from 1830 until the 1939–45 war. The first route to open was that between Dublin and Whitehaven which was begun by the *St Andrew* in 1830. Seven years later steamers began to ply between Dublin and Port Carlisle—later Silloth—and continued on this route until 1939, whereas the Whitehaven service closed down at the turn of the century.

At first, sailings between Dublin and Whitehaven were somewhat intermittent. For a time in the 1840s they were taken by the Isle of Man SP Co's *Mona's Isle* and *Ben-My-Chree*, which worked the route by extending some of their Dublin–Douglas sailings to Whitehaven. In the 1850s a thrice-weekly service was inaugurated by the Whitehaven SN Co who, at the time, also ran ships to Belfast (see Vol 1). The Whitehaven Co withdrew from the Dublin service in the early 1860s. This move, however, did not sever the passenger link between Dublin and Whitehaven, for vessels of the North British (Silloth) SP Co then began to call at Whitehaven on their way from Silloth to Dublin, a practice which was continued until the autumn of 1901.

The Port Carlisle passenger trade with Dublin began in 1837. The early sailings were taken by the Carlisle & Liverpool SN Co who generally employed its *Solway* on the crossing. In the mid-1850s the silting of the harbour at Port Carlisle got so bad that when the docks at Silloth were opened many of the Solway shipping services moved to the new port. In 1856 the railway between Carlisle and Silloth was completed and six years later it was leased to the North British Railway. Shortly afterwards the railway acquired an interest in the Solway Bay SN Co, an organisation which had been formed in 1856 to run steamers between Dublin and Silloth. In 1863 the railway obtained an Act of Parliament which authorised it to run its own steamers, as a consequence of which it formed the North British SP Co to look after its shipping interests. This action produced the paradox of a Scottish railway operating steamships on the Irish Sea from an English port. The railway did everything in its power to attract passengers to the route and advertised cheap fares between Dublin, Edinburgh and the Scottish Borders. Its vessels normally provided a twice-weekly service on which the single fares of 15s saloon and 6s steerage were charged.

In 1870 the Ardrossan SN Co took over the working of the railway steamship services. The close relationship between rail and sea was maintained, through bookings were continued, viz Dublin–Newcastle

28s 6d and 12s 9d, and the notices advertising the service contained the phrases 'Ardrossan SN Co in connection with the North British Railway' and 'Via Silloth (Waverley Route)'. In 1891 the service passed into the hands of Wm Sloan & Co who continued to operate it with the former Ardrossan steamer *Caledonian*. Two years later this vessel was replaced by the *Yarrow*, a steamer which remained in the Dublin–Silloth trade until the 1939–45 war.

PS *St Andrew*, PS *Solway*, PS *Cumberland*, PS *Newcastle*

These steamers worked between Port Carlisle and Dublin in the 1830s. The service was opened by the *St Andrew* (Capt M. Banks) in 1830. This vessel was built in 1826 and spent a fair amount of her early days cruising (see Vol 1).

PS *Earl of Lonsdale*, PS *Whitehaven*, PS *Queen*

The Whitehaven SN Co used these steamers on its Belfast–Whitehaven and Dublin–Whitehaven services at different times over the years 1837–61.

SS *Silloth*

This vessel was built for the Solway Bay SN Co in 1856. She normally ran between Silloth and Liverpool, but on occasions went to Dublin.

PS *Prince of Wales*, PS *William McCormick*, SS *Torch*, PS *Princess Alice*, PS *Ariel*, SS *Kittiwake*

In the 1860s the first four vessels were chartered by the North British SP Co to work between Dublin and Silloth. The *Torch* at one time worked between Liverpool and Dublin. The *William McCormick* had been built originally for the Derry cross-channel trade and the *Prince of Wales* and *Princess Alice* were at one time employed on the Belfast–Fleetwood crossing (see Vol 1). The *Ariel* was acquired by the company in 1862 and replaced by the *Kittiwake* four years later.

PS *Waverley*, PS *Waverley*

The two steamers of this name went into service in 1864 and 1865. The first *Waverley* made her initial crossing to Dublin in September 1864 but her stay on the route was short for she was replaced after a year. She then received a thorough overhaul, after which she was sold to owners in the north of Scotland who renamed her *St Magnus*. The second *Waverley* spent about three years plying between Dublin and Silloth. She was then sold to the London & South Western Railway for that company's Channel Islands service, an occupation in which she lost in June 1873.

SS *Countess of Eglinton*, SS *South Western*, SS *North British*, SS *Midland*, SS *Caledonian*

These steamers started their careers working between Belfast and Ardrossan; full accounts of them are given in Vol 1. In their Silloth days they generally ran twice a week to Dublin and made calls at Whitehaven and Douglas on their way. They took about twelve hours to get from Dublin to Whitehaven and an additional two hours to reach Silloth.

SS *Yarrow/Assaroe*

This steamer was built for the Dublin, Douglas & Silloth SS Co, an associate of Wm Sloan & Co, in 1893. In 1929 she passed into the hands of the Dublin & Silloth SS Co, a company which was managed by Palgrave, Murphy & Co of Dublin. At the hand over her name was changed to *Assaroe* and her funnel colours altered to buff with a green band and black top. The change did not upset her sailing programme of two round trips each week between Dublin and Silloth, calling at Douglas on the way; a schedule she had maintained from the turn of the century. The same cannot be said of her fares, for in 1900 a single passage cost 10s saloon and 5s steerage whereas in 1939 a saloon passage cost 20s with an additional 2s 6d for a berth or 5s for a single-berth room! The close liaison with the railway was still maintained, for notices advertising the route stated that further details could be obtained from the London & North Eastern Railway.

Dublin–Fleetwood

On Tuesday 9 March 1844 a bi-weekly service was opened between Dublin and Fleetwood. It was advertised as a joint venture of the City of Dublin SP Co and the North Lancashire SN Co. It was worked by the City of Dublin SP Co's *Hibernia* and the Fleetwood-owned *Princess Alice*. They sailed from Dublin on Tuesday and Saturday and called at the Isle of Man en route; the Tuesday steamer went on to Port Carlisle after her Fleetwood stop, thereby providing a service between Dublin and the Cumberland coast. The route was closed at the end of the year.

Page 53 (above): TSS *Scotia* (1902), first-class ladies' cabin. Note the oil lamp for emergency lighting
(below): TSMV *Leinster* (1969), two-berth cabin with private shower. Note the 'clinical' appearance of the room

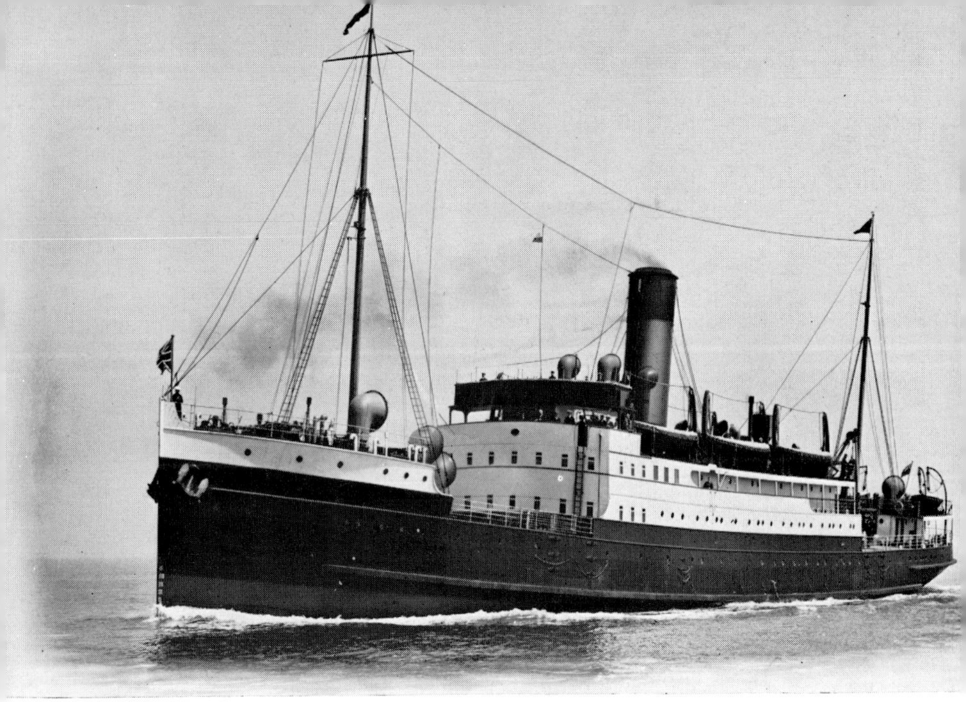

Page 54 (above): SS *Lairdscastle*, ex-*Lady Limerick*, at sea, c 1932
(below): SS *Lairdscastle*, ex-*Lady Limerick*, saloon passenger accommodation. There were also three single- and twenty-two double-berth staterooms on the main deck; this deck is not shown on the plan

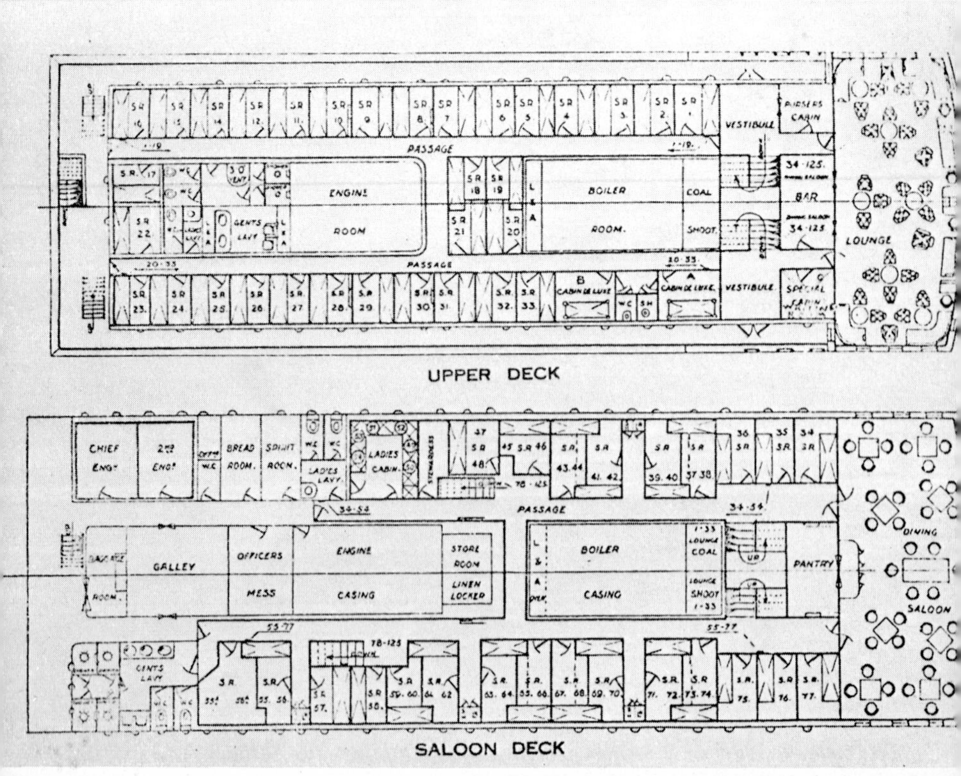

Dublin–Glasgow

The Dublin–Glasgow service opened in 1826. In the autumn of that year John Gemmill, who ran a steamer between Belfast and the Clyde (see Vol 1), put his *Erin* on the Dublin–Glasgow route and for the next 142 years steamers plied regularly for passengers between the capital of Ireland and the Clyde. The vessels at first ran once a week; in 1829 they sailed thrice weekly and by 1880 daily sailings were in operation. After this the number of sailings per week fluctuated between five and six until the service temporarily closed down during the 1914–18 war. In the years before and after the 1939–45 war a thrice-weekly service was provided which continued until the passenger sailings were suspended in February 1968. In the days of the *Erin* passengers were charged 34s 6d saloon and 10s deck for a single passage. Just before the close down in 1968 a saloon ticket cost 70s, steerage cost 45s and those who wanted a berth had to pay berth fees which ranged from 10s for a berth in the steerage dormitory to 30s for a single-berth cabin in the saloon.

In the 1830s the *Erin*, and her consort *Scotia*, were advertised under the name of the Dublin & Glasgow Sailing & Steam Packet Co, a company which retained its separate identity in the Dublin–Glasgow trade for over seventy years. During this time its steamers ran in competition, first with the vessels of the St George SP Co, and then with an independently owned steamer called the *Irishman*. This small screw vessel began a weekly service in 1854. She generally sailed from Dublin on Thursdays and took about twenty-one hours for the crossing. The steamers of the Dublin & Glasgow S & SP Co were scheduled to get over in fifteen hours and charged their passengers 15s and 6s, whereas the fares for cabin and steerage accommodation on the *Irishman* were 10s and 5s. In 1873 the *Irishman* was acquired by the Glasgow & Londonderry SP Co (later Laird Line) who replaced her in 1878 by the former Glasgow–Derry cross-channel steamer *Thistle* (see Vol 1). This vessel also ran for a time as a 'cut rate' steamer but, by 1880, an agreement was reached between the rival companies and in January of that year Laird steamers sailed from Dublin on Tuesday, Thursday and Saturday and the Dublin & Glasgow Company's vessels ran on Monday, Wednesday and Friday. This close association continued after the Dublin & Glasgow S & SP Co changed its name to the Duke Line in 1892 and survived the Duke Line's absorption by G. & J. Burns in 1908. The latter operated the Dublin–Glasgow service through an associated company known as the Burns Steamship Co. In 1922 G. & J. Burns and the Laird Line amalgamated to form Burns & Laird Lines Ltd. The new combine continued to work the route as a passenger carrying service until the suspension of passenger sailings on 10 February 1968.

In the years 1880–1908 many of the larger Laird Line steamers were used on the crossing. The vessels regularly employed since 1908 included the *Magpie* (*Lairdsgrove*) 1908–35; *Ermine* 1912–14; *Moorfowl* (*Lairdsmoor*) 1921–37; *Lairdshill* (ex-*Ardmore*) 1930–57; *Lairdsburn* 1936–57; *Lairdscastle* 1936–9; *Irish Coast* 1953–68; and the *Scottish Coast* 1956–67. The *Ardmore* is described on page 115 and more information about the other vessels can be found in Vol 1. The vessels of the St George SP Co are described in Chapter 6. A very complete account of the working of the Dublin & Glasgow Sailing & Steam Packet Co was published in *Sea Breezes* for November 1969.

PS *Erin*, PS *Scotia*

These vessels were used by John Gemmill for the opening of his Dublin–Glasgow service. The *Erin* arrived in the autumn of 1826 and early in the following year had a particularly rough crossing in a severe gale. She ultimately arrived safely at Dublin, when the passengers immediately published a testimonial to the master, Captain Newton, complimenting him on his good seamanship in getting them safely over the channel. In 1834 she was sold to the St George SP Co, who used her for a time on its Dublin–Bristol service. In 1845 she was sold to Wexford owners and was broken up six years later.

The *Scotia* joined the *Erin* late in 1828. Shortly after her arrival the frequency of the service was increased to three sailings a week and calls were made at Peel in the Isle of Man. The steamers generally took from twenty-four to thirty-six hours for the crossing and their sailings were advertised under the heading 'War Office and Commercial SP Co'.

PS *Arab*, PS *Mercury*, PS *Eagle*

The first two steamers arrived at Dublin in 1836. The *Arab* was outstanding. She made her début on the Belfast–Greenock route in 1835 when she set up a record of 9hr 5min for the crossing (see Vol 1). In 1836 she was acquired by the Dublin & Glasgow Co who retained her until her sale to other Scottish owners in 1844. Her consort, the *Mercury*, remained with the company from 1837 to 1846. This vessel had at one time worked between Belfast and Glasgow and had been chartered for a few runs to the Port Rush SN Co (see Vol 1). During the time these vessels were with the Dublin & Glasgow S & SP Co the company took up the challenge of the St George SP Co by extending some of its workings from Dublin to Cork and Bristol, see page 103. The Cork sailings continued for about ten years but the Bristol service was given up after a few months.

The *Eagle* belonged originally to G. & J. Burns, who used her on the Liverpool–Glasgow service from 1835 until her sale to the Dublin company in 1839. She remained for nine years on the Dublin–Glasgow run.

PS *Vanguard*, PS *Viceroy*, PS *Ariel*, PS *City of Carlisle*

The first three vessels were acquired by the Dublin & Glasgow S & SP Co in the 1840s. The *Vanguard* spent about twenty years with the company. She was then sold to the Aberdeen & Leith SP Co who disposed of her for breaking up some five years later. In her Dublin days she often worked to Cork and, when on one of these extended runs in December 1844, she was driven ashore at Roches Point at the entrance to Cork harbour during a severe gale. Her passengers and crew were taken off by the Cork owned *Ocean*. The vessel, herself, was ultimately refloated and towed to Passage West for repair.

The *City of Carlisle* was chartered for a few runs in 1840.

PS *Havelock*, PS *Herald*

These paddle steamers were capable of 14 knots. Their speed was their undoing, for they were sold to be blockade runners in 1862.

PS *Lord Clyde*, PS *Lord Gough*, PS *Lord Clyde*, PS *Earl of Carlisle*

These four vessels were built for the Dublin & Glasgow S & SP Co in the early 1860s. They had clipper bows, turtle-deck forecastles and single funnels. They were all fast steamers and returned optimum times of about twelve hours for the passage from Dublin to the Clyde. The first *Lord Clyde* was sold as a blockade runner in 1863 and never returned to the United Kingdom. Two of the three remaining vessels had more than their fair share of misfortune. The *Lord Gough* ran down a schooner off Greenock in 1864 and in 1869 collided with the *Marquis of Abercorn*. In 1864 the *Earl of Carlisle* collided with the *Guy Fawkes*, a small steamer which belonged to a gun powder company; the accident took place in November! The second *Lord Clyde* arrived as a replacement for her namesake early in 1864 and remained with the company for about twenty-five years during which time she suffered no serious mishap.

The departure of the first *Lord Clyde* left the Dublin & Glasgow S & SP Co with no steamers of its own, so it had to charter the Fleetwood-owned *Prince of Wales*, the City of Dublin SP Co's *Eblana*, the Dundalk SP Co's *Emerald Isle* and the Drogheda SP Co's *Colleen Bawn* to maintain its Dublin–Glasgow service.

PS *Earl of Dublin/Duke of Edinburgh*, PS *Marquis of Abercorn*

Langmuir & Duckworth in their *Clyde and Other Coastal Steamers* refer to the *Earl of Dublin* as 'one of the most unlucky channel steamers ever launched'. She arrived at Dublin in 1867 but on her second trip went ashore during a fog off the Co Down coast. She was ultimately salvaged and two years later was re-purchased by her former owners, who changed her name to *Duke of Edinburgh*. Her second career was also short for she was wrecked on Ailsa Craig in January 1870.

The *Marquis of Abercorn* was purchased as a replacement for the *Duke of Edinburgh* in 1867. She was sunk after being involved in a collision with the *Lord Gough* in May 1869.

PS *Duke of Leinster*, PS *Duke of Argyll*

These were the last paddle steamers built for the Dublin & Glasgow SP Co. They differed from their predecessors in having plain stems instead of elaborately decorated clipper bows surmounted by bowsprits. The *Duke of Leinster* was sold to the Dublin & Manchester SS Co in 1898 who used her on a new passenger/cargo service to Manchester until her sale for breaking up in 1911. The *Duke of Argyll* had an uneventful career which ended in 1905. By this time she had become the last paddle steamer to be regularly employed on a night service from the Clyde.

In their mid-careers the steamers were scheduled to leave Glasgow at 2 pm and then wait at Greenock until 6.30 pm so that passengers could join them off the late afternoon train from the city. On the return journey they called at Greenock in the early hours to allow those in a hurry to join an early train for Glasgow.

SS *Duchess of Marlborough*, SS *General Gordon/Duke of Gordon/Wren*, SS *Duke of Fife/Sparrow*

The *Duchess of Marlborough* was a cargo steamer with very limited passenger accommodation. She was the first screw steamer owned by the company.

The *General Gordon* was the company's first passenger steamer to have screw propulsion. She came into service in 1885 and ten years later was raised to the peerage by being created *Duke of Gordon.* She remained with the company until after the Burns's takeover in 1908 when her name was changed to *Wren.* In 1913 she was sold to Constantinople owners who renamed her *Eureuk,* after which she traded in the Eastern Mediterranean until about 1920.

The *Duke of Fife* was built in 1892 but only survived for two years after the Burns's takeover in 1908. She then went to Smyrna where she was renamed *Arcadia.* In 1933 she became the *Chios,* and was employed in the Mediterranean under Greek ownership until her demise in 1940.

SS *Duke of Rothesay/Puma/Lairdsford,* SS *Duke of Montrose/Tiger/Lairdsforest*

These vessels were built by the Caledon SB Co in 1899 and 1906 respectively. They spent the greater part of their careers on the Dublin–Glasgow crossing and survived to adopt the Burns & Laird names of *Lairdsford* and *Lairdsforest* in 1929. In 1931 the *Lairdsford* was transferred to the British & Irish SP Co, who renamed her *Lady Louth* and then used her as a cattle boat on the Dublin–Liverpool run until her sale for breaking up in 1934. The *Lairdsforest* remained with the company until she was broken up in 1934.

The two steamers were very similar in appearance, with long plated bridge decks which housed the greater part of their saloon accommodation. The *Duke of Montrose,* in the guise of Burns's *Tiger,* worked the Belfast–Ardrossan daylight service for a time in the 1920s and provided additional emergency sailings between Cork and Fishguard in September 1922 (see page 119).

TSMV *Irish Coast,* TSMV *Scottish Coast*

These two motor vessels were built for Coast Lines in 1952 and 1957 respectively. The *Irish Coast* spent the greater part of her time on the Dublin–Glasgow run and was also used as a relief steamer, when required, on the other Coast Lines routes to Ireland. In 1968 she was sold to the Epirotiki SN Co of Piraeus and sailed from the Mersey for the Mediterranenan on 22 August of that year. The *Scottish Coast* was used at times as a relief steamer on the Dublin–Glasgow crossing. In the summer of 1969 she was employed on the overnight tri-weekly service between Belfast and Glasgow. Later in the year she was sold to Greek owners who renamed her *Galaxias* and on 1 December she left Birkenhead for Piraeus. The two vessels are described in Vol 1.

PS *Express*, PS *Jupiter*, PS *Juno*, PS *Minerva*, PS *Ocean*, PS *Sirius*

The St George SP Co entered the Dublin–Glasgow trade with its *Jupiter* in July 1836. The vessel made a round trip between Glasgow and Dublin every five days and at Dublin was scheduled to make a connection with one of the company's steamers which shuttled between Dublin and Cork. The Dublin & Glasgow S & SP Co replied to this challenge by extending some of its sailings to Bristol and Cork. After a time reason prevailed and, by the late 1840s, both companies had given up poaching in one another's territory. Among the steamers employed in the Dublin–Glasgow service of the St George SP Co were those mentioned at the top of this paragraph; more information about some of these vessels is given in Chapter 6.

PS *Irishman*, PS *Lancefield*

These two vessels ran in opposition to the Dublin & Glasgow S & SP Co. The *Irishman* was employed on the Dublin–Glasgow crossing from 1854 to 1877. After this she went north and was renamed *Dunmurry*. In 1889 she went to Odessa. The *Lancefield*, which at one time had worked as a 'cut rate' steamer between Belfast and the Clyde (see Vol 1), made a few runs between Dublin and Glasgow in 1862.

Dublin–Isle of Man

Regular, summer-only, passenger services between Dublin and the Isle of Man began in the latter part of the nineteenth century. These have continued to the present day and have always been worked by the Isle of Man SP Co.

Dublin–Manchester

A passenger/cargo service operated between Dublin and Manchester (Pomona Dock) for a few years at the turn of the century. It was worked by the Dublin & Manchester SS Co, who employed the former Dublin–Glasgow steamer *Duke of Leinster* and the *Hare*, a vessel which at one time was owned by G. & J. Burns (see Vol 1). The service was mainly for cattle but a limited number of passengers were carried.

Dublin–Morecambe/Heysham

This service was operated by the Laird Line. It commenced in 1889 when there were three sailings a week in each direction. At the opening of Heysham harbour in 1904 the English terminal was moved to the new port and a daily service was begun. The steamers were advertised to sail from Dublin and Heysham at 7.30 pm and 9 pm respectively. The service was suspended during the 1914–18 war but was revived on a tri-weekly basis in 1919. In 1926 it was closed down.

The Laird practice, of switching steamers from one route to another, was followed so that most of the larger vessels of this company worked at some time in their careers on the crossing. The steamers, themselves, are described in Vol 1.

4: NORTH-EAST COAST OF LEINSTER

At the turn of the century the ports on the north-east coast of Leinster were busy. Passenger steamers plied regularly between Drogheda and Liverpool. At Dundalk the Dundalk & Newry SP Co maintained five sailings a week to Liverpool and at least one sailing a week to Ardrossan. At Newry the same company operated twice-weekly services to Liverpool and Ardrossan. At Greenore a London & North Western Railway cross-channel steamer sailed for Holyhead every weekday evening. The railway also kept a small paddle steamer on Carlingford Lough which plied between Greenore, Greencastle and Warrenpoint, and acted as a feeder to the company's cross-channel steamers. Further up the Lough small steamers ran between Rostrevor, Warrenpoint and Omeath (see Chapter 8). Today there are no passenger services other than the ferries between Warrenpoint and Omeath and no passenger cross-channel steamers now operated from either Drogheda, Dundalk, Newry or Greenore.

Drogheda–Ardrossan

In the late 1850s the Dublin & Liverpool Screw SP Co's steamers *Mail* and *Times* plied for a short time between Drogheda and Ardrossan via Dundalk. The service was advertised as run in connection with the Dundalk & Enniskillen and the Glasgow & South Western Railways.

Drogheda–Glasgow

A passenger service was operated by the Drogheda SP Co between Drogheda and Glasgow from September 1876 until the company was taken over by the Lancashire & Yorkshire Railway in 1902. At first a weekly service was operated in summer and a fortnightly one in winter but by the turn of the century the vessels sailed at infrequent intervals whenever occasion demanded.

Drogheda–Liverpool

In the late 1840s there was a daily service between Drogheda and

Liverpool. This was worked by the Drogheda SP Co, which was founded in 1826 and taken over by the Lancashire & Yorkshire Railway in September 1902. The service opened on 26 November 1826, when the paddle steamer *Town of Drogheda* sailed for Liverpool which was reached some fourteen hours later. For the next three years a weekly service was operated with the steamer sailing from Drogheda on Fridays and returning on Tuesdays. In 1829 the company chartered the *Liffey* and the *Mersey* from the City of Dublin SP Co and increased the number of sailings to three per week. Later in the same year it acquired the *Fair Trader* and returned the chartered steamers to their owners. Traffic continued to grow and by the late 1840s five sailings each week were required, and in 1849 a daily service was introduced. After a short time, however, the frequency of the sailings was reduced to five. There were four sailings a week in the late 1870s and this number of weekly sailings was maintained until after the takeover by the LYR. The railway put on new steamers; it provided free transport between Collingwood Dock and Exchange Station at Liverpool and maintained fares at about the same level as they had been since 1849—10s saloon and 4s deck—but passenger traffic continued to fall and, within a few years, only two weekly sailings were required. The passenger service was never revived after its suspension during the 1914–18 war but the cargo and cattle workings continued to be taken by railway steamers until the goodwill of the crossing was acquired by the British & Irish SP Co in 1928.

Drogheda is the only port of consequence on the east coast of Ireland which has no railway sidings on its quays. This is because of the considerable difference in level between the harbour and the Dublin–Belfast main line, which crosses the Boyne on a high viaduct immediately east of the town. The absence of rail facilities has meant that the greater part of the goods traffic passing through the port has generally been consigned to places in the immediate vicinity of the town. Before the advent of the motor lorry, traffic for places further afield had generally to be transported by horse-drawn carts to the railway, a process which involved double handling and considerable expense. Several attempts were made to overcome this handicap by making efforts to develop water-borne traffic on the Boyne, for the cross-channel steamers could be off-loaded direct into lighters and the latter towed to Navan and other places on the river. The carriage of livestock, however, was little affected by lack of railway facilities on the quays, for Drogheda is within 'cattle walking' distance of the fat grazing lands of Meath. The company encouraged this traffic by providing a reliable service at competitive rates and by giving free transport to drovers and others in charge of the animals.

During the mid-nineteenth century Drogheda was one of the ports through which thousands of Irishmen passed on their way to England and the New World. In the spring of 1849 the Drogheda–Liverpool steamers carried an average of 200 deck passengers per trip, a number which gave them third place in the Liverpool cross-channel trade. Dublin was first, with 670, and Cork second. The expansion of the Irish railway system killed the steerage passenger traffic of the port. The new mode of transport, which was centred on Dublin, enabled harvesters and emigrants to get conveniently and cheaply from their homes in the Midlands to join a steamer at the capital, whereas previously they had walked to Drogheda which had been their nearest port in the pre-railway era. Saloon traffic was never heavy and efforts made by the LYR to stimulate it met with little success.

The Drogheda SP Co never owned a screw steamer, yet it had a great reputation for being ahead of the times. It was the first company in the Irish trade to provide sleeping accommodation for ordinary steerage passengers. Its *Colleen Bawn* of 1862 was the first steamer on the Irish Sea to have a compound engine and its *Tredagh* (1876) was the first to have steam steering gear and steam cargo winches. Its *Kathleen Mavourneen* (1885) was the first steamer working from Liverpool to Ireland to have electric light. In contrast, its *Iverna* was the last paddle steamer to be built for the Irish cross-channel trade. The railway replaced the paddle steamers in 1903 by the twin-screw 17 knot vessels *Colleen Bawn* and *Mellifont*, but the arrival of the new vessels could not halt the decline of the cross-channel passenger trade through the port.

PS *Town of Drogheda*

On Monday 13 November 1826 the *Town of Drogheda* arrived at her home port having come over from the Clyde in twenty-seven hours. A glowing description of her was given in the *Drogheda Journal*, which contrasted the crimson and gold silk lace in the ladies' cabin with the blue cloth upholstery covering the berths reserved for gentlemen, and an account was given of the commodious holds which could take 100 cattle or 500 sheep! In the autumn of the next year she worked for a time between Cork and Bristol but returned to Drogheda where she was employed on the Liverpool crossing until 1846. She was then laid up and two years later was sold. After conversion to sail, she went to the Mediterranean where she foundered in May 1849, about a hundred miles east of Gibraltar.

PS *Fair Trader*, PS *Green Isle*, PS *Irishman*, PS *Grana Ueile*

All these four vessels came from the Clyde. The *Fair Trader* arrived in October 1829 and the other three in the mid-1830s. Like all Drogheda steamers they had commodious accommodation for cattle, which extended over two decks.

PS *Faugh-a-ballagh*, PS *Brian Boroimhe*, PS *St Patrick*, PS *Leinster Lass*

The *Faugh-a-ballagh* was the first iron steamer owned by the company. She arrived at Drogheda in February 1845. During her thirty years with the company she was often let out on charter. In 1853 she was chartered by the Midland Railway for its Morecambe–Belfast service and later in the same decade was stationed for a time at Derry.

The *Brian Boroimhe* and the *St Patrick* arrived in the summer of 1846. The former spent the greater part of her career at Drogheda, but the *St Patrick* was away for a time at the Crimean War, where she was employed as a troop ship by the French. Throughout her war service she received no damage either by storm or enemy action. Her master at the time was Captain Branigan, who afterwards became manager of the Drogheda SP Co.

The *Leinster Lass* gave her owners over thirty years of faithful service. Like the *Brian Boroimhe* she was built by Robert Napier at Port Glasgow and had the conventional two-cylinder side-lever engines of her day which were operated by steam at a pressure of 10psi.

PS *Colleen Bawn*

The *Colleen Bawn* was a graceful ship with a clipper bow and two funnels placed aft of her paddle boxes. On board she had such revolutionary features as an engine room telegraph, a wheel amidships and a compass which was repeated in the captain's cabin. She spent most of her career at Drogheda and was broken up in 1901.

PS *Tredagh*, PS *Nora Creina*, PS *Lord Athlumney*

The first two vessels, although not sisters, were very similar to one another. The *Tredagh* went into service in June 1876 and the *Nora Creina* followed two years later. The arrival of the *Tredagh* caused quite a stir, for she was the first cross-channel steamer working to Ireland to have steam steering gear, steam winches for cargo handling and a steam capstan for her anchor. She had also sleeping accommodation for steerage passengers, who were provided with a bar for those 'who liked to be afloat in the double sense of the word'. Her saloon accommodation was good, with berths for over fifty passengers. She was economical on fuel and needed only 25 tons of coal for a round trip. She spent her whole career at Drogheda and was broken up in 1904.

The career of the *Nora Creina* was very similar to that of her consort. She survived until 1912, when she was sent to France for breaking up. The *Lord Athlumney* had accommodation for over 500 cattle; she was wrecked in 1888.

PS *Kathleen Mavourneen*

The career of this vessel was short, for she entered the service in 1885 and was broken up in 1903. She was the first cross-channel steamer working to Ireland to have a steel hull and one of the first steamers in the British Isles to have electric light.

PS *Iverna*

The *Iverna* was one of the very few cross-channel steamers to be built with a diagonal triple-expansion engine. She was also the last paddle steamer to enter the Irish cross-channel trade. She was launched on 22 August 1895 by Mrs Archer, the wife of the secretary of the Drogheda SP Co. Like all other post-1870 Drogheda steamers she could carry about 500 cattle in well-ventilated cattle decks, but the feature which seems to have impressed the local newspapers was that she had a 'steam radiator' in her ladies' cabin!

TSS *Colleen Bawn*, TSS *Mellifont*

These 17 knot vessels were built for the LYR at Barrow in 1903. The *Colleen Bawn* went into service in August and the *Mellifont* followed later in the year. After the withdrawal of the passenger service the *Colleen Bawn* continued as a cattle boat on the Drogheda–Liverpool run until the British & Irish SP Co took over this trade in 1928. After this she was transferred to the Dublin–Holyhead cargo service on which she remained until her withdrawal for breaking up in 1931. The *Mellifont* was moved to her owner's Hull–Zeebrugge passenger/cargo service in 1906 and remained on this until 1912 when she returned to Drogheda to replace the *Iverna*. In 1928 she was transferred to the Greenore–Holyhead cargo trade, in which she remained until withdrawn in 1933.

Dundalk–Liverpool

Passengers were carried between Dundalk and Liverpool from September 1826 until the end of the 1914–18 war. At first the service was operated by the St George SP Co but, in the late summer of 1837, a local company, known as the Dundalk SP Co, began to run steamers and shortly afterwards the St George Company withdrew. The Dundalk–Liverpool service was mainly for livestock, a trade which reached its zenith about 1860 when some 120,000 cattle, sheep and pigs went by this route. In 1880 the number of livestock carried still exceeded 100,000 but by the turn of the century the trade was in a rapid decline, due mainly to competition from the Greenore–Holyhead steamers.

During the livestock boom in the mid-1850s there was considerable discontentment among cattle shippers who maintained that the rates charged by the Dundalk SP Co were exorbitant. Mr Peter Russell took advantage of this ill-will by forming the Dundalk & Midland SP Co in 1856. The new company, which was generally known as *Russells*, owned two steamers. These provided a twice-weekly service for cattle, cargo and passengers between Russell's Quay, Dundalk, and Collingwood Dock, Liverpool, whereas the Dundalk SP vessels ran three times a week from the Steam Packet Quay at Dundalk to the Clarence Dock at Liverpool. The new company tried by every means, fair and foul, to capture the livestock trade. It is claimed it hired ruffians to waylay cattle on their way to the Dundalk Co's steamers and then drive them on to its own vessels. The Dundalk Co retaliated by employing even tougher rogues. Local tradition maintains that the directors of the two companies once met when directing their respective 'cattle men' and that a board room rough house developed in which the weapons were fists and cows' tails. In the end the Dundalk SP Co won and bought out its rival in August 1858. A year previously the Dundalk Co had acquired a firm footing in the Newry–Liverpool and Newry–Glasgow trades by the purchase of the Ulster Canal Carrying Co. In 1862 it made overtures to the Drogheda SP Co for a takeover but this did not materialise. In 1871 it consolidated its position at Newry by amalgamating with the Newry SP Co, after which it changed its name to the Dundalk & Newry SP Co. The fortunes of the company were now at their peak for, after the opening of the Greenore–Holyhead route by the LNWR in 1873, a slow decline set in. The deterioration was accelerated by the partition of Ireland in 1921, and ended when the company was absorbed into the British & Irish SP Co on 28 October 1928.

When the Dundalk–Liverpool service opened in 1826 there were generally two sailings a week. This frequency was increased to three in the early 1830s. In the late 1850s and early 1860s five or six sailings were operated each week at busy times. After this the number of sailings settled down to four or five per week and remained at this until the 1914–18 war. The crossings were generally made overnight and the fares charged varied from 12s 6d to 18s saloon and from 2s to 3s steerage. During the competition between the Dundalk and Russell companies in 1856–8 the steerage fare came down to 6d.

There was always a close association between the Dundalk & Enniskillen Railway and the Dundalk SP Co. In the 1850s the Earl of Erne was chairman of both companies and many of the people living in Fermanagh and South Monaghan travelled via Dundalk when going to England. This patronage was little affected either by the absorption of the DER into the Great Northern Railway in 1878 or by the superior accommodation provided on the Greenore–Holyhead steamers. Nevertheless, passenger traffic was light for Fermanagh and Monaghan have always been thinly populated; on the other hand these counties have rich grazing lands for the cattle which, at one time, provided a regular supply of fat livestock for shipment through Dundalk.

A very complete, illustrated, account of all the steamers which have traded regularly from Dundalk has been written by Mr Allan B. Swan and published in the 1968 Edition of *Tempest's Dundalk Annual.*

PS *Cumberland*, PS *Solway*

These vessels worked in the 1830s between Dundalk and Liverpool. They were owned by the Carlisle & Liverpool SN Co and worked at times between Silloth and Dublin.

PS *Glasgow*

This was the first vessel acquired by the Dundalk SP Co after its incorporation on 17 July 1837. In mid-September of that year the *Glasgow* began to run twice weekly between Dundalk and Liverpool, thereby challenging the St George Company, who at that time were operating three sailings a week. The *Glasgow* was a wooden paddle steamer which had been built in 1828 for the Glasgow–Liverpool service of G. & J. Burns.

PS *Finn McCoull*

This was the first steamer built for the Dundalk SP Co. She was launched at Dumbarton in 1838 and during the next eight years worked regularly between Dundalk, Liverpool and Ardrossan. In August 1844 she made an unsuccessful, short-lived attempt to break into the Newry–

Liverpool trade. In 1845 she made a few trips for the Port Rush SN Co between Portrush and Liverpool. Early in the next year her boiler exploded. She survived and, in 1847, was involved in a collision with an American brig off Liverpool. This mishap she also survived but her end came in June 1848 when she was wrecked on the Tuskar Rock off the coast of Wexford (see page 129).

PS *Corsair*, PS *Dundalk*, PS *Pride of Erin*, PS *Emerald Isle*

The *Corsair* was built for the Belfast–Liverpool trade in 1827 (see Vol 1). She was employed by the Dundalk SP Co for several trips between Dundalk and Liverpool in 1837.

The other three vessels were acquired by the Dundalk SP Co in the 1840s.

PS *Earl of Erne*

This vessel is one of the immortals of the Irish Sea. She was built in 1855 and carried cargo and passengers between Ireland and Great Britain from 17 July 1855 until her sale to Piraeus owners in June 1918. She was then renamed *Sophia Inglessi* and worked in the Eastern Mediterranean where she was wrecked eight years later. In her last few years at Dundalk she was the sole surviving paddle steamer in the Irish cross-channel trade.

During her sixty years at Dundalk she made one attempt at salvage and was involved in three collisions. Her first was in 1869 when she collided with the schooner *Wye* off the Mersey Bar; in 1909 she ran into a trawler and in 1917 collided with the 3,000 ton steamer *Clan Macfadden*. At the time of her last mishap she and her victim were both running without lights owing to the suspected presence of U-boats.

The *Earl of Erne* had an iron hull 219ft long and a single funnel. When she first went into service she had a simple two-cylinder engine which was replaced by a compound one in 1888. She had berths for forty saloon passengers and was one of the first cross-channel steamers to have a dormitory for her steerage passengers. It is probable the latter was provided for cattle men, as she was principally a cattle boat. Nevertheless, in her youth she was capable of 14 knots and of getting from Dundalk to Liverpool in eleven hours. As she grew older she became an institution and was ultimately the subject of a poem by J. Bray which was reprinted in *Tempest's Dundalk Annual* of 1927. This described a race between the *Earl* and the Drogheda steamers *Nora Criena* and *Iverna*.

Down the Chief goes to the stokehold
And says, 'Boys let her go.
There are two Drogheda steamers by us
They won't pass us I know.
Nora Criena and *Iverna*
Think that by us they can walk,
But we'll show them they're just nowhere
With this old craft from Dundalk.'

PS *Independence*, PS *Enterprise*

These steamers were owned by the Dundalk & Midland SP Co. The *Independence* went into service in 1856 but was sold after only four years at Dundalk. The *Enterprise* remained in the Dundalk–Liverpool trade until her sale for breaking up in 1899. She was a good-looking vessel with sleek lines; her two funnels were placed one forward, and the other aft, of her paddle boxes.

PS *Emerald Isle*, SS *Amphion*, SS *Bessbrook*

The *Emerald Isle* was the last paddle steamer to be built for the Dundalk SP Co. She went into service in 1862 and remained with the company until sold for breaking up in 1898.

The *Amphion* was the first screw steamer owned by the Dundalk SP Co, who obtained her as a replacement for the *Mystery* in 1869. For the next twenty-three years her time was spent plying between Scotland, Newry and Dundalk. After this she was acquired by the Ayr SS Co who used her as a cargo steamer until her sale to French owners in 1895.

The *Bessbrook* had an active life of over fifty years, all of which was spent under the flag of the Dundalk & Newry SP Co. She was built in 1877 and was designed to make the crossing from Newry to Ardrossan in nineteen hours.

SS *Iveagh*

This was the first vessel built for the Dundalk & Newry SP Co to have a steel hull and triple-expansion engines. She went into service in 1892 and survived to join the British & Irish SP Co's fleet in 1930.

The *Iveagh* had accommodation for seventy saloon passengers, who enjoyed the amenities of a dining saloon panelled in oak and polished teak. She also carried 300 steerage passengers and had accommodation 'of a most comfortable kind' for cattle drovers, which was quite separate from that provided for livestock.

Page 71 (above): The quays at Drogheda. The photograph was taken from the railway viaduct at the turn of the century and shows PS *Kathleen Mavourneen* and two other paddle steamers of the Drogheda SP Co

(below): TSS *Mellifont*

Page 72 (above): SS *Argo* in the Avon Gorge; SS *Reginald* is in the background
(below): TSS *Great Western* (1933) at Waterford, 1956

TSS *Dundalk*

The whole career of this vessel was spent with the Dundalk & Newry SP Co. She went into service in 1899 and had the distinction of being the only twin-screw steamer to be built for the company. In December 1917 she had a running fight with a U-boat in which she used her speed, power of manoeuvre and single gun to such good effect that she escaped. Ten months later, however, she was torpedoed, and sank with the loss of her master, Capt O'Neill, and several of her crew. She met her fate on 14 October 1918 and was the last cross-channel steamer to be sunk in the Irish Sea in the 1914–18 war.

Newry–Liverpool

The passenger service between Newry and Liverpool opened in 1823 and continued until the 1914–18 war. Throughout this period the number of sailings varied between two and four per week, and the fares were generally of the order of 10s to 15s saloon, and 2s to 3s steerage. In 1850 and again in 1870, during bouts of sharp and bitter competition, saloon fares came down to 5s and steerage to 1s; indeed in the late summer of 1850 the steerage fare on the *Hercules* was reduced to 6d. At first the steamers sailed from Warrenpoint as it was difficult at that time to get up the river to Newry. The rebuilding of the ship canal, which culminated in the opening of the Victoria Lock at Fathom in April 1850, made the passage to Newry comparatively easy. Nevertheless, for several decades after the opening of the lock, many of the cross-channel steamers continued to use Warrenpoint as their Irish terminal.

The Newry–Liverpool passenger trade may be divided into four phases. The first was in the summers of 1823 and 1824 when Langtry's steamers, *Waterloo* and *Belfast*, had an absolute monopoly. In the second phase, which lasted from 1825 to about 1845, the War Office SP Co and its successor, the St George SP Co, dominated the route. The third was an age of transition. When it began there was only one steamer on the crossing. This was the *Hercules*, a vessel which was ultimately acquired by the Ulster Canal Carrying Co in 1851. In 1857 the Carrying Co was taken over by the Dundalk SP Co, a transaction which gave the latter three additional cross-channel steamers, four canal tugs, fifty lighters and a lease of the Ulster Canal. Throughout the fourth, or final phase which lasted from 1871 until the 1914–18 war the Dundalk & Newry SP Co enjoyed a monopoly of the Newry–Liverpool passenger trade.

Over the years 1826–68 the established companies were continually challenged by 'outsiders'. In 1826 the *George IV*, a steamer owned by the Liverpool & Newry SP Co, challenged the War Office SP Co's *St David*. The *St David* responded immediately by withdrawing to Dundalk and thereby becoming the first steamer to work regularly between that port and Liverpool. After a few months she returned to the Newry–Liverpool run. Other challengers in the first half of the century included the *Henry Bell* (1826–37), *Londonderry* (1826), *Eclipse* (1833), *Fingal* (1834), *City of Carlisle* (1837), *Victoria* (1838–40), *Antelope* (1840), *Iron Prince* (1849) and the Dundalk SP Co. The latter sent one of its steamers to work on this route in 1844. In the latter half of the century the only interlopers were the *Fairy Queen* (1868), *Newry* (1869–71) and *Garland* (1880). The first two of these belonged to the Newry SP Co, who joined forces with the Dundalk SP Co in 1871 to form the Dundalk & Newry SP Co. The *Garland* was a freelance steamer owned by the Warrenpoint SP Co. She was originally built for the Laird Line (see Vol 1). In the summer of 1880 she made a few trips between Warrenpoint and Clarence Dock, Liverpool.

PS *Waterloo*, PS *Belfast*

These two steamers were owned by George Langtry of Belfast. They 'specialised' in opening cross-channel routes to Ireland. In 1819 the *Waterloo* opened the Belfast–Liverpool service, a crossing on which she was joined by the *Belfast* shortly afterwards. In 1820 she opened the Dublin–Liverpool route and after a short time again had the *Belfast* as a consort. A year or so later she spent a few months in the Derry–Glasgow trade. She came to Newry in April 1823 and on the twenty-ninth of that month sailed from Warrenpoint for Liverpool. For the next six months she maintained a weekly service between the ports after which she was withdrawn for the winter. On her return in the following spring she was joined by the *Belfast*. Both vessels left Newry in the autumn of 1824.

When engaged on the Newry–Liverpool run the *Waterloo* had the dubious distinction of charging the highest fares ever imposed on passengers to the province of Ulster in the nineteenth century. In 1823 her first cabin single fare was 31s 6d, second cabin 15s and deck was 5s. Those who brought their carriage with them had to pay 84s for its transport, plus a 'slinging charge' of 10s 6d.

PS *St David*

This steamer spent sixteen years working from Newry and Dundalk.

She arrived at Newry early in May 1825 when she was described as 'fitted in an elegant style for the accommodation of passengers . . . and with good stabling for horses'. Deck passengers did not fare so well, for on a bad night in March 1839 three of the 150 'deckers' on board died from exposure.

On the arrival of the *George IV* in the late summer of 1826 the *St David* was immediately transferred to Dundalk, from whence she made her first sailing to Liverpool on 4 September. After a few months she returned to Newry where she remained until the early 1840s.

PS *George IV*, PS *Henry Bell*

The *George IV* sailed from Warrenpoint at 6 pm on Sunday 10 September 1826 on her first crossing to Liverpool. She remained at Newry for eleven years. In her early days she ran against the steamers of the War Office and St George SP Cos, and later in her career competed with the *Henry Bell* for the Liverpool traffic. Finally, her owners—Liverpool & Newry SN Co—came to an agreement with the owners of the *Henry Bell* whereby *George IV* took the Wednesday sailings from Warrenpoint and the *Henry Bell* sailed on Saturdays.

The *George IV* had good passenger accommodation with a 'spacious dining cabin detached from the sleeping quarters'. The latter included a 'cabin near the centre for ladies and a large stateroom for the convenience of private families and invalids'.

The *Henry Bell* first came to Newry in 1829 when she was six years old. After a few weeks she was sent to Scotland. In 1831 she was sold to James Little & Co who sent her back to Newry where she remained until 1837.

PS *Lord Blayney*

This vessel is the ghost ship of Carlingford Lough. She was owned by the St George SP Co and had spent some time on charter to Portuguese owners before coming to Newry. She sailed from the Lough for the last time on Wednesday 18 December 1833, and next day was wrecked near Prestatyn when all on board were drowned. Since this time she has made several appearances at Carlingford, all of which have taken place immediately before the loss of a local ship. She was seen before the wreck of the schooner *Robert Burns*, and before the sinking of the cross-channel steamer *Connemara* in 1916. On the latter occasion the relatives of the sole survivor saw the 'ghost ship' on the afternoon of the disaster.

In her earthly days the *Lord Blayney* was a wooden paddle steamer of about 200 registered tons.

PS *Eclipse*, PS *Fingal*, PS *Antelope*, PS *Victoria*

These vessels worked between Newry and Liverpool in the period 1830–40. The *Victoria* ran on a circular route on which she made calls at Belfast, Ardglass, Newry and Liverpool. The other three vessels had all worked between Belfast and Glasgow before coming to Newry (see Vol 1).

PS *Hercules*

The *Hercules* was built for the St George SP Co in 1835. Six years later she began to ply three times a week between Newry and the Clarence Dock at Liverpool. At first she ran in competition with the *Devonshire*, *Magnet* and *Shamrock*, but by 1846 all the opposition had retired and the *Hercules* had a monopoly of the passenger trade. In July 1850 the Ulster Canal Carrying Co, which had begun to carry passengers in the late 1840s, made a serious bid for a larger share of the passenger trade by introducing the free transfer of baggage between the railway station and its steamers at Warrenpoint. The *Hercules* replied by reducing fares from 10s and 2s 6d to 5s and 6d; the Carrying Co's *Sea Nymph* replied by charging 5s and 1s. The fare war continued until March 1851 when the Carrying Co took over the *Hercules* and at the same time restored passenger fares to their 'prewar' level. The *Hercules* was sold to the LNWR in the mid-1850s, after which she was employed on the Dublin–Holyhead service.

St George SP Co, War Office SP Co

The following steamers of these two companies ran on a twice-weekly service between Newry and Liverpool from 1825 until 1843—*Britannia, Erin, Hercules, Lee, Liffey, Lord Blayney, St David, St George, Severn, William IV* and *William Huskisson*. The same owners also operated regular services between Dundalk and Liverpool from 1826 to 1837. At first its steamers ran twice a week but in 1832 the frequency was increased to three. The vessels working on the route included the *Earl of Roden*, *Erin*, *Magdalena* and *William IV*.

The *Hercules*, *Lord Blayney* and *St David* are described in this chapter. Accounts of some of the other vessels and the dimensions of the St George steamers are given in Chapter 6 and its associated fleet list.

PS *Devonshire*, PS *Magnet*, PS *Shamrock*

These vessels were at Newry in the early 1840s from where they maintained a thrice-weekly service to Liverpool.

PS *Sea Nymph*, PS *Eagle*, PS *Mail*, PS *Pearl*, PS *Despatch*

These vessels worked for the Ulster Canal Carrying Co at different times between 1846 and 1857. The *Sea Nymph*'s career began in the Derry cross-channel trade in 1845 (see Vol 1); it ended on the railway service from Holyhead to Ireland (see Chapter 1). In 1857 the *Despatch*, *Eagle* and *Mail* were transferred to the Dundalk SP Co, who kept the former on her old routine of two sailings a week between Newry and Liverpool until her sale in 1863. The *Mail*, which at one time worked between Dublin and Liverpool, was lost after going aground near Dundalk in 1859. Details of the Ulster Canal Carrying Co are given in Vol 1.

SS *Mystery*

In 1857 the Newry, Glasgow & Preston Steamship Company announced that its steamer *Mystery* would commence a service between Newry, Glasgow and Preston. In 1859 she came into the hands of the Dundalk SP Co who retained her on the Newry–Glasgow run. She was engaged on this when she ran aground and became a total wreck in 1868.

PS *Fairy Queen*, SS *Newry*

The *Fairy Queen* was the first vessel operated by the Newry SP Co. She was chartered in the summer of 1868 and worked between Newry and Liverpool until replaced by the *Newry*.

The *Newry* began her career in 1866 as the *Earl of Belfast*, when she was employed on the Belfast–Ardrossan crossing. Early in 1869 she was acquired by the Newry SP Co and arrived at Victoria Lock, Fathom, in the evening of 25 March 1869. She received a great welcome for not only was the Newry SP Co a locally owned company but, at the time, the inhabitants of Newry were somewhat disgruntled at the poor service given them by the Dundalk SP Co. The latter had such a strong hold on the Newry–Liverpool trade that its steamers did not bother to go up the river beyond Warrenpoint. The *Newry Commercial Telegraph* was lyrical in its praise of the new steamer and emphasised that her master, chief engineer and mates were all teetotallers. For the next two years the *Newry* maintained a twice-weekly service between Newry (Albert Dock) and Bromley Dock, Liverpool. On the outward journey passengers were permitted to join the steamer at Victoria Lock, if they so desired, and to land at Warrenpoint on the homeward run. The fares were 5s cabin and 1s steerage, compared with the 10s and

3s charged on the Dundalk Company's vessels. In 1871 the Dundalk and Newry Companies amalgamated to form the Dundalk & Newry SP Co and the *Newry* became the property of the new company with whom she remained until 1911.

Newry, Dundalk and Scotland

Sailings between Newry and Glasgow began late in 1829. They were taken by the Derry–Glasgow steamer *Britannia*, but after a few crossings she was withdrawn. After this, sailings between Newry, Dundalk and Scotland continued to be intermittent for the next thirty years. In this period four different Glasgow-owned steamers—*Eclipse* (1833), *Londonderry* (1836), *Rover* (1837) and *Antelope* (1840)—were tried, but none of them remained for more than a few months on the crossing. In 1857 the Newry, Glasgow & Preston SS Co used its steamer *Mystery* to start a weekly service between Newry and Ardrossan. This time the effort was successful and in due course, the *Mystery* was acquired by the Dundalk SP Company who kept her at work between Dundalk, Newry and Scotland until her wreck in 1868. After this the route was worked by the *Amphion* and later by other steamers of the Dundalk & Newry SP Co until the passenger service closed down in the early 1900s. Just before the close down, two sailings a week were operated and some of the vessels proceeded from Newry to Ardrossan via Dundalk. Passenger traffic was generally light except during Glasgow Fair Week. The fares charged were of the same order as those between Newry and Liverpool and through rail and steamer tickets were available between Newry and Glasgow.

Newry–Preston

This service was operated for a short time by the Newry, Glasgow & Preston SP Co in 1857–8, who used the steamer *Mystery* for the crossing.

Newry–Swansea

In 1870 a steamer named *Elaine* was advertised as maintaining a weekly service between Newry and Swansea, with a call at Whitehaven on the way. The time for the passage was not stated but the single fares were given as 12s 6d and 5s.

Greenore/Warrenpoint–Isle of Man

From 1877 to 1884 the Isle of Man SP Co ran a weekly service between Greenore and Douglas during the summer. This working had the support of the LNWR who issued circular tickets which covered the journey from any station on their system to Greenore via Holyhead and return on the IOMSP steamers via Douglas and Liverpool. Passengers holding circular tour tickets were given free transport on the railway paddle steamer, which at that time ran between Greenore and Warrenpoint.

The same company also ran a similar service between Warrenpoint and Douglas in the summers of 1878 and 1879.

Warrenpoint–Holyhead

The London & North Western Railway operated a twice-weekly service between Warrenpoint and Holyhead in August and September 1873. It was probably run as a sop to the inhabitants of Newry, who at that time were somewhat indignant at the delay in the building of the railway between Newry and Greenore, and the inconvenience of having to go by local steamer from Warrenpoint to reach the Holyhead cross-channel steamer at Greenore.

5: SOUTH-EAST IRELAND

New Ross–Bristol/Liverpool

In March 1832 the St George SP Co began a service between New Ross, Bristol and Liverpool. Its *William IV* was advertised to sail from New Ross for Liverpool on one Friday and on the next Friday to go to Bristol. In May the company's *William Huskisson* was employed and the Bristol SN Co's *City of Bristol* also started on the New Ross–Bristol/Liverpool run. Both vessels were withdrawn during the summer. The service was revived in the winter of 1878–9, when the *Earnholm* operated a weekly service for a short time. The *Earnholm* had previously been stationed at Limerick.

Rosslare–Fishguard

This is the shortest sea route to the Republic of Ireland. It is worked by the Fishguard & Rosslare Harbours & Railways Co, an organisation which was acquired by the Great Western and Great Southern & Western Railway at the turn of the century. The building of the harbours at both terminals involved some very heavy engineering work. At Fishguard over a million tons of rock had to be blasted from the cliffs to make a clearing for the quays and railway station, and to provide material for building the breakwater which is half a mile long. At Rosslare a jetty over 1,000ft in length was built out into the sea and this was connected to the mainland by a bridge which carried two railway tracks but no road for vehicles. This meant that motorists shipping their cars had to put them on to railway flats for the quarter-mile journey from the quayside to an unloading dock on the shore. In 1965 one of the railway tracks was replaced by a roadway so today motorists can drive their cars from the ship to any part of Ireland.

The Rosslare–Fishguard route was intended to provide a more convenient service to the south of Ireland than that given via Holyhead. Fishguard itself is 261¼ miles by rail from Paddington, whereas Holyhead is 263¾ miles from Euston; furthermore, the crossing from Fishguard is only 54 nautical miles compared with the 58 nautical miles between Holyhead and Dun Laoghaire. At the opening of the route in 1906 all the 'best' transatlantic liners called at Cobh which was three hours closer to London via Fishguard than by any other route. This was at a time when the Cunard and White Star Liners had their home port at Liverpool, so, when the White Star vessels began to call at Holyhead to save a few hours in getting the mail more quickly from New York to London, the Cunard replied by calling at Fishguard. The first Cunarder to stop was the *Mauretania* which anchored off Fishguard breakwater at 1.15 pm on 30 August 1909, a call which enabled her American mail to reach Paddington at 6.40 pm on the same evening. So successful was the experiment that within a short period the Cunard liners substituted the Fishguard call for that made at Cobh, a practice they continued until the 1914–18 war. Steamers of the Booth and Blue Funnel Lines also called at Fishguard in the years before World War I.

When the service opened there were two sailings each day. The steamers left Fishguard at 2.15 am, and at the same time in the afternoon; on the return journey they sailed from Rosslare at 12.30 pm and 11.45 pm. The time allowed for the crossing was 2hr 45min. The connecting trains from Paddington did the journey in about five hours. On the Irish side the GSWR ran morning and evening boat trains to Cork via Waterford and Mallow which took about four hours for the 135 miles. Special rolling stock was built for these trains, which were the first standard gauge expresses in Ireland to carry first- and third-class passengers only. Hitherto, practically all standard gauge trains in the country had carried three classes of passenger, the principal exception being the limited mails many of which had no third-class accommodation.

In the inter-war years there was only one sailing a day throughout the year. This was made by the night boat which left Fishguard at 2.15 am having waited for the 7.55 pm train from Paddington. On the way back the steamer sailed from Rosslare at about 11.30 pm, having taken on board those who had travelled by the 6.30 pm boat train from Cork. A boat train also came from Dublin—this left Harcourt Street station at 6.30 pm and called at Bray, Wicklow and Wexford en route. The service was suspended in January 1942 and was resumed in 1946 when the same general pattern of sailings were followed in summer, but in winter the steamers ran only three times a week. The crossing was badly patronised and in the 1950s there were persistent rumours of probable closure. In the summer of 1961 an experimental daylight service was worked for a few months, which was intended for motorists as no trains ran in connection with the sailings. The venture was successful and in subsequent years a daylight service was worked at peak periods in summer. The *St David* was modified to become a side-loading car carrier and in 1965 the summer timetable was recast to meet the needs of motorists. There were now three sailings a day, two of these were taken by the *St David* and the third by the *St Andrew*, on to which passengers' cars had to be loaded by crane. In 1967 the *St Andrew* was replaced by the *Duke of Rothesay* which had been converted to a side-loading car carrier in the previous winter.

Today the Rosslare–Fishguard route is flourishing. Car-carrier trains run from London in connection with the sailings. At both ports everything is geared to get passengers and their cars on and off the steamers and through the customs with a minimum of fuss, so that in high summer it is possible for the vessels to turn round in under two hours. In winter the crossing is slack, the steamers sail on alternate nights and there are no car-carrier trains in service.

TrSS *St David/Rosslare*, TrSS *St Patrick*, TrSS *St George*

These vessels were specially built for the service. At the beginning of their careers in 1906 they were the largest railway-owned steamers employed in the Irish cross-channel trade, with a length of 350ft, a beam of 41ft and a gross tonnage of 2,500 tons. They had direct drive turbines which gave them a speed of 23 knots at their trials and enabled them to do the crossing in the scheduled time of 2hr 45min. In May 1913 the *St George* was sold to the Canadian Pacific Railway who disposed of her to the Great Eastern Railway in 1919; after this she worked between Harwich and the continent until her sale to the shipbreakers in 1929. The *St David* (renamed *Rosslare* in 1932) was sold for breaking up in 1933. The *St Patrick* was badly damaged by fire in 1929, after which she was sold for scrapping.

Accommodation on board was designed for day and night crossings. The first-class smoke room and lounge were on the shelter deck. The latter was a large room 50ft long and 21ft wide with a well in its centre to admit additional light to the dining saloon which was immediately below on the main deck. All the forty-seven first-class cabins had port holes. Steerage passengers had thirty-six berths at their disposal. Cargo facilities included electric winches and a refrigerated hold. An illustrated article and cabin plans of the *St David* and *St Patrick* were published in *Engineering*, Vol 82 (July 1906).

TrSS *St Andrew/Fishguard*

This steamer was built in 1908. She is virtually a sister ship of the 1906 trio. During the 1914–18 war she was a hospital ship, otherwise her entire working life was spent at Fishguard. She was sold for scrapping in 1933. It is interesting to note that the cross-channel steamers built in the early 1900s for the north of Ireland services had some single-berth cabins but the four Fishguard vessels had only two- and four-berth rooms. On the other hand, passengers desiring the exclusive use of a cabin on the Fishguard steamers could get one by paying a comparatively small supplement.

TSS *St Patrick*, TSS *St Andrew*, TSS *St David*

These vessels came into service in the early 1930s. The *St Patrick* was sunk by enemy action in June 1941 when engaged on a normal Rosslare–Fishguard crossing. Although she was owned by the FRHR she spent a great part of her time on the Weymouth–Channel Islands service of the GWR.

The *St Andrew* and *St David* were well-proportioned vessels. They had single-reduction geared turbines which gave them a speed of 21 knots. Their passenger accommodation was good; their first-class single cabins were the largest and best furnished single rooms ever provided on the crossing to Ireland. The *St David* was lost off Anzio in January 1944 when employed as a hospital ship; the *St Andrew* was also a hospital ship but she survived to return to Fishguard for the reopening of the service in 1946. She was scrapped in 1967. Both vessels could roll, a habit which did not endear them to bad sailors who had to cross St George's Channel in winter.

TSS *St Patrick*, TSS *St David*

These vessels were built by Cammell Laird in 1947. After a short time the *St Patrick* was transferred to the Weymouth–Channel Islands service. In 1959 she was taken over by the British Transport Commission, who moved her to the Straits of Dover in 1965. The *St David* spent over twenty years at Fishguard and was transferred to Holyhead at the end of the 1969 season. Five years previously she had been converted to a side-loading car-ferry after which she was booked to make two round trips every twenty-four hours between Rosslare and Fishguard during the holiday season. In winter she was often the only steamer stationed at Fishguard, for the winter service of three round trips each week can be maintained by one vessel.

The arrival of these two steamers at Fishguard during the post-war austerity was like a return to Eden for cross-channel passengers. The staff were attentive, the vessels new, the paintwork fresh and the bed linen wholesome. Furthermore, there was no rationing in the Republic so there was food in plenty on board. Regulars always went straight to the dining saloon for a supper which consisted of thick Limerick ham, fresh fried eggs, Irish bread and real butter; it was no wonder that an hour later many were somewhat puzzled to find they felt distinctly unwell even though the sea was calm!

TSS *Duke of Rothesay*, TSS *Caledonian Princess*

The Belfast–Heysham steamer *Duke of Rothesay* came to Fishguard in 1967. Previous to her transfer she was given an extensive refit which included removing all her cabins from D deck and converting this deck into a garage which could be entered through doors on the side of her hull. Like her consort—*St David*—she is allowed 3hr 15min for the crossing. The *Duke of Rothesay* does not spend all her time at Fishguard, for each winter she returns to Heysham to relieve the other *Dukes* when they are away for their annual surveys.

The Larne–Stranraer car-ferry *Caledonian Princess* was stationed at Fishguard during the summers of 1969 and 1970.

Rosslare–Le Havre

A weekly, summer only, car-ferry service between Rosslare and Le Havre began in June 1968. The crossings are taken by the *Leopard*. The vessel is owned by the French company SAGA who operate it in association with Irish Shipping Ltd. The crossing takes about twenty-two hours. The service was due to have commenced on 18 May 1968 but was delayed for a month by strikes in France. Nevertheless, an attempt was made to fill the gap by arranging that the same company's *Dragon* would call at Rosslare on her trips between Southampton and Lisbon. The route has proved to be so popular that bi-weekly sailings have become necessary at peak periods.

Waterford–Aberdovey

A twice-weekly service for passengers, livestock and goods ran between Waterford and Aberdovey in 1887 and 1888. The first sailing from Waterford was made by the *Liverpool* on 19 April of the former year. After six months the *Liverpool* was replaced by the former Belfast SS Co's vessel *Magnetic*; this steamer is described in Vol 1.

The service was sponsored by the Cambrian Railway and worked by the Waterford & Aberdovey SS Co. It was run mainly for cattle and the notices advertising it pointed out that the 'cattle space on the

Magnetic is illuminated with electric light' and that on arrival at Aberdovey all beasts would be let into a field near the Cambrian Railway terminus where they could be rested after their journey. The notices advertising the crossing were headed 'SHORTEST AND MOST EXPEDITIOUS ROUTE to the Midland Counties and other parts of England'. The saloon fare was 10s, and for 5s one could either travel steerage in the *Liverpool* or second cabin in the *Magnetic*.

Waterford–Bristol/Liverpool

Steamers plied with passengers, goods and cattle between Waterford and Bristol from 1823 until the mid-1930s. In the early days the majority of the steamers were owned by the predecessors of either the Bristol SN Co or the Waterford SS Co but the two groups of proprietors were generally on such good terms that the service was virtually a joint one. After the withdrawal of the Bristol SN Co, in the mid-1870s, the Waterford SS Co continued to operate the service until the vessels and good will of the service passed to the Clyde Shipping Co in July 1912. The new owners continued to operate the route until its close down in the 1930s.

When the service first opened there was only one sailing a week but in the early 1830s this was increased to two, a frequency which was maintained until the turn of the century. At the latter time the vessels generally took about fifteen hours to get from one port to the other and they did not sail at a fixed time as they had to wait for a suitable tide to get down the river from Bristol. This was not too inconvenient, for if the steamer were due to sail before the arrival of the morning train from London, through passengers were permitted to spend the previous night on board. The single fares in the years preceding the 1914–18 war were 15s and 7s 6d. Through fares from Waterford to London cost 34s 9d and 17s 4d compared with 48s and 21s charged on the GWR steamers via New Milford.

The War Office SP (later Bristol SN Co) steamers, which ran between Waterford and Bristol, were also employed at times on the company's Dublin–Bristol and Cork–Bristol services. Indeed, almost all the vessels mentioned in the Fleet List of this company, on pages 190–1, visited Waterford at some time in their careers.

The Waterford SS Co was founded as the Waterford & Bristol SN Co in 1826 and acquired its first steamer—*Nora Creina*—late in that year. In 1836 the company was reorganised and registered as the Waterford Commercial SN Co, a title which gradually grew shorter as time went on until it became known as the Waterford SS Co. It was at its zenith in the years 1835–60. At the beginning of this period it was expanding rapidly and sent its steamer *Mermaid* to run for a short time as a 'pirate' between Dublin and Liverpool, the stronghold of the City of Dublin SP Co. Retaliation took the form of the arrival of the *Gipsy* and *St Patrick* at Waterford to work between Waterford and Bristol but within a short time this unwelcome competition ceased—the Waterford SS Co had purchased the two vessels! In 1850 the Waterford SS Co was involved in a bitter trade war with the British & Irish SP Co, the City of Dublin SP Co, the Cork Shipping Co and George Langtry of Belfast. All five rivals competed against one another whenever possible and their activities reached a climax when the Waterford SS put on a steamer to run between Belfast and Liverpool and George Langtry had a steamer working to Cork. In the end all parties came to terms. The Waterford SS Co continued to expand, so that by the early 1860s its cross-channel steamers were working from Waterford to Bristol, Liverpool and London, its deep-sea vessels engaged in foreign trade and its fleets of small paddle steamers plied on the Shannon and Suir Estuaries. The man behind the company was William Malcolmson who, at the time, was chairman of the Waterford & Limerick Railway and proprietor of the Neptune Iron Works at Waterford, a company which was engaged in iron foundry work and shipbuilding. Sixty years later the Neptune Iron Works had closed, the Waterford & Limerick Railway had been absorbed by the Great Southern & Western and the Waterford SS Co had been taken over by the Clyde Shipping Co.

The Clyde Shipping Co carried on the service between Waterford and Bristol but by now trade had declined and one sailing each week was sufficient for the traffic. The carrying of passengers was suspended during the 1914–18 war and revived on a limited scale in the 1920s. After this, passengers continued to be carried until the steamers were withdrawn during the trade depression and the penal British taxes on Irish cattle, which occurred simultaneously in the early 1930s.

Passengers could travel by steamer between Waterford and Liverpool from 1826 to 1957. For the greater part of this time the crossing was worked by the Waterford SS Co who disposed of the good will of the route to the Clyde Shipping Co in 1912. The latter continued to work the service until the sale of its last coastal steamer—the *Tuskar*—in 1968. Passenger carrying, however, had been suspended eleven years earlier. In the days before the 1914–18 war there were two sailings each week and toward the end of the nineteenth century there were often three sailings a week in summer; the fares in those days were 21s saloon and 7s 6d deck.

In the years after the famine of 1847, many of those evicted from their homes in East Cork, Kilkenny, Waterford and Carlow, made their way to England on the Waterford steamers. On one particular evening in August 1848 over 1,200 people left Waterford by ship and figures published in the Denham Report reveal that in April 1849 each steamer from Waterford arrived in Liverpool with 200 deck passengers on board. Many of these had received no food and had obtained little shelter throughout the whole of the thirty-hour crossing. In the preceding twelve months 300,000 'deckers' had passed through Liverpool from all parts of Ireland, about half of these went on to America and a third were 'paupers' who were described to be 'people in a starving condition, begging alms . . . asking their way to the relieving officer'.

There was a very close relationship between the Waterford–Bristol and Waterford–Liverpool services. Steamers were often moved from one to the other and on occasions even vessels belonging to the War Office SP Co of Bristol worked between Waterford and Liverpool.

PS *Duke of Lancaster*

On 11 September 1823, the *Duke of Lancaster* added to her number of firsts by being the first steamer to cross from Bristol to Waterford. She was a year old at the time and had already worked between Liverpool and the river Dee, Cork and Bristol, Dublin and Bristol, and had been the first steamer to run from Bristol to Chepstow (September 1822) and had opened the Bristol–Ilfracombe steamer service in March 1823. She was laid up immediately after her Waterford episode and did not resume active service until her acquisition by the Campbeltown & Glasgow SP Co in 1826.

The arrival of the *Duke of Lancaster* at Waterford was the event of the year. The *Waterford Mirror* commented very favourably upon her and observed that 'passengers and horses are provided with a degree of attention which would do credit to a first rate restaurateur'.

PS *St Patrick*, PS *Severn*

The Waterford–Liverpool service was opened by the *St Patrick* in 1826. She arrived at Waterford in mid-November, and was given a great send off, complete with military band on the quay, when she set off on her return journey. In December she was joined by the *Severn*, a vessel which normally worked between Bristol and Cork. The *St Pat-*

rick was built in 1825 and her career ended in 1831 when she was wrecked at the mouth of the Suir during a fog.

PS *Nora Creina*, PS *Water Witch*

The *Nora Creina* was the first steamer owned by the Waterford & Bristol SN Co. She was built in 1826 and went into service in December of that year. Her whole career was spent at Waterford.

The *Water Witch* was a wooden paddler. Like her consort she was built at Birkenhead but her career was short. She went into service in 1833 and in December of the same year was wrecked during a gale on a reef near Ballyhole on the Wexford coast.

PS *City of Waterford*

This Bristol-owned steamer spent her early career working between Waterford and Bristol. In May 1833, when she was four years old, she was chartered as a troop carrier for the Royalist forces in the Portuguese Civil War. She got to Oporto safely but later in the year ran ashore and became a total loss.

PS *St Patrick*, PS *Gipsy*

In February 1834 the *Waterford Mirror* reported that a steamer named *St Patrick* had come to the Suir to run against the *Nora Creina* and *City of Waterford* in the Bristol trade. After a few runs the steamer seems to have been taken off but she came back again a year or so later accompanied by the *Gipsy*, a wooden paddle steamer which had been built in Liverpool in 1828. In 1836 both vessels were advertised as providing a bi-weekly service between Waterford and Liverpool. The *St Patrick*, which was built in 1832, was wrecked near the mouth of the Suir in December, 1838, close to the place where her namesake was lost in 1831. In the late 1830s the two vessels became the property of the Waterford Commercial SN Co.

SS *Mars*

The *Mars* was unfortunate. She was built at Waterford in 1849 but when she went into service it was found she had a most alarming list. The list was remedied but local cattle shippers at first fought shy of her, for in those days it was believed that screw steamers were not sufficiently steady in a rough sea for cattle. On 31 March 1862, she set off on her last crossing from Waterford with fifty passengers on board as well as 178 head of cattle, over 300 pigs and 10 horses. Early next day she ran aground on Linney Head in Pembrokeshire. At the time she struck,

Page 89 (above): TrSS *St Patrick* and TSS *Great Southern* at Rosslare shortly after the opening of the harbour in 1906
(below): TSS *St Andrew* (1932) arriving at Belfast in 1956 on a special crossing from Fishguard to take home Territorials from their annual camp in Wales

Page 90
(above): SS *Innisfallen* (1896) in the River Avon
(left): TSMV *Innisfallen* (1948) leaving Cork
(below): TSMV *Innisfallen* (1969) arriving at Swansea, 1969

visibility was bad and a gale was blowing, yet she was driving along with all but one of her sails set. There were only four survivors, one of whom was a small boy who had climbed into a lifeboat during the crossing to keep warm. He subsequently fell asleep and awakened to find himself alone in the boat, which had floated away from the sinking steamer.

SS *Gipsy*, SS *Zephyr*, SS *Lara*

These steamers were built at Waterford over the years 1859–69. The *Gipsy* and *Zephyr* were virtually sister ships with straight stems, three masts and a single funnel placed between the main and mizen masts. The *Gipsy* went aground on the Avon in May 1878, she ultimately broke her back and became a total loss. The *Zephyr* foundered in the Bristol Channel in September 1889, but the *Lara* gave her owners, the Waterford SS Co, forty years of useful and comparatively uneventful service before her sale for breaking up in 1908.

PS *Camilla*, PS *Clonmel*, SS *Comeragh*, SS *Kincora*, PS *Mermaid*, PS *Nora*, PS *Victory*, PS *William Penn*

These vessels worked for the Waterford SS Co in the nineteenth century; their dimensions and dates of building are given in the Fleet List on pages 198–9.

The *Victory* was built in 1832 and after fourteen years' service, most of which she spent on the Bristol–Cork run, came to Waterford. She was lost off the Wexford Coast when on her way from Liverpool to Waterford in September 1853.

The *Mermaid* went into service in 1835 and in the next year baited the City of Dublin SP Co by running for a few months between Dublin and Liverpool. After this she returned to Waterford, where she spent her time working to Bristol with the occasional trip to Liverpool. When on one of the latter runs she was lost after going aground on the West Hoyle Bank off Liverpool.

The *Camilla* was built in London in 1844 for the Baltic trade. She arrived at Waterford in the early 1850s and for the next ten years was mainly used on the Waterford–Bristol run. In 1851 she went north for a few months where she was employed on the Belfast–Liverpool crossing (see Vol 1). She was sold in 1863 and it is said she ended her days as a blockade runner.

SS *Reginald*, SS *Dunbrody/Arklow*, SS *Clodagh/Coningbeg*

These Waterford SS Co's steamers were transferred to the Clyde

Shipping Co in 1912. The *Reginald* was over thirty years old at the time and two years later was sold to the Admiralty for use as a block ship at Scapa Flow; this was not her first term of resting on terra firma for there is a photograph in the York Collection at Bristol Museum and Art Gallery which shows her when she went aground in the Avon in 1896.

The *Dunbrody* was built with refrigerated cargo holds which were lit by electricity. Her passenger accommodation included a single-berth state room with a particularly wide bed for the use of one of her regular passengers, who was somewhat portly.

The *Clodagh* was the last vessel to be acquired by the Waterford SS Co. She had accommodation for eighty cabin and sixty steerage passengers as well as space for 500 head of cattle. After her transfer to the Clyde Shipping Co she was renamed after the Coningbeg lightship off the Wexford coast. Her subsequent career was short, for she was sunk with the loss of all on board in December 1917 when on her way from Liverpool to Waterford.

SS *Skerries*, SS *Rockabill*, SS *Tuskar*

The Clyde Shipping Co's *Skerries* and *Rockabill* were the last steamers to carry passengers between Waterford and Bristol and Waterford and Liverpool respectively. They had accommodation for twelve passengers. The *Skerries* gave up carrying passengers in the mid-1930s but she remained with the company until 1946 when she was sold to the Saorstat & Continental SS Co and renamed *City of Waterford.* She was sunk in a collision in April 1949. The *Rockabill* was built in 1931. In the inter-war years she was generally employed on the weekly passenger/cargo service to Liverpool and continued in this work until withdrawn for breaking up in 1957. The Waterford–Liverpool service then became cargo only and in its latter days was worked by the *Tuskar,* a vessel equipped to carry heavy loads. She was sold in 1968, after which the service was worked by steamers which were on charter to the Clyde Shipping Co.

Waterford–Milford/Fishguard

Passenger steamers plied intermittently between Waterford and Pembrokeshire from 1824 to 1959. In the former year the Post Office substituted steamships for the sailing packets which had previously carried the mail from Milford Haven. The steamers at first did not proceed beyond Dunmore, from which place passengers and mail had to travel ten miles by road to Waterford. In 1835 the pier at Hobbs Point in Milford Haven was completed and at about the same time the steamers began to go up the Suir to Waterford. In 1837 the mail services became an Admiralty responsibility, a commitment which it retained until the Government closed down the Port Patrick–Donaghadee and Milford–Waterford mail routes in 1848. After this there were no regular passenger sailings between Waterford and West Wales until after the completion of the railway to Neyland in 1856. In August of that year the London shipowners R. Ford & T. T. Jackson acquired the *City of Paris* and operated her in conjunction with the Great Western and the South Wales Railways. In February 1872, the GWR took over the steamers and continued the working of the passenger service to Waterford until the latter was suspended in the spring of 1959. A cargo and cattle service continued to operate but the change in the Irish beef trade from live cattle to carcass meat so reduced the demand for cattle boats that the steamers were withdrawn in 1966. In 1906 the Welsh terminal was moved from Milford Haven to the new harbour at Fishguard which was opened in August of that year.

In the days of the government mail steamers the vessels ran every weekday. Few passengers patronised the steamers as West Wales at that time was very inaccessible. Those who used them had to pay 30s for a single passage in the saloon and 5s for a crossing on deck. On the other hand dogs could travel free, whereas on the Holyhead route dog owners had to pay 2s 6d. This concession does not seem to have attracted many passengers for fewer than 2,000 people patronised the route each year; the total receipts from all non-government sources seldom exceeded £19,000 per year, which did not go far toward meeting the operating costs which were of the order of £150,000.

At the beginning of the Ford & Jackson era the steamers sailed from Hobbs Point, to which railway passengers crossed by ferry from Neyland. In 1857 a pontoon pier was built at Neyland and a covered way was constructed to enable passengers to go from the train to the steamer without getting wet. In 1859 the name of the station was changed to New Milford, a title it retained until the transfer of the cross-channel services to Fishguard, when it resumed its former name of Neyland.

At the re-opening in 1856 two sailings were made each week and early in 1857 the frequency was increased to three. In the mid-1870s a daily service was introduced which continued to operate until the 1914–18 war. In the inter-war and post-1939 war period the steamers usually ran three times a week. In the 1860s they sailed from New Milford at 7.45 pm on the arrival of the 9.15 am express from Paddington—third-class passengers were not permitted to travel on this train and had to leave Paddington at 6 am! The vessels berthed at Waterford shortly after 5 am. On the return journey they sailed from Waterford at 4.15 pm and passengers going to London arrived at their destination at 6.15 pm next day. In 1930 passengers left London at 5.55 pm and were due in Waterford at 8 am next morning. On the return journey a 5.30 pm departure from Waterford enabled London passengers to join the 3.55 am train at Fishguard, which was due in Paddington at 9.40 am.

PS *Ivanhoe*, PS *Meteor*, PS *Royal Sovereign*, PS *Vixen*, PS *Aladdin*, PS *Crocodile*, PS *Sibyl*, PS *Prospero*

The government mail was operated by these steamers. When steamers replaced sail in 1824 the service was at first operated by the *Ivanhoe*, *Meteor*, *Royal Sovereign* and *Vixen*, vessels which had worked at some time, or another, in their careers at Holyhead and which are described in Chapter 1. The *Prospero*, which was formerly the Belfast–Glasgow cross-channel steamer *Belfast*, arrived in 1837; this vessel is described in Vol 1. The *Sibyl* was the fastest steamer on the station with a record of 8hr 13min for the crossing from Neyland Point to Dunmore. In general the vessels were somewhat under-powered and took about twelve hours to get over but this time could be increased to thirty hours when conditions were bad.

The captains of the Milford mail steamers had a salary of £300 per year with few perquisites, whereas their colleagues at Holyhead had a larger salary and very generous extras. It seems probable the only happy crew members at Milford were the firemen, who received a ration of half a pint of spirits a day, an emolument not given on any of the other mail routes to Ireland.

SS *City of Paris*, PS *Malakhoff*, PS *Courier*, SS *Griffin*

These vessels were used by Ford & Jackson on the Waterford–Milford Haven crossing which was re-opened by the *City of Paris* and *Malakhoff* in August 1856.

The *City of Paris* was six years old when she came to Milford where she remained for eight years. In February 1860 she was in the news when the ill-fated Cork steamer *Nimrod*, see page 112, refused her offer of a tow.

The *Malakhoff* was built as the *Baron Osy* in 1851 and spent some of her early days working between London and Antwerp, after which she went trooping in the Crimean War. For the latter she was renamed

Malakhoff, a name she retained when acquired by Ford & Jackson in 1856. She survived on the crossing to be taken over by the GWR in 1872 and continued as a railway steamer until her sale for scrapping in 1884. J. Scott Russell gives a full and somewhat rose-tinted account of this vessel in his book *The Modern System of Naval Architecture*; he claimed she was the ideal cross-channel steamer—this was no wonder for he had designed and built her!

The *Courier* did some crossings in 1861; this vessel also worked to Cork. The *Griffin* was employed on the route in the early 1860s.

PS *Vulture*, PS *South of Ireland*, PS *Great Western*

These were the last steamers owned by Ford & Jackson who disposed of them, along with the *Malakhoff*, for £45,500 to the GWR in 1872. The *Vulture* was built in 1864 and was acquired by Ford & Jackson in 1870. The *South of Ireland* and *Great Western* were built for Ford & Jackson in 1867 and worked to Waterford until their transfer to the GWR Weymouth–Channel Islands route in 1878. The *South of Ireland* spent only five years on her new station, for she was wrecked off the Dorset coast on Christmas Day, 1883. The *Great Western* remained at Weymouth until her sale in 1890. She then went north and finally ended her days as David MacBrayne's *Lovedale*.

PS *Milford*, PS *Waterford*, PS *Limerick*

These three paddle steamers worked on the crossing from the early 1870s until the turn of the century. They were good sea boats with a single funnel placed aft of their paddle boxes. In December 1900, the *Milford* ran into such abominable weather that she took over forty hours to get to New Milford. This was in the days before radio, so those ashore had given up all hope for the vessel when she became hours overdue. She was so badly damaged by the buffeting she received that she was withdrawn shortly afterwards and broken up. The *Waterford* remained on the crossing until she was sent to Garston for scrapping in 1905. The *Limerick* was sold to foreign owners in 1892 and was broken up in Holland ten years later.

TSS *Great Western*, TSS *Great Southern*

These two old faithfuls spent over thirty years with the railway. They began their careers working from New Milford and transferred to Fishguard on the opening of the harbour in 1906. They had single funnels and were driven by four-cylinder triple-expansion engines which gave them a speed of 16 knots. Saloon passengers were accommodated amidships and steerage aft.

PS/TSS *Pembroke*, TSS *Waterford*

The *Pembroke* was built as a paddle steamer by Laird of Birkenhead in 1880 and was converted to twin-screw propulsion in 1896. Her first thirty-five years with the railway were spent on St George's Channel, after which she was transferred to the company's Weymouth–Channel Island service where she remained until replaced by the *St Helier* in 1925. She was the last paddle steamer to be built for the GWR and the first vessel with a steel hull to be owned by the company.

The *Waterford* was the only GWR steamer to have a quadruple-expansion engine. She was stationed at Fishguard from 1912 to 1924 and was used mainly for cargo and cattle on the Waterford service.

TSS *Great Western*, TSS *Princess Maud*

The *Great Western* came into service in 1934 and spent almost all her entire peacetime career working between Waterford and Fishguard. She generally sailed from the latter at midnight and arrived at Waterford about 8 am next morning. She was not a handsome vessel but she was steady and comfortable with large, well-ventilated, cabins; this and the fact that the last hour of the westbound journey was spent going up the Suir when breakfast could be enjoyed, and held, no matter how rough the seas had been in St George's Channel, made the route popular with those who knew it. Unfortunately there were few people in this category and in the spring of 1959 she ceased to carry passengers but continued as a cargo and cattle boat until the railway closed down the route in 1966. She then went to Heysham and was broken up in Belgium in 1967. The *Great Western*, like all the steamers previously employed on the Waterford–Milford/Rosslare crossing, was a coal burner.

In the 1950s when the *Great Western* was taken off for her annual survey she was generally replaced by the Holyhead relief steamer *Princess Maud*.

Wexford–Ayr

A passenger/cargo service ran on this route in 1860. It was worked by the *Colonist* and *Ayrshire Lass*. The former called at Liverpool on her way north.

Wexford–Bristol

Steamers ran between Wexford and Bristol from January 1857 until 1911. They were operated at first by the Bristol SN Co who disposed of its interests in the service to the Waterford SS Co in September 1890. The vessels generally ran once a week and took about sixteen hours for the crossing. The record, however, was 12hr 45min, a time which was made by the *Rosetta* in 1869. Fares on the route were remarkably consistent, the steerage single fare was always 7s 6d and the cost of a saloon passage varied between 15s and 20s. In the early days the steamers called at Milford Haven but shortly afterwards Tenby became the normal calling place en route, and at times the vessels stopped at Carmarthen.

The first few sailings were taken by the *Phoenix* which was replaced by the *Juno* later in the year. Both these vessels also worked between Dublin and Bristol. The *Firefly* replaced the *Juno* in 1858. This steamer began her career working between Belfast and Ardrossan and came south in 1855. Nine years later the *Briton* arrived. This vessel had spent the previous six years working between Waterford and Bristol and before this had worked on the Larne–Stranraer crossing. In 1890 she was transferred to the Waterford SS Co who retained her on the Wexford–Bristol run until she ran aground on the North Bar at Wexford in March 1892. The *Firefly* and *Briton* are described in Vol 1. The last vessel to be employed on the crossing was the Waterford SS Co's *Menapia* which worked the service until its close down in 1911.

In 1896 the Fishguard & Rosslare Harbours and Railways Co opened a service between Wexford and Bristol via Rosslare. The route, which was worked by the former Belfast SS Co's steamer *Voltaic*, had a life of only four years.

Wexford–Glasgow

At the beginning of September 1864, the Clyde Shipping Co opened this route with the *Oscar*, a vessel chartered for the crossing pending the completion of the *Saltee* which was being built specially for the route. On 17 September a notice appeared in the *Wexford Independent* stating the service had been withdrawn as the steamer had experienced difficulty in getting over the bar at Wexford. In November 1878, the Clyde Shipping Co revived the service with the *Rockabill*. This vessel set off for Glasgow on 23 November and arrived at her destination twenty-five hours later. After a few months she was withdrawn.

The *Oscar* carried passengers but the *Rockabill* did not. The former called at Dublin when southbound and at Dun Laoghaire on her way back to Scotland. Passengers travelling the full distance paid 10s and 5s, those going between Dublin and Wexford were charged 6s and

3s. Alan Cuthbert in his *History of the Clyde Shipping Company* claims that, as a result of the company's brief sortie into the Glasgow–Wexford trade, Wexford enjoyed low rates for freight to Scotland for very many years.

SS *Oscar*

This vessel was built in 1850 for Robert Henderson of Belfast and from 1858 to 1870 was owned by William Sloan & Co. She was then sold to the Dingwall & Syke Railway and shortly afterwards ran ashore near Applecross. After her salvage she was purchased by G. G. Mackay of Grangemouth, for whom she was working when she sank after a collision off Flamborough Head in July 1882. She seems to have spent a considerable time on charter; thus in the 1850s she frequently worked between Belfast and London, in 1856 she ran for a short time between Belfast and Sligo, in the early 1860s she plied between Dublin and Wexford and in 1864 was used by the Clyde Shipping Co in its first attempt to establish a line of steamers between Wexford and Glasgow.

Wexford–Liverpool

Steamers plied between Wexford and Liverpool from the late 1820s until about 1910. The *Kingstown* (page 99) was the first steamer on the route. She was replaced by the *Harriett* and *Ormrod* which competed with one another in 1833 and 1834. No fares were published in the local papers for the *Harriett* but a passage by the *Ormrod* cost fat cows and cabin passengers 10s, store cattle 6s, deck passengers 2s 6d and pigs 1s 6d. In 1834 some sailings were taken by the *Abbey* and later in the same year the *Fingal* (see Vol 1) was chartered to replace the *Ormrod*. The next vessels on the station were the *Antelope* and *Belfast*. These maintained a weekly service until the arrival of the locally owned, and locally built, *Town of Wexford*. The arrival of this steamer in August 1837 caused great excitement. On 6 September the *Wexford Conservative* reported, 'On Friday last as the steamers were about to sail from the Quay, a fine little boy happened to "Hurrah for the Antelope" when a ruffian seized the poor little fellow and threw him into the river. A boatman hastening to his relief was severely pelted with stones for his laudable exertions by some of the unfeeling rabble in the interests of the *Town of Wexford*.' Next week, the rival local paper, the *Wexford Independent*, stated the story was a fabrication.

In the mid-1850s the working of the service was taken over by John Bacon of Liverpool, who continued to work it until the withdrawal of the passenger service. In 1913 John Bacon amalgamated with F. H. Powell & Co and Samuel Hough Ltd to form the shipping combine which today is known as Coast Lines Ltd.

There was little serious competition on the Wexford–Liverpool crossing for the greater parts of the *Town of Wexford* and Bacon regimes but mild competition took place on two occasions. In 1857 the Bristol-owned *Firefly* ran for a time against Bacon's *Emerald* and *Montagu*. Both proprietors despatched their vessels from Wexford on Fridays and competed for the passenger trade by a mild cutting of fares to 7s 6d and 5s; in normal times single tickets cost 12s 6d saloon and 6s steerage. In 1860 the *Colonist*, which also ran between Wexford and Ayr, made a few competitive crossings to Liverpool. In normal times the steamers ran once a week. The service was run mainly for cattle and cattle men travelling with livestock were usually given a free passage. The number of passengers using the route was small and even in the post-famine exodus seldom exceeded twenty-five per trip.

The Bacon steamers working on the service included the *Eden Vale* (1889–1904), *Emerald* (1853–7), *Montagu* (1855–91), *Pharos* (1876) and *Troubadour* (1858–62). The last-mentioned vessel also worked occasionally from Wexford to Milford Haven and Bristol and opened the Cork–New Milford service in 1856.

Dublin–South-east Coast of Leinster and Waterford

A regular passenger service between Dublin and Waterford began in 1870. In this year some of the Glasgow–Waterford–Cork steamers of the Clyde Shipping Co began to call at Dublin on their way between Ireland and Scotland (see page 103). Previous to this there had been short-lived attempts, such as that made by the *Eclipse* in 1844, to establish passenger communications between Waterford and the capital.

The Dublin–Wexford service had a precarious existence for about fifty years. It began in 1826 when the *Marquiss Wellesley* and the *Kingstown* made some runs between the two towns. In 1857 the *Ellan Vannin* and *Troubadour*, which were working under the auspices of the South Wales SS Co, opened a weekly service between Dublin and Milford Haven with a call at Wexford en route. The service lasted for only a few months but, when it was in operation, one could get from Dublin to Wexford in five hours at a cost of 6s saloon or 4s deck. In the early 1860s the *Mars* (see page 141) plied once a week between Dublin and Wexford. On her departure to be a blockade runner, in 1862, her place was taken by the *Oscar*, a vessel which seems to have remained in this service until about 1870 even though she had difficulty in getting over the bar at Wexford. The completion of the railway to Wexford in 1872 should have killed any further attempts to maintain a passenger steamer service with Dublin. It did nothing of the kind, for the *Loch Nell* carried passengers and cargo for a time on this route in 1877 and in the next year she was joined by the *Henry Allen.* These two vessels worked closely with the Dublin–Glasgow steamer *Irishman* and the Wexford newspapers advertised that the cheapest way of sending goods to Glasgow was by the *Loch Nell* or *Henry Allen* and the *Irishman.* Later in 1878 both vessels were replaced by the *Clanalpine* but it is not clear whether this vessel carried passengers; the *Loch Nell* certainly did and charged her patrons 7s for a saloon passage and 3s 6d for a place in the steerage.

6: CORK AND THE SOUTH-WEST

CROSS-CHANNEL steamers have plied between Cork and Great Britain from July 1821 to the present day. The first route to be developed was that to Bristol. Four years later a service to Liverpool commenced and in 1837 steamers began to run between Cork and Glasgow. The Cork–New Milford service began in 1856, a few months after the extension of the railway to Neyland on Milford Haven. In 1906 the Welsh terminal on this route was transferred to Fishguard, where a new harbour had been opened by the Great Western Railway in August of that year. Drive-on car-ferries replaced the conventional cross-channel steamers on this crossing in May 1969, and at the same time the British terminal was moved to Swansea where special car loading facilities had been provided for the traffic.

The history of the Cork cross-channel trade is closely bound with that of the Clyde Shipping Co and the City of Cork SP Co. The former operated the long-distance passenger/cargo service to Glasgow over the years 1859–1962 (see Chapter 7) and the latter has had vessels, at one time or another, on most of the cross-channel routes working from Cork, and today maintains the car-ferry service between Cork and Swansea.

The City of Cork SP Co was formed as the St George SP Co in October 1821 by groups of businessmen in Cork, Dublin and Liverpool. In the mid-1830s it was one of the big shipping companies in the world and its vessels traded from Cork to Bristol, Glasgow and London, as well as between Dublin and Bristol. It also maintained services between Liverpool and Dublin, Dundalk, Newry and the Isle of Man, and was heavily involved in the deep-sea trade. The St George SP Co was never strong financially and was reorganised in 1843, when its South of Ireland interests passed to the Cork SS Co, a company formed in that year by Mr Ebenezer Pike. He set up the headquarters of the new company at Cork, where the head office of the City of Cork SP Co is situated today. In July 1871 the activities of the Cork SS Co were divided into deep-sea and coasting sections. The former continued to be worked by the Cork SS Co but the latter became the responsibility of the City of Cork SP Co, a company specially created to work this traffic. The new company became a member of the Coast

Lines Group in 1918 and in 1936 became a totally owned subsidiary of the British & Irish SP Co. On 1 January 1965 the Government of the Irish Republic purchased the BISP, an action which restored all the vessels of the City of Cork SP Co to Irish ownership. The Cork SS Co went out of business at the end of the 1914–18 war.

In the early days the vessels of the St George SP Co flew the St George's cross as a house flag. This custom was continued by the Cork SS Co, a practice which caused much consternation among ships of the Royal Navy, where the undefaced St George's cross is flown only by admirals. On several occasions masters of Cork SS Co's vessels were directed to haul down their house flag by senior naval officers, an order which they refused to obey. After one particular encounter in the Persian Gulf the Cork SS Co decided to placate 'Their Lordships' of the Board of Admiralty by altering its house flag to a St George's cross defaced by a blue star at its centre. The City of Cork SP Co was not affected by this decision for its vessels have always flown the St George's cross with the arms of the City of Cork at its centre.

Cork–Bristol

The Cork–Bristol passenger service began in July 1821 and ended at the beginning of the 1914–18 war. Throughout the nineteenth century it was worked by Bristol- and Cork-owned steamers, but from 1900 onwards all vessels regularly employed on the crossing were owned by the City of Cork SP Co, the direct descendent of the St George SP Co, one of the companies which worked the route in its early days. The majority of the Bristol steamers employed in the service belonged to the War Office SP Co, a Bristol shipping company which became the Bristol SN Co in 1877. Some twenty years later this company disposed of its interests in the Cork–Bristol service to the City of Cork SP Co. A very complete account of the Bristol SN Co's steamers is given in Grahame Farr's *West Country Passenger Steamers* and the Cork-owned vessels have been fully covered in a series of illustrated articles by W. J. Barry which appeared in the *Journal of the Cork Archaeological Society* over the years 1917–24, and were collected together in his book *History of the Port of Cork Steam Navigation*.

The first ten years of the Cork–Bristol services is just as confused as the early days of the Belfast–Clyde and Dublin–Liverpool routes. Steamers came, steamers went and owners changed in quick succession. The first sailings were taken by the *Ivanhoe* and *Talbot* in the summer of 1821. These vessels were well known at the time for, in the previous year, they had been the first steamers to ply regularly between Dublin and Holyhead. After a few visits to Cork they were withdrawn. In the following spring the *George IV* from Bristol and the Irish-owned *St Patrick* went into service and immediately initiated a period of vigorous competition. This reached its peak in 1826 when the *Superb* and *Severn* enticed patronage by cheap fares, brass bands and free commons. In the late 1820s there were usually two sailings each week, a frequency which remained fairly constant until the beginning of the twentieth century, when it was reduced to one, but by this time the faster and more convenient service via Milford Haven had creamed off the passenger traffic. The move of the Welsh terminal on this route from New Milford to Fishguard in 1906 so reduced the number of passengers travelling by direct steamer between Cork and Bristol that the vessels ceased to carry passengers as a normal practice at the beginning of the 1914–18 war.

Cork–Glasgow

In July 1836 the St George SP Co's *Jupiter* started to run between Glasgow and Dublin, where she made a connection with the company's *Innisfail* which, at the time, was working regularly between the latter city and Cork. The advertisement which appeared for the new service in the *Cork Constitution* was headed 'Communication with Glasgow' and stated that the vessels would leave Cork and Glasgow on every fifth day commencing on 2 July. In April next year the Dublin & Glasgow SP Co, who resented the entry of the St George SP Co into the Glasgow–Dublin trade, commenced a through working between Glasgow and Cork with its steamer *Mercury*. The St George SP Co immediately responded by extending some of its Cork–Dublin sailings to Glasgow. The vessels of each company provided a weekly service; passenger fares, which were originally 30s and 15s, soon came down to 15s and 5s. The steamers employed at this time by the Dublin & Glasgow SP Co included the *Arab* and the *Herald* whilst the *Juno* and *Ocean* were often used by the St George SP Co. The Dublin & Glasgow Co withdrew during the 1840s but the St George SP Co, and its successor the Cork SS Co, continued to work between Cork and Glasgow until about 1860. In the summer of 1837, a steamer called the *Grand Turk* made some runs between Cork and Glasgow, thereby providing a third competitor on the crossing.

In 1856 the Glasgow Screw SS Co, an associate of the Clyde Shipping Co, puts its *Vivandiere* on the Cork–Glasgow service. This steamer was very fast and is reputed to have overtaken, and steamed past, the

Cork SS Co's *Nimrod* on one of her early crossings. Shortly after her entry to the Cork–Glasgow trade she was joined by another Clyde SS Co's steamer called *Killarney*. At about the same time the Cork SS Co withdrew, thereby giving the Clyde SS Co a monopoly on the route, which it held until its withdrawal from the Cork–Glasgow trade in 1952. The Clyde steamers always carried passengers in peacetime, and in the years immediately after the 1939–45 war it was still possible to travel by steamer from Cork to Glasgow. More information about the Clyde Shipping Co's service to Cork can be obtained on page 123, and the steamers of the Dublin & Glasgow SP Co are described in Chapter 3.

Cork–Liverpool

The Cork–Liverpool passenger service lasted for nearly 140 years. It opened in October 1825 when the *Lee* made the first passage between the ports; the last sailing was taken by the *Glengariff* in December 1963. The crossing was always worked by the St George SP Co and its successors, who enjoyed a near monopoly for most of the time. Short-lived opposition took place in the Shipping War of 1850 when the Belfast-owned *Telegraph* plied for a time between the two ports. There was a brisk passenger traffic between the two ports in Victorian times which reached a peak in the post-famine exodus in the late 1840s. In 1849 each Liverpool-bound steamer sailed from Cork with an average of 250 deck passengers who had to brave a twenty-six-hour journey in a vessel which had little covered accommodation for those travelling at the minimum fare.

When the service opened there was only one sailing a week; this was soon increased to two and by the 1870s there were three sailings each week, a frequency which was maintained until the 1914–18 war. In the inter-war years there were often only two sailings, and when the service was resumed after the 1939–45 war one sailing was sufficient for the traffic. This was taken by the *Kenmare*, which was replaced by the *Glengariff* in May 1956. The latter usually sailed from North Victoria Dock in Liverpool at 6 pm on Wednesdays, and was due in Cork at 4 pm next day. On the return journey she left Penrose Quay, Cork, at 1 pm on Saturday and arrived in Liverpool at about 10 am on Sunday. She did not carry steerage passengers and those in the saloon paid 74s plus 12s 6d for a berth. In the days immediately before the 1914–18 war the saloon fare was 17s 6d, a sum which had remained unchanged from 1860. Over the same period the steerage had kept constant at 10s.

Throughout the nineteenth century the Cork company employed its larger steamers on the crossing. These included vessels such as the *Albatross*, *Cormorant*, *Lord Blayney* and *Sirius*. Toward the end of the century the New Milford crossing was gaining rapidly in importance as a route for passengers and, from 1896, the largest and fastest vessels of the company were allocated to this service, whilst the Cork–Liverpool crossing was pushed into second place.

Cork–Milford Haven/Fishguard/Swansea

The service between Cork and Milford Haven opened in September 1856 when the *Troubadour* began a twice-weekly service between the two ports. At first the steamers were worked by the London shipowners R. Ford & T. T. Jackson on behalf of the Great Western Railway but, in 1872, the railway acquired the vessels and in 1873 increased the number of sailings to three each week. The railway do not seem to have been able to make the service pay and in 1875 disposed of its interests in the crossing to the City of Cork SP Co, who have operated it ever since.

From the beginning the steamers have always run in close cooperation with the GWR. They used the railway pier at Milford Haven, and, when the railway opened the harbour at Fishguard in 1906, the City of Cork steamers changed to the new port. In May 1969 they moved to a new car-loading terminal at Swansea, but the railway tradition was maintained, for the City of Cork SP Co put on a bus to ferry its non-car-owning passengers from the docks to the High Street station in that city. Previous to the move to Swansea the steamers had always run overnight. At first they sailed from New Milford in the early evening, but as vessels got faster the departure time got later until, in the inter-war years, the Cork boats left Fishguard at midnight, having made a connection with the 5.55 pm train from Paddington. They arrived at Penrose Quay, Cork, at about 9 am next morning. The last hour of the journey was spent in sheltered water amid beautiful scenery, for the sail up the Lee to Cork rivals that up the Suir to Waterford as the most pleasant sea approach to a major city in Ireland. The approach was just as attractive in winter for the smooth passage up the river enabled passengers to enjoy the best possible convalescence after sea-sickness—a hearty breakfast. On the return journey the steamers left Cork in the early evening so that passengers could be in Paddington by 10 am next day. The service was suspended for a time during the two world wars, and in the mid-1960s it did not operate in the depth of winter. After the move to Swansea in May 1969 the car-ferry *Innisfallen* was scheduled to complete one round trip every twenty-four hours. She did this by crossing overnight from Swansea to Cork and returning during the hours of daylight, thereby establishing the first regular *daylight* service from Cork.

In the Ford & Jackson era vessels were frequently switched from the Milford–Waterford to the Milford–Cork routes and vice versa. This practice was continued by the railway, but was not followed by the City of Cork SP Co. The latter used to give its steamers reasonably long spells on the crossing. Thus, in the 1870s, the *Belle* and *Preussischer Adler* were assigned to the route and were followed in the 1880s by the *Shandon* and *Lee*. In the two decades before the 1914–18 war the *Innisfallen* and *Inniscarra* were each stationed for a time on the crossing. The service was closed for a time during the war and was resumed in January 1919 when the sailings were taken by the *Kilkenny*, which had been allocated to the company by the Ministry of Transport. In February the *Glengariff* returned to her peacetime owners and was immediately put on the crossing. She was replaced by the first post-war *Killarney* in July of the same year. This vessel had just been completed as the *Moorfowl* for J. & G. Burns, but had been sent to Cork for the Fishguard service for which her name had been temporarily changed to *Killarney*. In the summer of 1920 she returned to the north and for about a year the Fishguard sailings were shared between the *Bandon*, the Laird Line's *Maple* and the Belfast SS Co's *Logic*. The next vessel to be assigned to the route was the *Classic*, which arrived in June 1921. This vessel was stationed at Cork for nine years. In 1924 her name was changed to *Killarney*, a name she retained until she was scrapped in 1948. In 1930 she was replaced by the *Innisfallen*. This motor vessel was a great success and her name has since been used by the company in advertising the crossing which is now known as the *Innisfallen Route*. She was lost in the 1939–45 war and replaced in 1948 by a second *Innisfallen*, which worked the service until the move from Fishguard in 1968. The car-ferry working on the route today is also called *Innisfallen*. She is similar in appearance to the 1969 *Leinster* and like this vessel is also a one-class ship. Passengers pay 70s for a single crossing and 128s for a through ticket—second-class rail—from Cork to London. At the turn of the century the minimum fare via New Milford and the GWR was 21s 9d.

PS *St George*, PS *St Patrick*, PS *Emerald Isle*, PS *William Huskisson*

The *St George* was the first steamer owned by the St George SP Co. She was launched in April 1822 and went into service between Dublin

Page 107 (above) SS *Glengariff*, ex-*Rathlin* (1936), c 1960
(below): SS *Copeland/Toward* (1923), passenger accommodation. Note the piano in the dining saloon and the berths in the smoking room

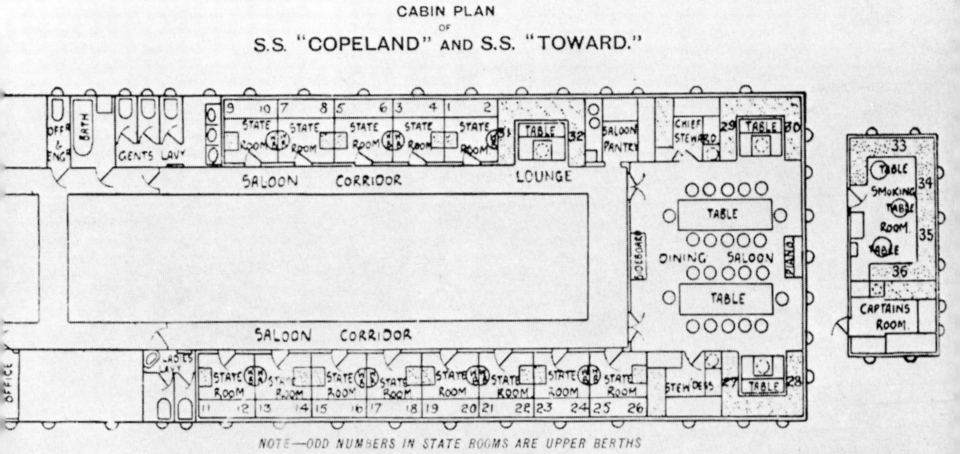

Page 108 (above): SS *Menapia*
(below): MV *Torr Head* at Toronto

and Liverpool later in the same year. She spent most of her career working between Liverpool, Dublin and the Isle of Man, and was wrecked on Conister Rock, off Douglas, during a gale in September 1830. She was a fast vessel and in her second season returned a time of 10hr 40min for the Liverpool–Dublin crossing. She worked occasionally between Dublin and London but never seems to have been to Cork.

The *St Patrick* was also built in 1822 and was the first steamer to trade regularly between Dublin and Bristol; later in her career she worked occasionally between Cork and Bristol. In 1824 she was sold to Portuguese owners who renamed her *Restaurado Lusitano*.

The *Emerald Isle* and *William Huskisson* were advertised as working between Dublin and Liverpool in 1823. The former was transferred to the Cork–Bristol route in 1825. The *William Huskisson* was named after the member of Parliament for Liverpool who was run over by a train at the opening of the Liverpool & Manchester Railway on 15 September 1830, an accident which made him the first person in the world to be killed on a public railway. The steamer bearing his name was employed on the Liverpool–Dundalk and Liverpool–Newry services of the company, until she was wrecked near Liverpool in January 1840. In 1919 parts of her hull were found during dredging operations at Burbo Bank at the entrance to the Mersey.

PS *Lee*

This was one of the early steamers owned by the St George SP Co. She was built at Chester and registered at Liverpool in June 1825. She was the first steamer to be employed in the Cork–Liverpool service, and most of her time with the company was divided between working on this route and on that between Liverpool and Newry.

PS *Severn*, PS *Superb*

The squabble between the Kilkenny cats was a nursery tea compared with the feud between these two vessels. In the early summer of 1826 the St George Co increased the number of its sailings to three each week and advertised 'During July and August the capacious holds of their vessels will be appropriated to the comfort of deck passengers.' The owners of both steamers then began a fare war. When this looked like ending in a scoreless draw, the *Superb* tried to attract passengers by parading a brass band through Cork. The *Severn* responded by stating, 'Each deck passenger per *Severn* will get a loaf of bread gratis.' Tradition maintains the practice was stopped after a 'decker' complained about the quality of the bread. Neither steamer contented itself with war on land so every crossing became a race, a race which the *Superb* generally won. Racing ended when the latter ran on to a mud bank on the Lee and had to wait for the tide to rise before she could get off. This enabled the *Severn* to 'win' and have her passengers disembarked several hours before her opponent arrived at the quays. In the late summer of 1826 the contestants came to terms and fares were restored to 'normal'. This action prompted a most irate Englishman to write to the *Cork Constitution* to complain about being charged 45s to get back to England whereas he had only paid 20s for a saloon ticket for his crossing to the Emerald Isle.

The *Superb* was owned by a group of Cork businessmen and the *Severn* was the property of the St George SP Co. The former made her maiden voyage on 6 May 1826 and ended in February 1835 when she was sunk near Liverpool when engaged in the Cork–Liverpool trade. The *Severn* went into service in 1826 and, after trading for a few years between Cork and Bristol, was moved to the Cork–Liverpool crossing in 1832. Toward the end of the 1830s she worked for a time between Dublin and Bristol, after which she made occasional trips to the Continent. In 1845 she was sold but remained in the British coastal trade until broken up in 1848.

PS *Express*, PS *Jupiter*, PS *William IV*, PS *Earl of Roden*, PS *Magdalena*

These vessels were owned by the St George SP Co. The *Express* is reputed to have worked on all the company's services from Cork and Dublin over the years 1832–43. In 1844 she went to the Orient where she is said to have found lucrative employment in the opium smuggling trade. The *William IV* was the vessel used in the unsuccessful attempt to open a service between New Ross and Bristol in 1832; later in her career she worked between Dundalk, Newry and Liverpool. The *Jupiter* spent most of her time on the Liverpool–Newry trade but on occasions worked to Glasgow and also to Bristol; when engaged in the latter in 1846 she ran ashore on the Avon but was salvaged. She was so badly damaged, however, that her owners disposed of her a year later. The *Earl of Roden* and the *Magdalena* worked between Liverpool and Dundalk, where the company's association with the port is still commemorated by one of the quays which carries the name 'St George's Quay'.

PS *Sirius*

At 10 am on 4 April 1838 this steamer set off from Cork Harbour and at 10 pm on 22 April arrived off the Battery, New York. She thus became the first vessel to steam all the way from Europe to America. She was commanded by Lieut Richard Roberts, RN, a native of Cork who lost his life when the *President*, another early steamer, disappeared during an Atlantic crossing three years later.

The *Sirius* made two round trips to New York, after which she commenced the work for which she was designed, the coastal trade of the St George SP Co. She normally plied between Cork, Liverpool and Glasgow and when engaged in the latter trade was wrecked on the Cork coast in January 1847. An artist's impression of the wreck appeared in the *Illustrated London News* for 30 January of that year. On her epic transatlantic voyage she had forty passengers on board, who were segregated into three classes and who paid 25, 20 and 8 guineas respectively for the passage. The passenger list included nine ladies, one of whom was travelling steerage.

The *Sirius* had a two-cylinder engine (60in × 72in) which took steam at 5psi. On her initial Atlantic crossing she consumed 450 tons of coal but required only 20 tons of water, for she was fitted with surface condensers which enabled her boilers to be fed with water condensed from steam.

PS *Ocean*, PS *Victory*

These vessels were among the St George SP Co's steamers transferred to the Cork SS Co on its formation in 1843. The *Ocean* spent most of her career at Cork working between that city and Glasgow via Dublin, and acted as tender to the *Sirius* when the latter set out to cross the Atlantic in April 1838. The *Ocean* was sold to the Chester & Holyhead Railway in 1853, for the latter's Holyhead–Dublin service. The *Victory* ran between Cork and Bristol over the years 1832–46, after which she was sold to Waterford owners for whom she worked until she was wrecked on the Wexford coast in September 1853.

PS *Ajax*, PS *Minerva*, PS *Nimrod*, PS *Sabrina*

These four steamers were used by the Cork Shipping Co in its attempt to break into the Belfast–Liverpool trade in the early 1850s.

The *Minerva* was employed on this intermittently throughout the whole of the time the Cork company was operating to Belfast. Before going north she had worked between Cork and Glasgow and after her Belfast venture was transferred to the Cork–Liverpool service, a crossing on which she was engaged when she was wrecked during a fog in August 1854. At the time there were 256 deck passengers on board, all of whom survived.

The *Ajax* made a few crossings from Belfast in 1851. She was a schooner-rigged vessel with an effigy of Ajax, the classical hero, as her figurehead. Her career ended in November 1854 when she hit the Mewstone Rock, off Portsmouth. Her master at the time was Captain Rochfort who had commanded the *Minerva* when she went down three months previously.

The *Nimrod* was the first iron cross-channel steamer at Cork. She was built at Liverpool in 1843 and spent most of her time trading between Cork and Liverpool. In 1851 she was sent to Belfast, but within a short time was back on her normal run. When so engaged she foundered near St David's Head on 27 February 1860 with the loss of forty-five lives. At the time her engines had broken down, but she was making way under sail and a short time before her end had refused a tow from the *City of Paris* (see page 94.)

The *Sabrina* was on the Belfast–Liverpool run in 1851. She was built in 1844 and normally worked between Cork and Bristol. She had an uneventful career which was relieved a little in 1848 when Michael Doheny, an Irish patriot on the run, disguised himself as a cattle drover and went on board with some bullocks. He got safely to Bristol and ultimately to America.

SS *Blarney*

This vessel had two firsts; the first cross-channel steamer to be built at Cork and first screw-steamer to be owned by the Cork SS Co. She went into service in 1846 and could be truthfully described as an iron-hulled auxiliary schooner. In 1853 she was advertised as working a fortnightly passenger/cargo service between Tralee and London, an assignment which should qualify her for a triple-first, for she was the first steamer to carry passengers regularly on this route.

SS *Albatross/Cymba*

This vessel spent a considerable amount of her time on the Cork–Liverpool and Cork–London crossings. She was built in 1850 and during the Crimean War was employed as a transport, carrying troops and stores between Batjeh and Balaclava. In 1866 she was sold to the Waterford SS Co who used her on its Dublin–London service. In the early 1870s the Waterford company transferred the goodwill of this route to the British & Irish SP Co, and with the goodwill went the *Albatross*. Her new owners renamed her *Cymba*, but after a time sold her to Norwegian owners.

SS *Cormorant*

The *Cormorant* was one of the eight steamers transferred from the Cork SS Co to the City of Cork SP Co at its formation in 1871. She was one of the first steamers in the world to have iron masts, a novelty which impressed Queen Victoria when she inspected the vessel at Portsmouth. At the time the steamer was on charter to the British government for the carrying of troops and military stores to the Crimea.

SS *Belle*, SS *Dodo*, SS *Lee*, PS *Preussischer Adler*, SS *Shandon*, SS *St Finbar*

These steamers were employed at times on the Cork–New Milford service before the arrival of the *Innisfallen* in 1896. The *Belle* was on the crossing in the years 1876–8, after which she was sold to the Chilean Government. The *Lee* was also sold to Chile, but her sale took place after she had been twenty-six years at Cork. The *Dodo* (1855–94) was a vessel which was somewhat unsteady in a beam sea and earned the unofficial title of the '*Rolling Dodo*'. The *Shandon* was one of the few second-hand steamers possessed by the City of Cork SP Co. She was built in 1864 as the *Principe Tomaso* and worked on the Adriatic before coming to Cork in 1880. In 1893 she was sold to Marseilles owners who changed her name to *Bastiais*. The *St Finbar* spent fourteen years at Cork after which she went to Leith, and was ultimately sent to Constantinople. The *Preussischer Adler* was built as a yacht for the King of Prussia. She had a dashing appearance with a clipper bow and single well-raked funnel. She never went into the Kaiser's service and spent her career as an Irish cross-channel steamer. She often worked between Cork and Bristol.

SS *Xema*, PS *Juno*

These were the last vessels of their respective companies to be regularly employed on the Cork–Bristol service. The *Xema* was owned by the City of Cork SP Co. She was a typical City of Cork steamer with three masts and machinery aft. In 1904 she was sold to a syndicate who used her in some rather peculiar treasure hunting—off South-West Africa, after which she was sold to Bombay owners. These changed her name to *Saifi* and, under this name, she traded on the Indian coast until the beginning of the 1914–18 war. The *Juno* was a two-funnelled paddle steamer which was built for the Bristol SN Co in 1868. She had quite a distinguished career. In 1873 she was the first vessel to pass through the new lock at the Cumberland Basin in Bristol and in

February 1877 she, and her eminent passenger, the Lord Mayor of Bristol, together opened the new docks at Avonmouth. She passed into the hands of the City of Cork SP Co in 1900 and was sold soon afterwards to be a coal hulk at Dartmouth.

SS *Bandon*, SS *Blarney*, SS *Glengariff*, SS *Kenmare*, SS *Killarney* SS *Lissmore*

The *Lissmore* was frequently employed on the Cork–Bristol run after the departure of the *Xema* in 1904. The *Blarney* and *Killarney* also worked occasionally on this route; both vessels were sold in 1910. The *Bandon* and *Kenmare* were lost during the 1914–18 war. The *Glengariff* was built in 1893. In 1919 she took some of the Cork–Fishguard sailings. She, and the collier *Pylades*, were the only City of Cork SP Co's steamers to survive the 1914–18 war.

SS *Innisfallen*, SS *Inniscarra*

These two-funnelled steamers were built in 1896 and 1903 respectively, for the Cork–Fishguard service. Both were lost by enemy action in May 1918. The *Innisfallen* was working at the time between Cork and Liverpool, a route to which she had been transferred on the arrival of the *Inniscarra* in 1903.

SS *Killarney*, TSS *Killarney*, SS *Bandon*, TSS *Logic*

The SS *Killarney* was employed on the Cork–Fishguard run for a short time in 1919. She had just been completed as the *Moorfowl* for G. & J. Burns but, owing to heavy losses sustained by the City of Cork SP Co in the 1914–18 war, was temporarily allocated to the Cork company. After about a year she was returned to her original owners and reassumed the name *Moorfowl*.

The TSS *Killarney* was formerly the Belfast SS Co's *Classic* (see Vol 1). She arrived at Cork as the *Classic* in May 1921 and immediately went into service on the Fishguard crossing. In August 1922 she was requisitioned to take the body of Michael Collins to Dublin after he had been killed in an ambush near Cork during the Irish Civil War. At this time the fighting in the Cork area was particularly heavy and all rail communication with Dublin had been cut by the Irregular Forces. In 1924 she was transferred to the City of Cork Co and renamed *Killarney*. She remained at Cork until replaced by the *Innisfallen* in 1930.

The *Bandon*, which was formerly the *Louth* of the City of Dublin SP Co, was stationed at Cork from 1920 to 1931. Shortly after her arrival at Cork she worked for a few months on the Fishguard crossing and from August to December 1922 ran on a special overnight service between Cork and Dublin (see page 119).

The *Logic*, which had been built for the Belfast SS Co in 1898 (see Vol 1), ran with the *Bandon* in the autumn of 1922. She was scheduled to make one round trip each week to Fishguard and also carried out a weekly sailing to Bristol. The latter seems to have lasted for only a few months.

SS *Ardmore*

This was the second *Ardmore* to run between Cork and Liverpool in the inter-war years. She was built, as the *Killiney*, for Tedcastle's Dublin–Liverpool service toward the end of the 1914–18 war but before her completion the Tedcastle steamers were all transferred to the British & Irish SP Co. The latter added the prefix *Lady* to her name and in 1923 sold her to the City of Cork SP Co, who renamed her *Ardmore*. She remained with her new owners, working the Cork–Liverpool crossing, until the night of 11/12 November 1940 when she disappeared off the south coast of Ireland.

SS *Kenmare*, SS *Ardmore/Lady Longford/Lairdshill*

These sister ships were built in 1921. *Kenmare* had a long association with the Cork–Liverpool service. Her career began in 1921 and ended when she made her last passenger sailing from Cork to Liverpool on Saturday, 12 May 1956. In the 1939–45 war she worked for a time on the 'hostilities only' cargo service to Fishguard and took the first passenger sailings between Cork and Fishguard when the crossing was reopened in August 1945. She was displaced from the route three years later by the *Munster*, which ran this service for a few months before taking up her permanent station trading between Dublin and Liverpool. In the meantime the *Kenmare* had returned to her old haunts, the Cork–Liverpool route, on which she opened the post-war passenger service in February 1948. She was a sedate vessel with a single funnel and accommodation for about sixty saloon passengers amidships. In her steerage she had a dormitory for ten ladies.

The *Ardmore* was the first Irish cross-channel steamer to have oil-fired boilers. She spent only a short time at Cork before being transferred to the Dublin–Liverpool route of the British & Irish SP Co where she worked under the name of *Lady Longford*. In 1930 she joined the Burns & Laird fleet and was renamed *Lairdshill*. Her new owners used her mainly on the Dublin–Glasgow run, a route on which she plied on and off for over twenty years.

SS *Glengariff*

This was the last steamer to be employed on the Cork–Liverpool passenger trade. She took over from the *Kenmare* in 1956 and was retired at the end of 1963, when her place was taken by the cargo-only diesel vessel *Glanmire*. The *Glengariff* was built for the Clyde Shipping Co as the *Rathlin* in 1936. During the war she was employed as a rescue ship, ie she was one of the small vessels which trailed at the back of a convoy to pick up survivors. She survived this hazardous occupation and returned to her owners' coastal trade. In 1953 she was sold to Burns & Laird and three years later was transferred to the City of Cork SP Co, who gave her the name *Glengariff*.

TSMV *Innisfallen*, TSMV *Innisfallen*

These motor vessels went into service on the Cork–Fishguard crossing in 1930 and 1948 respectively. They were members of Coast Line's successful class of three island, 3,000 ton, cross-channel ships, of which the *Ulster Monarch* (1929) was the first and the *Scottish Coast* (1957) the last. The 1930 *Innisfallen* was lost during the air raids at Liverpool on 20 December 1940. All 143 passengers on board were saved but two of the crew and two cattle men lost their lives. At the time the vessel was on the Cork–Liverpool crossing owing to the wartime suspension of the Cork–Fishguard service. The *Innisfallen* of 1948 was the last vessel employed on the Cork–Fishguard crossing, a route from which she was withdrawn in November 1968. After this she was sold to the Isthmian Navigation Co of Cyprus and given the name *Innisfallen I*.

The main difference in appearance between the two *Innisfallens* was that the earlier vessel had two funnels and the post-war 'steamer' had only one.

TSMV *Innisfallen*

This vessel opened the Cork–Swansea service in May 1969. She is almost identical in hull design and interior layout to the *Leinster* (see page 44), but her engines are more powerful. These enable her to attain a speed of 24 knots, which makes her one of the fastest car-ferries in Western Europe.

PS *Troubadour*, PS *Pacific*, SS *Griffin*, PS *Courier*

The *Troubadour*, which normally worked between Wexford and Liverpool, was chartered to open the Milford–Cork service of Ford & Jackson in 1856. In September of that year she was advertised to sail from Milford to Cork on Tuesdays and from Milford to Dublin on Fridays; in both cases she awaited the arrival of the 9.40 am train from Paddington, which meant she sailed between 7 and 8 pm.

In 1857 the frequency of the Cork sailings was increased to two each week which were taken by the *Pacific* and, in the same year, the Dublin sailings were dropped. The *Pacific* was an ocean-going vessel of about 1,500 gross tons. She was built at Millwall for the Sydney & Melbourne SS Co in 1854, and was registered in Sydney in the next year. She had a streamlined hull designed by her builders to make her the fastest steamer in the world, a title she failed to acquire for she seldom exceeded 14 knots. After a few years she returned to England, and was ultimately acquired by Ford & Jackson in 1857. In 1858 she was chartered to the Galway Line (see page 134) who retained her until 1861. Ten years later she was wrecked on the coast of the Shetland Islands.

The *Griffin* was chartered by Ford & Jackson over the years 1859–65. She was then sold to the London & South Western Railway who used her on its Southampton–Channel Island and Cherbourg crossings. In 1895 she went to French owners who renamed her *Le Georges Croisé*. Her career ended in March 1900 when she was lost at sea.

The *Courier* was chartered for a few runs in 1861.

Cork–Manchester

In the years immediately after the 1914–18 war the docks at Liverpool became so congested that the City of Cork SP Co opened a Cork–Manchester service. This was intended primarily for goods and cattle but passengers were carried on occasions. The service began in August 1919 and ended about the middle of 1921. The sailings were usually taken by the *Cumbria*, an ex-Tedcastle steamer. When this vessel was away for her annual survey the service was generally worked by the *Eblana*. Nearly a quarter of a century earlier a company called the Munster & Manchester Line advertised that its SS *Liverpool* would run between Cork and Manchester via the newly opened ship canal. It is probable that this steamer carried cargo only, for there is no mention of passenger fares in the advertisement which appeared in August 1896. The *Liverpool* was over forty years old at the time of her Manchester venture and in her earlier career had worked between Dublin and Barrow (see page 47).

Cork–South-West Munster

A local steamer service operated between Cork and Dingle from the late 1850s until 1905. The first steamer on the route was called the *South Western*; she was followed by the *Rio Formosa* which was acquired by the Clyde Shipping Co, when the latter took over the service in 1876. At first the steamers ran intermittently from Cork but, by the 1890s, they had settled down to one round trip each week from Cork to Dingle with calls at Schull, Castletownbere, Bantry, Kenmare, Sneem and Cahirciveen if, and when, cargo demanded. In 1900 the sailings were taken by the *Fastnet*, which sailed from Cork on Tuesday, and was due back on Sunday. A limited number of passengers were carried, who were charged 22s 6d, exclusive of food, for the round trip. In November 1901 the Congested Districts Board (see Vol 1) began to pay an annual subsidy of £500 to the Clyde Shipping Co for the maintenance of the service which provided the only economic means of transport to parts of south-west Munster in the pre-motor age. The subsidy was discontinued in 1904 and a few months later the service closed down.

Other steamers employed on the route included the Clyde Shipping Co's *Rockabill*, *Skelligs* and *Valentia*. The same company chartered the *Viking* and *Agate* for a few trips in 1878.

Cork Shipping in the Civil War

In the summer and autumn of 1922 there was heavy fighting in County Cork between the army of the newly formed Irish Free State and the armed supporters of those who opposed the established government. The latter were known initially as the Irregulars and were later called the IRA. During the fighting, the railway viaduct at Mallow on the Dublin–Cork main line was blown up, as were numerous bridges on the other lines in the district. Indeed, during part of August and September large areas in Cork, Kerry and Limerick were without rail services. The Irregulars also sealed off the port of Cork by sinking two block ships in the river near Passage and attempted to isolate Cobh by destroying Belvelly Bridge, which carried the railway from Cobh to the mainland. The destruction of the bridge did not completely isolate Cobh for an enterprising businessman began to operate a motorboat service between the town and Cork with the *Nellie* and *Flora*, two former ships' lifeboats which, in normal times, generally ran short excursions from Cobh.

Toward the end of August the block ships were removed and shortly afterwards the City of Cork SP Co began a thrice-weekly steamer service between Cork and Dublin with the chartered *Lady Kerry*. In mid-September she was joined by the *Bandon* and the number of sailings was increased to give a nightly service, a frequency at which it remained until the end of the year. In January the sailings were decreased to alternate nights and were advertised to be taken by the *Lady Kerry* and *Lady Carlow*. The service was suspended at the end of March. The number of sailings on the Cork–Fishguard route was temporarily increased to give a nightly service in September 1922; the additional sailings were taken by the *Logic* and J. & G. Burns's *Tiger*, which had been sent to Cork for this purpose.

Throughout the 'war' the steamers of the Clyde Shipping Co continued to provide regular services between Dublin, Waterford and Cork (or Cobh) and its Glasgow–Limerick steamers were diverted from the west coast to run via Dublin and Cork, where calls were made for passengers and goods. The company's steamers working to Limerick at this time included the *Aranmore*, *Eddystone* and *Sheerness*.

The inconvenience of travel at this time is illustrated by a journey made by the schoolfriend of the author who had to go from Cobh to Callan, a town about ten miles west of Kilkenny. He started his journey by going to Cork by launch, where he joined the *Bandon* for the overnight run to Dublin. He then made the eighty-mile journey from Dublin to Kilkenny by rail and finally arrived at his destination by jaunting car having taken about twenty-four hours to cover the eighty miles which separate Cobh and Callan geographically.

The 'war' of 1922 was not confined to land forces, for in August the Free State Army used the *Arvonia* (page 30) and the *Lady Wicklow* in an attempt to get troops to Cork. The soldiers had to be put ashore at Passage, for the block ships in the fair way prevented them from getting up the river. Earlier, during the British withdrawal in April, the British Ordnance vessel *Upnor* was held up shortly after leaving Cobh when her cargo of arms and ammunition were removed to the tug *Warrior* which had been 'commandeered' by the Irregulars a few hours before the hold up. After this all vessels carrying munitions were given an escort by the Royal Navy. In contrast, the *Lady Wicklow* had a completely uneventful journey when she evacuated the last of the Royal Irish Constabulary from Cork to Dublin later in the same month.

Cork–Welsh Bristol Channel Ports

In the latter half of the nineteenth century the City of Cork SP Co's steamers, which plied between Cork, Cardiff and Newport, carried passengers. The frequency of the service varied between one and three sailings weekly, which were taken by vessels such as the *Bitterne* and the *Pelican*. The latter vessel had a gross tonnage of 650 tons, yet on a voyage, made in February 1851, she conveyed 609 deck passengers from Cork to London. One of the 'deckers', a child, died from exposure, but, by the standards of those days, the 'deckers' were comfortable and not overcrowded for she had accommodation for 612 deck passengers, who were provided with 434 square yards of covered accommodation, 143 of which were under canvas.

Youghal–Bristol/Liverpool

The St George SP Co's vessel *Lee* made a few runs between Liverpool and Bristol via Youghal in March 1829.

Cork–Dublin/Waterford

Passengers could travel by steamer between Cork and Dublin from the late 1820s until the outbreak of the 1939–45 war. At first the Dublin workings were taken by the St George SP Co who used its *Innisfail*, *Manchester* and *Mona* to maintain weekly sailings. In latter years the service was provided by some of the Cork–Glasgow steamers of the Dublin & Glasgow SP and the Cork SS companies making a call at Dublin. The latter continued this practice until the Clyde Shipping Co took over the working of the route in the late 1850s. In the 1930s the service was provided by the company's *Fastnet* which called at Dublin on Wednesday, at Waterford on Thursday and arrived at Cork on Friday. No service was given in the opposite direction as the *Fastnet* sailed direct from Cork to Glasgow (see page 123). In the winter of 1922–3, when direct rail communication between Cork and Dublin was interrupted by the Civil War, an overnight passenger/cargo service between the two cities was provided by the City of Cork SP Co.

In the latter half of the nineteenth century passenger workings between Cork and Waterford were usually provided by certain of the Cork–Glasgow and Cork–London steamers making a call at Waterford.

7: LONGER CROSSINGS AND COASTAL CRUISING

AT one time some of the 'long-distance' steamers working between Great Britain and Ireland used to carry a limited number of passengers. Until the 1939–45 war the steamers of the Clyde Shipping Company worked between Glasgow, Plymouth and London via Belfast and Waterford, and William Sloan's vessels called at Belfast en route from Glasgow to Bristol. In the North, the Antrim Iron Ore steamers operated a fortnightly service between Belfast and Stockton via the north of Scotland. In the South, the British & Irish SP Co carried passengers on its Dublin–London steamers. Passengers on these 'long-distance' vessels were usually accommodated in four-berth cabins, many of which opened off the dining saloon. Ventilation was natural, ie by port hole and mushroom ventilator. The latter consisted of a pipe about two feet long with a screw-lid which opened on to the deck above. When the sea was rough the lid had to be screwed down and passengers got their 'fresh air' via the dining saloon; failure to close the lid meant the occupants of upper berths got a cold, sea water bath every time a wave came on board. In reasonable weather travel by these steamers could be exceedingly pleasant and in summer all available places were booked well in advance. The replacement of the older steamers by vessels with well-ventilated cabins placed amidships made for greater comfort but did nothing to destroy the happy family atmosphere on board. The stringent conditions laid down in recent years by the Board of Trade for the carriage of passengers, the better accommodation and greater space given to the crew and the difficulty in getting suitable catering staff have all contributed to the ending of this pleasant mode of travel around the coasts of the British Isles.

Antrim Iron Ore Company

This company was formed in 1872 for the conveyance of iron ore from Co Antrim to Tees-side. No passengers were taken at first but, on the arrival of the *Glendun* in 1903, the company entered the passenger trade. Three years later a second passenger/cargo steamer, the *Glenravel*, joined the fleet. This vessel was built at Troon and became a war casualty in August 1915. Her place was taken by the *Plousa*, which was renamed *Glentaise*. In August 1929 the company withdrew from shipping and the *Glendun* and *Glentaise* were sold to Coast Lines, who renamed them *Aberdeen Coast* and *Antrim Coast* respectively. For many years the *Glendun* was commanded by Capt Andrew Agnew, the master mariner who was captain of the *Fanny* and *Clyde Valley* when they ran guns to Ulster in April 1914.

The round voyage from Belfast to Stockton generally took about twelve days and calls were made at Stornoway, Dundee, Leith and Newcastle. On the outward run, when carrying iron ore, the vessels could be very stiff in a choppy sea and on the way home, when lightly loaded, they could be exceedingly lively, especially in the Pentland Firth. They generally carried about twelve passengers who were accommodated in two-berth rooms. The round trip fare was £6, exclusive of food. The latter could be paid for either by the meal, or at 7s 6d per day. The helpings were enormous and the fish and chips served at high tea were superb.

Belfast–London

In August 1826 the *Erin* made her first trip from Belfast to London, a voyage which inaugurated a direct passenger service between these two cities which lasted until the 1939–45 war. The *Erin* had a short career, which ended when she foundered with the loss of all on board off the Pembrokeshire coast in February 1833.

The service was at first worked by the Belfast SN Co but, by the late 1830s, it was operated as a joint undertaking by the British & Irish and the City of Dublin SP companies. In the 1850s the sailings were taken by the *Aurora* (see Vol 1), *Malvina*, *Oscar* and *Temora*, vessels which were advertised under the name of the Belfast Screw SS Co. A decade or so later, the Clyde Shipping Co acquired the route and, by 1887, its vessels were providing a twice-weekly service. The number of sailings reached a peak in the years immediately before the 1914–18 and 1939–45 wars when three calls were made each week at Belfast, by the company's Glasgow–London steamers. Some of these vessels also called at Waterford thereby providing a Belfast–Waterford service, a service which had been started originally by the Belfast Screw SS Co in the 1850s. In 1852 single tickets from Belfast to London by sea cost 20s saloon and 10s deck. The corresponding fares for the combined rail and steamer journey via Fleetwood and the London & North Western Railway were 54s 4d first and 22s 2½d steerage and third rail.

The Clyde Shipping Company

The Clyde Shipping Co at one time operated a fleet of passenger/cargo steamers from Glasgow. Its vessels, which had black hulls and funnels, used to be a familiar feature at many Irish ports and traded regularly as far west as Limerick. The company started business as tug owners in 1815 and entered the coastal passenger trade in 1856. Since this time the passenger trade expanded and reached its peak in Edwardian times when on each day of the week at least one Clyde steamer set off from Glasgow for either London, Southampton or an Irish port. The passenger/cargo services were curtailed somewhat in the inter-war years yet, in the summer of 1937, the following passenger sailings were operated from Springfield Quay, Glasgow:

Monday	London via Belfast, Waterford and Plymouth
Tuesday	London via Belfast
Tuesday	Cork via Dublin and Waterford
Friday	London via Belfast

In addition, a steamer was scheduled on Tuesdays to sail direct from Ardrossan to London, which was reached three days later. The vessels generally carried about forty passengers, the majority of whom were making a round trip. These coastal cruises were good value for money; thus passengers could leave Glasgow by the Cork steamer on Tuesday, spend Wednesday in Dublin, Thursday in Waterford and arrive at Cork on Friday. The return journey was commenced on Saturday and ended at Glasgow late on Sunday night. The round trip fare, exclusive of meals, was 60s. Those who wanted to economise could rough it by occupying 'made up' berths in the dining saloon and smoke room and thus qualify for a 5s reduction in fare. Corresponding round-trip tickets were issued for all the other routes and single tickets were also available.

The company's early passenger steamers had their cabins aft but, from the arrival of the *Ballycotton* in 1911, passengers were accommodated amidships. The final innovation was the placing of a glass shelter at the forward end of the boat deck, this improvement was incorporated in the *Beachy* and *Rathlin* which went into service in 1936. These were the last passenger/cargo steamers built for the company. After the 1939–45 war a gradual withdrawal from the coastal trade took place and by the mid-1960s only the Waterford–Liverpool cargo service was left. This was worked by the *Tuskar*, a vessel which maintained the Clyde Shipping Co's tradition of being named after a lighthouse or a lightship. The company now confines its activities to towing on the Clyde, where it maintains a fleet of tugs which have the prefix *Flying* in their names.

The CSC seldom acquired second-hand steamers and generally disposed of its coastal vessels when they were about twenty-five years old. So well had they been built that the majority of them gave their new owners many years of useful service.

The history of the Clyde Shipping Co was written by Alan D. Cuthbert and published privately in Glasgow in 1956.

Cork–London and the South Coast of England

Passengers could travel by steamer between Cork and London from 1826 until the 1914–18 war. The service was opened by the *Erin*, which earlier in the year had been the first steamer to trade regularly between Belfast and London. In December she was joined by the *Shannon*. Other steamers employed on the crossing in its early days included the *William Fawcett* and the *Thames*, vessels owned by the British & Irish SP Co, and which often plied between Dublin and London. From the mid-nineteenth century the route was worked by the Cork SS Co and its successor, the City of Cork SP Co, who continued to operate it until the withdrawal of the passenger service at the beginning of the 1914–18 war. The passenger service was never revived.

Dublin London

British & Irish SP Co

The British & Irish SP Co, which today is generally associated with the Dublin–Liverpool crossing, was at one time heavily involved in the Dublin–London passenger/cargo trade. The latter was the first passenger cross-channel steamer working in the world. It was opened by the paddle steamer *Thames* in the late spring of 1815 and closed down in the mid-1960s. At first the steamers worked somewhat intermittently but, after the formation of the Dublin & London SP Co, a reliable service was established and, by the late 1820s, the *Shannon, City of Londonderry* and a second steamer named *Thames* were working regularly between the two capitals. Notices advertising the service stated, 'These vessels are each provided with a qualified surgeon with every requisite means of treating with promptitude with any illness which may arise during the passage.' They also contained the information, 'No pigs or horned cattle are carried.' The latter announcement

Page 125 (above): TSS *Pioneer* (1896) at Warrenpoint with members of the Irish Railway Clearing House on board, 1896
(below): PS *Audrey* leaving Custom House Quay, Dublin, c 1910

Page 126 (above): SS *Duras* in Galway Bay, c 1895
(below): PS *Albert* (1881) and TSS *Rostellan* at Cork, c 1900

was probably for the benefit of deck passengers, for in those hard times 'deckers' used to try to keep warm during the voyage by sheltering among the livestock. The Dublin & London SP Co went into liquidation in 1837 and its place on the crossing was taken by the British & Irish SP Co, which was itself absorbed by Coast Lines in the early 1920s. In January 1965 the British & Irish SP Co returned to Irish ownership when it was purchased from Coast Lines by the government of the Irish Republic.

The original BISP fleet consisted of the paddle steamers *City of Limerick*, *Devonshire* and *Shannon*. In 1845 the company obtained its first screw steamers, which were named *Rose* and *Shamrock*, and by the turn of the century it was employing vessels such as the *Lady Olive* and *Lady Roberts* on its Dublin–London crossing. These steamers had a single screw and a speed of 13 knots. They could sleep 120 saloon passengers and 50 in the second class. Single fares for the four-day trip were 27s 6d saloon and 19s 6d second. Food was not included, but passengers could either pay for each individual meal or buy a contract ticket for all meals which cost 23s first and 17s second. Guinness stout was available at 4d a bottle and a basin of soup cost 4d; the latter beverage was available to second-class passengers only! Notices advertising the route were generally headed 'Grand Summer Cruises' and those appearing in the years immediately before the 1914–18 war contained the information that 'motor cars are carried at reasonable prices between ports.' This was at the time when the service was at its peak, with four sailings a week between Dublin and London.

Sailings were resumed in the inter-war years but their frequency was gradually decreased until in the 1930s there was only one sailing a week. Sailings were revived once more after the 1939–45 war. The route was then worked by Coast Lines who employed passenger/cargo motor vessels such as the *Caledonian Coast* and *Hibernian Coast*. These carried eleven passengers who were accommodated in single and two-berth cabins and who paid £50 for a ten-day round trip from London to Liverpool via Dublin.

PS *Duke of Argyle/Thames*

This was the first steamer to go from Dublin to London. She was built as the *Duke of Argyle* at Port Glasgow in 1814 and ran for her first season between Glasgow and Greenock. In April 1815 she was sold to R. Cheesewright & Co of London, who renamed her *Thames*. After her move to England she spent the rest of her time working on the Thames below London Bridge until she was sold for breaking up in 1835. She is now remembered for her passage from the Clyde to London via Land's End, an adventure which gave her the distinction of being the first steamer to leave the shelter of coastal waters and brave the open sea.

She set off on her epic voyage from Glasgow toward the end of May 1815. Her master was Captain George Dodd and she carried an engine room staff of one engineer and one fireman. The vessel reached Dublin on 24 May after a rough crossing and set off for Wexford at noon on Sunday 28 May with two passengers on board—Isaac Weld, secretary of the Royal Dublin Society and his wife. The latter, in spite of seasickness and the warning that the vessel was unseaworthy, insisted on going with her husband. Her persistence had its reward, for Mrs Weld became the first woman to make a cross-channel passage in a steamboat. On 29 May the vessel arrived at Wexford. The crossing of St Georges Channel to St Abbs Head was made in comparative calm, but there was trouble with the paddles which had to be remedied by removing a float from each of the wheels. On arrival within the shelter of the Welsh coast a halt of several hours was made to rest the 'stoker' and enable the engineer to oil his engines. After this the rest of the voyage became a triumphal procession which reached its climax at Portsmouth. Here a court martial on board HMS *Gladiator* was adjourned so that the members could see the curiosity which had arrived at the port and shortly afterwards the Commander-in-Chief, accompanied by three admirals and a retinue of captains, went for a cruise in the vessel. The voyage ended at Limehouse, London at 6 pm on Monday 12 June, the steamer having done the 760 nautical miles from Dublin in 122 hours of actual steaming at an average speed of just over 6 knots.

The *Thames* had a carvel hull 76ft long and 25ft over her paddles which were each 9ft in diameter. Her funnel combined the dual purpose of chimney and mast and her engine had a single vertical cylinder (22in × 36in) which took steam pressed to 2psi.

Senator Screw Schooners

In the middle 1840s passengers travelling by sea from Dublin to London could go either by the British & Irish SP Co or by the Senator Screw Schooners. The latter were described as steam schooners and were named *Citizen*, *Ranger*, *Senator* and *Tribune*. They usually sailed from Dublin on Wednesdays and were scheduled to leave London on Saturdays. Passengers travelling cabin could pay either a basic 21s or an all-in fare of 42s, which included the cost of food and steward's fee; deck passengers had no such option, their basic fare was 7s 6d.

The easy-going ways in which some steamers were run in the mid-nineteenth century is illustrated by the way in which the *Tribune* was wrecked on Carnsore Point on 27 October 1847. At the subsequent enquiry it was revealed that neither had the vessel's compass been checked at any time for local variations nor had she been given the appropriate set of charts for her passage. The lack of appropriate charts was also the main cause for the loss of the *Finn MacCoull* near the same place a year later (see page 69).

Galway–Liverpool/Glasgow

For a few years round about 1860, and at the turn of the century, passengers could travel by steamer between Galway and Liverpool. A weekly service was usually provided and in the 1860s some of the sailings were extended from Galway to Westport. The route was opened by the West of Ireland SN Co who employed the *Tubal Cain* and *Vigilant* on the crossing. The former steamer had previously worked between Bristol and London. She ended her career as a most unsuccessful blockade runner, for she was captured off the coast of Carolina on her first run in July 1862. The service was revived for a short time at the turn of the century by the Limerick SS Co.

In the latter half of the nineteenth century, some of the Limerick–Glasgow steamers made occasional calls at Galway on their outward and return journeys, thereby providing a direct steamship service between Glasgow and the capital of Connaught.

Limerick–Glasgow

A passenger service operated between Limerick and Glasgow from the middle of the nineteenth century until the outbreak of the 1914–18 war. The first mention of the working was made in a general advertisement inserted by the London & Limerick SS Co in the *Limerick Chronicle* in January 1854. In this it was stated that its *Rose* would provide a fortnightly service to Glasgow and that passengers would be carried who would be charged 15s and 7s 6d. The service seems to have operated for only a few months, after which facilities for passenger travel by sea between the two ports seems to have been suspended until June 1874, when Mr Hugh McPhail of Glasgow put the *Earnholm* on the crossing. In September 1878 Mr McPhail withdrew from the Limerick–Glasgow trade which was then taken over by the Clyde Shipping Co. The new operators continued to provide a weekly passenger/cargo service between the two cities until the passenger-carrying side of the business was given up in the early 1920s. The steamers plying on this route had to sail up the west coast of Ireland where they were often exposed to the full fury of winter Atlantic gales. On one such voyage in December 1894 the Clyde SS Co's *Inishtrahull* disappeared on her way between Glasgow and Limerick. Some time later the wreckage of a lifeboat, which was presumed to have come from the stricken vessel, was washed up near Kilkee on the Clare coast.

At the turn of the century the Clyde Shipping Co used to issue combined rail and steamer tickets from Glasgow to Killarney and other resorts in the south of Ireland. One such ticket provided steamer travel from Glasgow to Limerick, rail to Waterford by the Waterford, Limerick & Western Railway and return to Glasgow by the Clyde Shipping Co's Waterford–Glasgow steamer. This circular tour cost 33s 4d (saloon on steamer and second rail).

SS *Earnholm*

This vessel was owned by Hugh McPhail of Glasgow. She was built in 1874 and on 2 June of that year arrived for the first time at her berth at Mount Kennedy Quay, Limerick. She had a two-cylinder surface-condensing engine which gave her a speed of 12 knots. Saloon and steerage passengers were carried, who paid 15s and 4s respectively for a passage to Glasgow. She generally sailed from Glasgow on Monday and, after a call at Greenock, reached Galway on Wednesday and arrived at Limerick on Thursday. She set off on her return journey on Friday. Local passengers were carried between Galway and Limerick; these were charged 7s saloon and 3s 6d deck for a single passage. In September 1878 Mr McPhail withdrew from the Limerick–Glasgow trade and later in the year the *Earnholm* was employed on a short-lived service between New Ross and Liverpool. In 1882 she was sold to the Aberdeen, Leith and Moray Firth SS Co and was lost during the 1914–18 war. In her Limerick days notices advertising her sailings were headed 'Clyde and West of Ireland Direct Steamer' and stated she had a 'good larder and capital steward'.

SS *Fairholm*, SS *Antona*, SS *Clutha*

These vessels were employed by Hugh McPhail in the west of Ireland trade in the 1870s. The *Fairholm* originally carried cargo only, and worked between Limerick and Glasgow until replaced by the *Earnholm* in 1874. After this she was advertised as plying to those 'other ports on the West Coast of Ireland as may be agreed upon'. Her career ended when she went aground on Tory Island off the Donegal Coast.

The *Antona* and *Clutha* were built for William Sloan & Co for the Bristol–Glasgow trade in the early 1860s. They were chartered by Mr McPhail in 1878 when the frequency of the Limerick–Glasgow sailings was increased for a short time to two sailings each week.

Limerick–Liverpool

Passengers could travel by steamer between Limerick and Liverpool over the years 1854 and 1910. At first the service was very intermittent and worked by the London & Limerick SS Co's *Rose*, *Secret* and *European*. These were followed by the same company's *Mangerton*, which was employed on the route just before the temporary suspension of sailings in 1860. The crossing was reopened in 1874 by the *Holyrood*, a vessel which was owned by J. N. Russell & Sons and which had previously worked as a cargo steamer between Limerick and Glasgow. After her move to the Liverpool route she was advertised as having accommodation for steerage passengers. A few years later the service was taken over by the Limerick SS Co who generally provided a fortnightly service for passengers and cargo until the end of the Edwardian era. The steamers generally ran to Bramley Dock at Liverpool and passengers paid 17s 6d saloon and 7s 6d deck for a single journey. The vessels often called at Cahirciveen and Baltimore on the outward journey and at Tralee on the way home. Accommodation for saloon passengers was very limited. Nevertheless, the crossing was advertised as a convenient one for tourists desiring to visit Killarney.

Limerick–London

A passenger/cargo service was run intermittently between Limerick and London in the middle of the nineteenth century. It was opened in the mid-1840s by the Dublin-owned auxiliary screw schooners *Tribune* and *Waterwitch*. These vessels were withdrawn after a short time and there was no direct sailing until 1854 when the *Brandon*, *Holyrood* and *Mangerton* were advertised to provide a weekly service between the two ports. The service continued until about 1865 and was worked by a variety of steamers which included the three already mentioned and the *Express*, *European*, *Rose* and *Victory*. The fares by direct steamer were 21s for a berth in the 'state cabin' and 10s 6d steerage, prices which compared favourably with 41s and 20s 4d charged for a combined rail and steamer ticket via Waterford and Bristol.

William Sloan & Company

In 1851 William Sloan of Glasgow became agent for a screw steamer called *European* which, at that time, plied between Glasgow and London. Later in the same year he acquired a steamer of his own and in 1858 entered the Glasgow–Bristol trade with his *Brigand* and *Corsair*. These vessels were scheduled to sail from Glasgow on Wednesday and set out from Bristol on the return journey a week later. Calls were made en route at Belfast and one or more of the Bristol Channel ports. The frequency of the service gradually increased until in the days before the 1914–18 war there were five sailings a week between Glasgow and Bristol, all of which included a call at Belfast. In the days before the 1914–18 war the round trip fare from Belfast to Bristol cost 22s 6d. Passengers continued to be carried until 1932 when the passenger accommodation was removed from the company's four remaining passenger/cargo steamers—*Annan*, *Beauly*, *Brora* and *Findhorn*. In April 1968 the company, which by this time was a member of the Coast Lines Group, withdrew from the Glasgow–Bristol cargo trade.

The Sloan steamers had similar silhouettes to those of the Clyde Shipping Co. The similarity was increased by their black hulls, but the Sloan vessels had black funnels with a white band whereas those of the Clyde Shipping Co were all black. From 1880 onwards all Sloan steamers were named after rivers.

A monograph entitled *A History of William Sloan & Co* has been written by G. E. Langmuir and G. Somner; it was published by the World Ship Society in 1961.

Tralee–London/Liverpool

In 1853 the Cork SS Co's *Blarney* was advertised to run once a week between Tralee and London. In the latter half of the nineteenth century certain of the Limerick–Liverpool steamers also called at Tralee.

Ulster Steamship Company (Head Line)

In August 1877 the Ulster SS Co's first steamer was registered at Belfast. This was the *Bickley*, a vessel of about 600 gross tons with a single screw. In 1879 the management of the company was taken over by G. Heyn & Co of Belfast, and in the same year it acquired the *Fair Head*, the company's first steamer to be named after an Irish Headland.

Since this time all the Head Line steamers have had 'Head' in their names. The vessels themselves are easily identified by their black funnels which carry a white shield embellished with the red hand of Ulster. In 1917 the company absorbed the Belfast-owned Lord Line. One of the results of the merger was that the 5,000 ton deep-sea cargo steamers *Lord Antrim* and *Lord Downshire* joined the Head Line Fleet.

The company traded at first in the Baltic but, by the turn of the century, it had extended its activities to include the North Atlantic, a route on which it still carries mixed cargoes and a limited number of passengers. Today its Atlantic passenger service is worked by the *Inishowen Head*, *Carrigan Head*, *Roonagh Head*, *Torr Head* and *Rathlin Head*. These vessels have a gross tonnage of the order of 10,000 tons and can accommodate a few passengers in single and two-berth rooms. The crossing to Montreal or Norfolk (Virginia) takes about ten days and costs about £70.

A full account of the steamers owned by the Head Line has been written by John McRoberts and was published in *Sea Breezes* for June 1954.

Waterford–London and the South Coast of England

In the years between the 1914–18 and 1939–45 wars, Clyde Shipping Co steamers ran weekly between Waterford and London. The vessels sailed from Glasgow on a Monday, called at Belfast on Tuesday and left Waterford on Wednesday afternoon. On Thursday they arrived at Plymouth, where they remained for twenty-four hours, and reached their destination on Sunday. On the return journey they left London on a Wednesday and arrived at Waterford on Saturday, having made a call at Plymouth on the way. The fares charged were 45s and 22s 6d, exclusive of food. The service, which started in the mid-1830s, closed down in the early 1950s but the carrying of passengers was never revived after World War II.

The route was opened by the *St Patrick* and *Margaret* in the mid-1830s. Shortly afterwards the St George SP Co took over the working of the service, which was usually maintained by including a Waterford call in the schedule of its Cork–London sailings. The Waterford stop was omitted at about the time of the entry of the Malcolmsons of Waterford into the Waterford-London trade. In the early 1880s this part of Malcolmsons' business was taken over by the Clyde Shipping Co, who continued to work it until the close down seventy years later.

Crossing the Atlantic

In the nineteenth century crossing the Atlantic meant emigration to the average Irishman. In the period 1847–51 over a million and a quarter people left Ireland, the majority of whom went to the New World. Cobh was the principal port for the emigrants, but many went to Liverpool and Glasgow to join 'liners' which were to take them to a new life.

In the mid-nineteenth century there were two Irish transatlantic steamship companies—the Atlantic SN Co and the British & Irish Transatlantic SP Co. The former was established in 1858 to carry emigrants from Galway and to provide a fast means of communication between Europe and North America. This was in the days before the Atlantic submarine cable was in operation so the company planned to carry urgent messages between Galway and St Johns, Newfoundland, from which place they could be transmitted by land telegraph to their destinations. The company had a most unfortunate career. It was weak financially, it was over-ambitious and it had to depend either on chartered steamers which broke down or on its own vessels which were not strong enough for the North Atlantic. The crossing was seldom made within the six days stipulated by the mail contracts which the company had obtained from the British and Newfoundland governments. The company changed its name to the Atlantic Royal Mail SN Co in 1859 but continued to advertise as the *Galway Line*. It finally went out of business in 1862.

In its five 'seasons' the Galway Line employed sixteen steamers which made a total of fifty round trips. Six of the vessels were involved in serious accidents and five made either only one round trip for the company or foundered on their first crossing. Only one made more than ten round trips, this was the *Prince Albert*; her nearest rival was the *Circassian* which made eight. The company's *Adriatic* was the last wooden paddle steamer built for the Atlantic passenger trade; she was launched at New York in 1856 for the Collins Line. She is remembered in philatelic circles as the vessel whose picture was reproduced on the USA 12 cent green postage stamp issued in 1869. The *Pacific* made three round trips. Previous to her Atlantic venture she had worked for a short time on the Cork–New Milford cross-channel service.

Its ships may not have been a success but the company did make two real contributions to Atlantic travel by introducing through fares from inland towns in the British Isles to inland destinations in America and its presence forced some of the more well established ocean liner companies to call regularly at Irish ports. The latter practice reached its peak in the inter-war years when liners called at Belfast, Cobh, Derry, Dublin and Galway. A short account of the Galway Line is given in *North Atlantic Seaway* by N. R. P. Bonsor and more technical descriptions of some of the company's vessels are published in *Transatlantic Paddle Steamers* by H. P. Spratt.

The other Irish transatlantic company was also active in 1858. This was the British & Irish Transatlantic SP Co who chartered the British & Irish SP Co's *Lady Eglinton* for two round trips between Galway and the St Lawrence in the autumn of that year. The vessel had previously made two Atlantic crossings. These were carried out in 1853 when she had been chartered to the Canadian SN Co to run between Liverpool and Montreal.

In 1850 the Dublin–Glasgow steamer *Viceroy* was chartered for a voyage from Galway to Halifax and New York. On her way home she was lost off the coast of the USA. Her venture had the backing of the Midland Great Western Railway which, at the time, was interested in developing Galway as an Atlantic packet station.

8: LOCAL INSHORE SERVICES

Bantry Bay

IN 1881 the Cork, Bandon & South Coast Railway reached Bantry and three years later the small screw steamer *Countess of Bantry* opened a thrice-weekly service between Bantry and Castletownbere. The vessel was owned by the Bantry Bay SS Co, a local company in which the CBSCR owned 3,375 £10 shares. In 1906 the Congested Districts Board built a pier at Glengariff and commenced to pay a subsidy to the Bantry Bay SS Co which, in return, opened a steamer service between Bantry and Glengariff. The new route provided an attractive way of getting to Killarney for, after a forty-minute sail from Bantry, the journey could be continued by road through some of the finest scenery in Ireland. The Castletownbere service closed down before the 1914–18 war and that to Glengariff ceased operating in 1936 but for many years after this a notice board remained at Glengariff Pier which was headed BBSC.

The Bantry Bay SS Co also owned the small screw steamers *Princess Beara* and *Lady Elsie*. These vessels arrived in the early 1900s and spent over thirty years with the company. In 1905 the Shannon steamer *Lady Betty Balfour* spent a season at Glengariff after which she went to Warrenpoint.

Blackwater

In the nineteenth century small coasters used to get to Lismore by going up the Blackwater to above Cappoquin, where they entered a canal for the last two miles of their journey. The canal is no longer used and steamers today only go up river as far as Killahala where they frequently load timber for pit props. Passenger services operated intermittently on the river from 1843 until the 1914–18 war. The 1843 service ran for a few years and was worked by a steamer named *Star*. After this there was no passenger service until the early 1860s when the Cork & Youghal Railway advertised the *Daisy* (see page 160) would ply between Youghal and Cappoquin. This vessel was replaced a few years later by the *Fairy*, which remained on the Blackwater for about ten years after which the passenger service lapsed. It was revived in 1893 by the *Sibyl*, which worked on the river for a few years. After this again the service lapsed but was started once more in July 1907 by the *Dartmouth Castle*. This vessel generally took about two hours for the sixteen-mile journey on the 'Irish Rhine' from Youghal to Cappoquin. Unfortunately the river was not navigable at low tide and this prevented the steamer from keeping to a fixed timetable. Nevertheless, round-trip tickets costing 6s 6d were issued from Cork, which enabled tourists to go to Youghal by train and thence by steamer to Cappoquin where the train was joined for Cork via Mallow. The service closed down at about the beginning of the 1914–18 war and has never been revived.

A small steamer named *Ness Queen* worked 'shilling cruises' from Youghal in the summer of 1896

PS *Star*, PS *Countess*

The *Star* was advertised to run on alternate days between Cappoquin and Youghal in the late summer of 1843. Three classes of passenger were carried who paid 1s 4d best cabin, 8d second cabin and 4d deck. The vessel was owned by Capt Villiers Stewart MP who often used her as a yacht. On these occasions her place on the Blackwater was taken by the *Countess*.

PS *Dartmouth Castle*

This small paddle steamer was built in 1885 and spent her first twenty years working on the River Dart in Devon. In 1907 she was acquired by the Youghal & Blackwater Tourist Steamer Co who used her as a summer-only tourist boat on the river. At the end of her first season she received an extensive overhaul, in the course of which the height of her funnel was reduced.

Carlingford Lough

The inshore services on Carlingford Lough may be divided into two classes. One was operated by the London & North Western Railway to provide feeders for its cross-channel steamers at Greenore, the other was based at Warrenpoint and provided the ferry services to Omeath and short cruises for holidaymakers in summer.

SS *Pioneer*

The Ulster Canal Carrying Company owned this tug and generally used her for towing lighters between Newry and Lough Neagh. In the summer of 1850 she was employed on an experimental market service between Carlingford and Warrenpoint, where a connection was made with the trains for Newry. This enabled shoppers to leave Carlingford on Tuesdays and Thursdays at 9.30 am and to be in Newry at 10.45 am; on the return journey they left Newry by train at 4 pm.

PS *Dodder*, PS *Mersey*

The *Dodder* worked between Greenore and Warrenpoint from 1873 to 1876. At Warrenpoint, where the railway station was beside the harbour, her passengers transferred to the railway for the four-mile journey to Newry. Her sailings were suspended on 21 August 1876 when the direct railway was opened between Greenore and Newry. She then left the lough and was converted to be a floating coal stage for the railway steamers at Holyhead. The vessel, herself, was built for the LNWR at Dublin in 1866 and spent her early days working between Dublin and Dun Laoghaire.

The *Mersey* was owned by the LNWR who sent her to Greenore in 1880; she was replaced by the *Greenore* in 1896.

PS *Greenore/Cloghmore*

This was the last paddle steamer owned by the LNWR. She was built on the Tyne in 1896 and for the next twenty-four years she was stationed at Greenore. She ran throughout the year when her summer schedule included two trips daily to Warrenpoint in addition to the usual two or three crossings to Greencastle. She generally took about an hour each way for the long trip and about fifteen minutes to get to Greencastle. She was a one-class vessel, the fares charged for the trip from Greenore to Warrenpoint were 1s single and 1s 6d return, guests staying in the railway hotel at Greenore travelled free.

After the close down of the local service in 1920 she was sold to the Ribble Passenger Transport Company who renamed her *Ribble Queen* and used her in an unsuccessful attempt to revive cruising on the Ribble at Preston. She was taken out of service in August 1923 and was broken up two years later.

The *Greenore* was an ugly 'double ended' paddle steamer with a short mast and a single upright funnel situated amidships. When she first went on the Lough she would not steer properly and had to be lengthened by 12ft by the Dublin Dockyard Company. In 1912 her name was changed to *Cloghmore* to enable the name *Greenore* to be transferred to one of the new LNWR cross-channel steamers.

TSS *Pioneer*, SS *Pilot*

These vessels were operated by the Pleasure Steamers of Ireland Ltd. The *Pioneer* was an experimental steamer which was built and owned by Henry Barcroft of Newry. She commenced to work local trips from Warrenpoint in 1896 and is reputed to have carried 13,000 passengers during her first two months. She had Barcroft's semi-submerged propellers which were driven by a conventional high-speed steam engine through a 3:1 reduction gear. The propellers had diameters of 4ft 10in and were set with their bosses at surface level so that they were never more than half submerged. She could do six knots. A description of this peculiar craft was published in the *Proceedings of the Institution of Mechanical Engineers* for 1897. The *Pilot* ran on short excursions from Warrenport at the turn of the century. On her evening cruises she often carried an eight-piece band.

SS *Lady Betty Balfour*, SS *Countess of Mayo*, TSMV *St George*

The *Lady Betty Balfour* and *Countess of Mayo* were former Shannon steamers which were employed on excursion work at Warrenpoint in 1906 and 1908 respectively. Accounts of these vessels are given in Chapter 10.

The motor launch *St George* was stationed at Warrenpoint in the inter-war years.

Omeath Ferry

The ferry service between Omeath and Warrenpoint has been in operation for many years. At one time it was worked by rowing boats but today open motor boats are used for the ten-minute crossing. The service is well patronised in summer, especially on Sunday afternoons.

Clear Island

A motor boat runs between Baltimore and Clear Island off the southwest coast of Cork. The *Dun an Oir* was used on the service from 1930 to the early 1960s when her place was taken by the Arklow-built *Naomh Ciaran*. The latter vessel is powered by two 40hp diesel engines which give her a speed of 8 knots. In her forecastle she has accommodation for a crew of three and a small cabin for passengers under a raised poop.

Dublin Bay

Local steamships have operated intermittently at Dublin for over

150 years but few have enjoyed success for long. The vessels were employed either in cruises along the coast to such places as Lambay and Wicklow, or in attempts to work regular passenger services between Dublin and Dun Laoghaire. The former began in 1816 when the *Hibernia* took a party for a cruise from Howth and have continued to the present day. Attempts to operate regular services between Dublin and Dun Laoghaire took place during the years 1830–70. The custom of running excursions for special events such as regattas or Royal Naval visits began in 1828 when the cross-channel steamers *Innisfail*, *Kingstown* and *Mersey* took spectators to the regatta at Dun Laoghaire in July of that year. In the mid-nineteenth century everything that could float from tugs to cross-channel steamers took passengers on these special occasions. Thus in the 1860s and 1870s the tug *Integrity* cruised round the fleet as did the *Royal Charlie* in 1864. The former Belfast–Holywood steamer *Wonder* was similarly employed in the 1870s and the tugs *Knight of the Cross*, *Knight Errant* and *Knight Templar* took passengers to see the fleet on its numerous visits to Dublin in the Edwardian era.

PS *Hibernia*

In September 1816 two steamers arrived at Howth with the intention of opening a cross-channel service to Holyhead. One of the vessels was named *Hibernia*. She had a length of 77ft and a beam of 24ft; nevertheless, there were three cabins on board, one with 'beds' for eight gentlemen, a similar one for ladies and a steerage cabin with room for fourteen passengers. In addition there was room for six horses and eight carriages so she must have been like Noah's ark when fully laden! The other steamer had similar accommodation but none of the Dublin papers mentioned her name.

The service never materialised, for on 6 September a notice appeared in both *Saunder's Newsletter* and *Freeman's Journal* stating the steamer sailings had been postponed 'as some forms must be gone through at the Customs House before they are permitted to proceed on their voyages'. During their Irish visit the steamers made occasional excursions from Howth. Thus, on Thursday 5 September, the *Hibernia*, with Captain Turner in command, took a party of guests for a short cruise during which she steamed four miles in three-quarters of an hour.

No vessel under the name of *Hibernia* was given in the list of steamers published in the *Fifth Report on the Roads to Holyhead* (*1822*). It is possible, however, that the two vessels which visited Howth in 1816 were the *Caledonia* and *Britannia*. The former went from Glasgow to London via Land's End in 1816 and was sold to Copenhagen owners two years later. The *Britannia* was used at one time on the Derry–Glasgow run (see Vol 1) and made a few trips between Dublin and Liverpool in the early 1820s. Burtt, in his book *Cross Channel and Coastal Paddle Steamers*, claims the *Britannia* was one of the vessels at Howth in 1816 and states the other was named the *Hibernia*.

PS *Glasgow*, PS *Eclipse*

These vessels were employed in the Dublin–Dun Laoghaire service. The *Glasgow* was registered at Greenock in 1827 and in 1829 was mentioned in a Government Report as regularly employed making several round trips daily between Dublin and Dun Laoghaire. The *Eclipse* was the second steamer of this name to be owned by Robert Napier. She arrived at Dublin in July 1830, having previously been employed in the Belfast–Clyde cross-channel service (see Vol 1). She generally made one round trip each day between the Custom House Quay at Dublin and the Old Pier, Dun Laoghaire.

PS *Arran Castle*, PS *Isle of Bute*

These two vessels came from the Clyde, where they had been employed on the Greenock–Rothesay service. They arrived at Dublin in 1845 and 1846 respectively and remained until about 1852. During their stay in Ireland they generally worked between Dublin and Howth, a route on which they maintained a 'shuttle' service on Sundays in midsummer. The run was particularly popular for fares were cheap—6d and 4d—and the Hill of Howth has always been an exceedingly pleasant place on a warm summer afternoon. The vessels also ran to resorts south of Dublin and took racing enthusiasts to Wicklow for the race meetings.

PS *Loch Goil*, PS *Mona*, PS *Mars*

These vessels made occasional trips to Lambay and other resorts over the years 1846 to 1860. The outings generally lasted all day and there would often be a band on board to entertain the passengers. The fares charged varied according to the trip, that for the Lambay excursion being 2s. The *Loch Goil* was at Dublin in 1846. She was built in 1835 and should not be confused with the *Loch Goil* of 1853, which was stationed for a time at Derry where she traded under the name of *Lough Foyle* (see Vol 1). The *Mona* (see page 42) was employed as a tug at Dublin. The *Mars* made some excursions in the early 1860s. She was normally employed working between Dublin and Wexford (see page 99) and left Ireland to become a blockade runner in the American Civil War; she was wrecked whilst on active service off the coast of Florida in 1863.

PS *Kingstown*, PS *Dublin*, PS *Anna Liffey*, PS *Dodder*

In the early 1860s the Dublin & Wicklow Railway was so unpopular on account of the poor service and high fares it inflicted on the public, that a company called the Dublin & Kingstown SP Co was formed to run steamers between Dublin, Kingstown and Wicklow. In July 1861, it took delivery of the *Kingstown* and *Dublin*. Toward the end of the month, the former began to ply between Custom House Quay, Dublin, and Dun Laoghaire, and the latter started working to Wicklow. The Wicklow sailings were soon disbanded but the Dun Laoghaire service prospered and within a short time the *Kingstown* was joined by the *Anna Liffey*. The two vessels provided a good service with hourly sailings at holiday periods. The fares charged were reasonable, return tickets cost 9d saloon and 6d deck, while tickets bought in lots of a hundred were given a 25 per cent discount. The *Kingstown* was a double-ended vessel which was built on the Tyne in 1861.

In 1866 the London & North Western Railway entered the fray with its small paddle steamer *Dodder* but by this time the Dublin–Dun Laoghaire sea-borne traffic was in decline. In 1867 the Dublin & Kingstown SP Co withdrew from the trade and sold its two steamers, the railway company also withdrew and a few years later sent the *Dodder* to Carlingford Lough.

After this general withdrawal there were no inshore passenger steamers regularly stationed at Dublin for about twenty years.

PS *Erin's King*, TSS *Duke of Abercorn*, PS *Audrey*, SS *Storm*, SS *Alderney*

In 1891 the Wallasey ferry *Heather Belle*, appropriately renamed *Erin's King*, came to Dublin where she remained for nine years, employed in the dual role of tender and excursion steamer. At the time of her building in 1862 she was the first Mersey ferry to have two funnels and passenger saloons on her fore- and after-decks.

The *Duke of Abercorn* was built as the *Britannia* in 1888 and was stationed at Morecambe until she was acquired by the Duke Shipping Co, who changed her name to *Duke of Abercorn*. She began her career on the Liffey in April 1909, where she remained until going to Scotland to join the David MacBrayne fleet in 1913. Her only adventure when

Page 143 (above): PS *Shannon* at Limerick, c 1900. The tug with two funnels is the *Flying Huntsman*
(below): PS *Dartmouth Castle* at Cappoquin, c 1910. Note that all adults in the photographs are wearing either hats or caps

Page 144 (above): SS *Countess Cadogan* on Lough Derg, c 1898
(below): TSMV *St Brendan* at Athlone, c 1960

in Ireland occurred on 10 August 1909, when she ran aground on Dalkey Island during a fog. All her passengers were landed safely in the ship's boats and the steamer herself got away at the next high tide.

In the years immediately before the 1914–18 war afternoon cruises were sometimes made by the Cork-owned *Audrey*, by the Duke Shipping Co's *Storm* and by the Preston & Dublin SP Co's *Alderney*. In this period the cross-channel steamers of the Dublin & Glasgow SP Co used to make occasional short trips in Dublin Bay, thereby establishing a custom which was followed by the Dun Laoghaire mail boats and the British & Irish SP Co's steamers in the years between the two world wars.

PS *Cynthia*, TSS *Royal Iris*, TSS *John Joyce*

The *Cynthia*, which had spent the greater part of her career on the Foyle (see Vol 1), was acquired by Hewett's Travel Agency of Dublin in November 1931. After an extensive overhaul she made her first passenger trip in Dublin Bay on 25 March 1932, and continued on excursion work throughout the summer. In October she was laid up in Dun Laoghaire harbour but never sailed again for she was driven from her moorings during a gale in February 1933 and became a total wreck. During the Eucharistic Congress held at Dublin in June 1932, she acted as a tender to the liners anchored in the Bay, a task in which she was assisted by the ex-Mersey tender *Royal Iris*. The latter had been purchased by Messrs S. R. & R. F. Palmer in February 1932, who used her as an excursion steamer and tender for the Cunard Line at Dublin until moving her to Cork in May 1937. A second Mersey tender, the *John Joyce*, arrived in the winter of 1936–7 and was employed as an excursion steamer and Anchor Line tender until her transfer to Cork in 1939. The Dublin Bay cruises in the 1930s had a carnival air about them. People went either to see the sea or to 'take the waters'. There was singing, music and dancing on board and the proceedings were sometimes enlivened by good-natured 'drunks' explaining that Dublin was the centre of the universe.

TSMV *Larsen*, TSMV *Clearwater*, TSMV *Tara*, TSMV *Western Lady II*

Excursion traffic was revived after the 1939–45 war with the arrival of the converted landing craft *Larsen* in 1946. After two years she went to Greece where she was lost several years later. In 1954 a converted trawler ran trips for a time and in 1959 an unsuccessful attempt was made to revive cruising with a former German submarine tender called the *Clearwater*. In 1955 the ex-naval launch *Western Lady II* cruised from

Custom House Quay and Dun Laoghaire as did the *Tara* some ten years later.

ML *Jest*, ML *Rhodera*, ML *Merry Golden Hind*

The *Jest* and *Rhodera* were motor launches which did short trips from Dun Laoghaire in the 1930s and the *Merry Golden Hind* was similarly employed in the 1950s.

Galway Bay

Local passenger steamers have operated in Galway Bay for about a hundred years. They commenced in 1872 when the paddle tug *Citie of the Tribes* began to carry passengers between Galway and Ballyvaughan. At the latter place those who wanted to go to Lisdonvarna Spa could proceed by horse-drawn brake via the Cork Screw Hill, while naturalists usually went westwards by jaunting car or bicycle to explore the plant life in the Bureen country of West Clare. Through tickets by rail and steamer from Dublin to Ballyvaughan were issued by the Midland Great Western Railway. The steamer service, which only operated in summer, continued until the 1914–18 war.

In February 1891 the Galway Bay SB Co began to operate an all-year-round service between Galway and the Aran Islands. The sailings were subsidised by the Congested Districts Board in the hope that regular transport with the mainland would encourage the fishing trade in the islands. In 1951 the Aran steamer was acquired by the CIE who have continued to provide a bi-weekly all-year service to the islands with additional sailings during the summer. The steamer usually leaves Galway in the morning and returns in the evening. A stop of several hours is made at Kilronan on Inishmore which is the largest of the islands. Calls are also made at Inishmann and Inisheer where there are no harbours and where goods and passengers are ferried to and from the steamer in canvas covered rowing boats called *curraghs*; cattle have to swim and are hoisted on board by the ship's derrick. The steamers also used to go occasionally to Kilkieran Bay in Connemara.

From time to time Galway has been a port of call for transatlantic liners. From 1858 to 1862 it was the home port for the ill-fated North Atlantic SN Co (see page 134). In the inter-war years liners often called in Galway Bay to pick up passengers, who had to be ferried from the quayside to the ship by tender. The Galway Harbour Commissioners facilitated the liner calls by obtaining the former Birkenhead ferry *Lancashire* which they renamed *Cathir-na-Gaillimhe*. She arrived in the winter of 1929–30 and acted as a tender until the liner traffic began to decline. Liners ceased to call in 1939, after which there was no tender work until the Holland Amerika Line revived the custom of calling at Galway in the mid-1960s. In the summer of 1964 the former Southampton tug/tender *Calshot* arrived, resplendent in Holland Amerika colours and bearing the name *Galway Bay* on her bows. The newcomer remained at Galway employed on tender work and on running excursions to the Aran Islands until the Holland Amerika Line gave up its Galway call in 1968.

PS *Citie of the Tribes*

Galway is called the *City of the Tribes* after the fourteen Anglo-Norman families which at one time dominated the city. It was therefore appropriate that a paddle steamer bearing this name should have been used to open the steamer service between Galway and the Aran Islands in February 1891. The vessel was owned by the Galway Bay SB Co who obtained her as a tug in 1872. The company also used her on a summer-only passenger service between Galway and Ballyvaughan, which commenced soon after the steamer first arrived at Galway. In 1903 the *Citie of the Tribes* was sold to Middlesbrough owners who finally disposed of her for breaking up in 1912.

SS *Duras*

This small steel steamer was specially built for the Galway Bay trade in 1892. She was named after the residence of Major J. Wilson Lynch who at the time was chairman of the Congested Districts Board. Passengers could travel in her from Galway to Aran at a single fare of 3s saloon or 2s 6d deck. On the Ballyvaughan run she was a one-class ship charging her passengers 2s for a single journey but their bicycles were carried free!

SS *Dun Aengus*, SSMV *Nabro*, SSMV *Ros Breasil*

The *Dun Aengus* was named after the great prehistoric fortress in the Aran Islands. She was an austere vessel with a low freeboard to facilitate the loading of cargo and passengers to and from *curraghs* at Inishmann and Inisheer. Her passenger accommodation was adequate but spartan and the only refreshments obtainable on board were tea and buns. Nevertheless, for forty-six years she provided the recognised link between the islands and the outside world. During this time she continually plied on some of the most exposed waters in the British Isles, she also survived two world wars and on several occasions was literally on the rocks. After each mishap she was soon repaired and back at work so that when she was transferred to the CIE in August 1951 she qualified for the distinction of being the oldest railway-owned steamer in regular employment in Western Europe. She was finally broken up in 1958.

In her latter days the motor fishing vessels *Nabro* and *Ros Breasil* took her place when she was away for her annual surveys.

SSMV *Naomh Eanna*

This vessel is named after the patron saint of the Aran Islands. She was built in the same Dublin shipyard as the *Dun Aengus*. She has a gross tonnage of 500 tons and is propelled by a 650hp Boland diesel engine which gives her a service speed of 10 knots. Her passenger accommodation is vastly superior to that provided in earlier steamers and includes a sick bay for conveying patients between the islands and the mainland. On the other hand her comparatively high freeboard makes her facilities for cargo handling to and from *curraghs* much inferior to that of the *Dun Aengus*.

Shannon Estuary

From 1829 until the 1914–18 war inshore steamers plied between Limerick and the towns on the Shannon Estuary. The first vessels were owned by the City of Dublin SP Co but in the early 1850s a rival service was started by William Dargan who was the principal shareholder in the Limerick & Foynes Railway. Traffic at this time must have been brisk, for a third competitor, *Cardiff Castle*, arrived on the estuary and operated a pirate service for several months in the summer of that year. The City of Dublin SP Co withdrew from the Shannon trade toward the end of the 1850s, an action which gave the Dargan steamer a monopoly in the estuary trade. In 1861 Dargan disposed of his holdings (£33,000) in the LFR to William Malcolmson who at the time was chairman of the Waterford & Limerick Railway and the proprietor of the Waterford SS Co. In the next year he became chairman of the LFR and shortly afterwards replaced Dargan's steamer with vessels specially built for the Shannon estuary at his Waterford shipyard. In 1907 the Waterford SS Co's Shannon steamers were transferred to the Limerick SS Co who continued to operate them until the 1914–18 war. Attempts made to revive the passenger sailings in 1922 and 1924 were unsuccessful, as were attempts to put the former Isle of Wight car ferries *Fishbourne* and *Hilsea* on a cross-estuary car-ferry service in 1964. In 1966 the ex-Severn car-ferries *Severn King*, *Severn*

Princess and *Severn Queen* were purchased for a car-ferry service between Killimer and Tarbet but the service never materialised. Finally, on 29 May 1969, a ferry service was established between these two places by the Dartmouth-built ferry *Shannon Heather*.

The Shannon steamers were mainly passenger carriers and in their early days ran all year round. In the 1870s they ceased to operate in winter but in summer continued to make the four-hour journey between Limerick and Kilrush (Cappa Pier) calling at Foynes, Cahiracon, Redgap, Glin and Tarbet on the way. At Cappa passengers could board a four-horsed conveyance for Kilkee, the seaside resort on the Atlantic Coast of Clare. After the opening of the railway between Kilrush and Kilkee in 1892 a special train called the 'Steamer Express' ran non-stop from Cappa to Kilkee, thereby giving its patrons the longest non-stop run (8 miles) on the West Clare Railway. Through tickets were issued from Limerick to Kilkee which cost 4s first and 2s 6d deck and third rail. The steamers also provided a fast means of getting from South Clare to Kerry. At the turn of the century one could go from Kilkee to Tralee in five hours, a time which cannot be bettered by public transport today. Whereas in 1969 the journey was made by bus via Limerick, the 1900 expedition involved a rail journey by narrow-gauge train (3ft) from Kilkee to Cappa, the sea trip across the Estuary to Tarbet and thence by horse bus or jaunting car to Listowel where the standard-gauge (5ft 3in) train could be joined for Tralee.

PS *Clarence*

The *Clarence* was the first steamer on the Shannon estuary. She was built in 1827 and, in 1829, was reported as working between Limerick and Clare Castle, near Ennis. Trade must have been bad, for in 1833 she was back on the Clyde working from Gareloch.

PS *Garryowen*

The *Garryowen* was outstanding. At the time of her launch at Laird's of Birkenhead in 1834 she was the largest iron ship in the world. She was also the first steamer in the world to have iron bulkheads, an innovation which saved her from destruction when she broke away from her moorings at Kilrush during a gale in January 1839. She also acted for a short time as a research ship, for she was used by the Admiralty for an investigation into the behaviour of magnetic compasses in iron ships. The experiments were carried out in October 1835 in Tarbet Bay and the results were communicated to the Royal Society by Captain (later

Admiral) Francis Beaufort, the Irish-born sailor who devised the Beaufort wind scale.

The *Garryowen* spent twenty-four years plying between Limerick and Kilrush. In summer an itinerant fiddler named Paddy O'Neill was always on board to entertain passengers by his singing and wit. He made up ballads about his patrons and about the *Garryowen* herself—the latter, sung to the tune of Garry Owen, contained the couplet:

> She's an iron boat that flies like shot
> Against the strongest storm.

When her owners, the City of Dublin SP Co, left the Shannon the *Garryowen* is reputed to have been sold to the west coast of Africa where she probably ended her days.

PS *Erin-go-bragh*, PS *Dover Castle*

The *Erin-go-bragh* spent twenty years on the Shannon. She was built for the City of Dublin SP Co in 1841 and arrived on the Shannon in April of that year. The *Dover Castle* spent twelve years on the south coast of England before her acquisition by the City of Dublin SP Co in 1845. She remained on the Shannon until about 1860.

PS *Koh-i-norr*, PS *Kelpie*

These steamers were operated by William Dargan. The former used to work on the Clyde and was chartered by Dargan for his first attempt to break into the Shannon Estuary trade. The attempt failed and the *Koh-i-norr* foundered off the south-west coast of Ireland on her way back to the Clyde in March 1855. The *Kelpie* was purchased by Dargan in 1858 when he was making his second bid for the Shannon traffic, immediately after the opening of the railway to Foynes. Previous to this the *Kelpie* had worked between Largs and Millport. In September 1862 she was sold as a blockade runner, an occupation in which she was lost later in the same year. The *Kelpie* was certainly a good buy, for in her first four months she carried 14,000 passengers between Foynes Pier and Kilrush and her takings (£80 per week) accounted for 30 per cent of the total revenue of the Limerick & Foynes Railway.

SS *Erin*, PS *Rosa*, PS *Vandaleur*

These three vessels were owned by Mr William Malcolmson. The *Erin* was purchased by him for £23,000 from the Citizens River Steamer Co of Cork as a replacement for the *Kelpie* in 1862. After about a dozen years on the Shannon she was transferred to Waterford where she spent the rest of her career. The *Rosa* and *Vandaleur* were built at Waterford for the Shannon estuary in 1863 and 1866 respectively. The *Rosa* spent all her working life on the river but the *Vandaleur* ultimately returned to Waterford.

PS *Elwy*

In 1867 the general discontent about the poor service provided by Malcolmson's steamers reached such a pitch that Mr P. Tait, Mayor of Limerick, chartered the *Elwy* to run between Limerick and Kilrush. At the time the Malcolmson steamers plied between Kilrush and Foynes Pier, from which place Limerick-bound passengers had to continue their journey by train. After a few weeks of fare cutting the *Elwy* was withdrawn.

PS *Mermaid*, PS *Flying Huntsman*

These steamers came from the Clyde. The *Mermaid* was built in 1864 as the *Largs* and, after working on the Clyde, was acquired by the Waterford SS Co in 1875. The rest of her working life, which ended in 1903, was spent on the Shannon.

The *Flying Huntsman* was built as a tug for the Clyde SS Co in 1881. In 1885 she was acquired by the Limerick Towing Co who sold her to the Waterford SS Co in 1893. In 1907 she was transferred to the Limerick SS Co with whom she remained until just before the 1914–18 war. She was an ugly vessel with two funnels placed abreast forward of her paddle boxes. She was used mainly for towing but was pressed into passenger service at peak periods.

PS *Shannon*

This vessel was built in Belfast in 1892. Her entire peacetime working life was spent on the Shannon.

PS *The Mermaid*

In 1922 Mr L. E. Elton obtained this vessel and used her in an attempt to revive cruising on the Shannon estuary. After a few trips she was requisitioned by the Irish Free State Government to act as a 'troopship' in the Civil War. She was 'derequisitioned' in 1924, after which another unsuccessful attempt was made to revive cruising at Limerick. She was then laid up at Limerick and was ultimately sent to Preston for scrapping in 1927.

QSMV *Shannon Heather*

This drive-through car-ferry was built by Phillip & Son of Dartmouth. She began to work between Killimer and Tarbet in May 1969. She maintains an hourly service and is scheduled to sail from Tarbet on the hour. She can carry thirty cars, which are charged 20s for a passage; passengers on foot pay 2s 6d. The vessel is owned by the Shannon Car Ferry Co Ltd of Kilrush.

Suir

Waterford at times has been an exceedingly busy port. In addition to deep-sea and cross-channel shipping there was also a lively river trade between Waterford and the towns on the Suir and the Nore, a trade which lasted from the 1830s until the opening of the railways to New Ross and Rosslare in 1904 and 1906 respectively. Throughout these seventy years steamers left Duncannon and New Ross on weekday mornings and returned from Waterford in the afternoon. The deck fare from either place to Waterford was 6d and the cabin fare 1s. No passenger steamers ventured up river to Carrick-on-Suir but there was a barge trade on the Suir as far as Clonmel.

PS *Shamrock*, PS *Duncannon*, PS *Maid of Erin*, PS *Repealer*, PS *Tintern*

The first two vessels were used for the opening of the services to New Ross and Duncannon respectively in 1837. The *Shamrock* spent most of her time on the New Ross run. At one time in the mid-1840s she had the Cork Harbour steamer *Maid of Erin* as a running mate and a vessel called the *Repealer* as a rival. The latter retired after a few months.

The *Duncannon* was built by Laird of Birkenhead in 1837 and on 1 May of the same year opened the Waterford–Duncannon service. She seems to have been a versatile steamer for she was also employed at times on the Waterford–Liverpool cross-channel service and filled in her idle moments by acting as a tug on the Suir. She was replaced by the *Tintern* in 1861. The latter was built at the Neptune Iron Works at Waterford earlier in the same year and was a smaller edition of the *Ida* and *Vandaleur*. The *Tintern* was also employed occasionally on cross-channel work and returned to this on the arrival of the *Vandaleur* in the mid-seventies.

PS *Taff*, SS *Erin*

The *Taff* was launched at Bristol in 1840 where she was the first iron steamer to be built at that port. She spent her first few years working local services on the Severn. She was then acquired by the Waterford & Duncannon SN Co who employed her as a consort for the *Duncannon* on the Waterford–Duncannon service. She seems to have been a most unsatisfactory steamer for in 1851 she was converted to be a coal hulk at Waterford.

Mr Malcolmson used the *Erin* as a maid of all work at Waterford in the 1870s. She was really a cargo steamer but at times carried passengers.

PS *Vandaleur*, PS *Ida*

These steamers were sister ships. They were built for Mr William Malcolmson at his Waterford shipyard (Neptune Iron Works) in 1866 and 1868 respectively. The *Vandaleur* spent her early days on the Shannon estuary but returned to the Suir in the mid-1870s after which she spent her time working between Waterford and Duncannon. At her launch she was described as 'a beautiful new river steamer . . . with a very commodious saloon cabin fitted up with all the elegance of a modern drawing room'. The *Ida* made her maiden voyage to New Ross in company with the *Shamrock* on 31 January 1868. In spite of bad weather she did the journey in 1hr 10min. She spent her entire career working between this port and Waterford. On the opening of the railway between New Ross and Waterford in 1904 she was taken out of service and broken up at Bristol in 1909. She was a popular little steamer and is still spoken of with affection by the older inhabitants in the area, one of whom still recalls her trips on the *Ida* which took her from New Ross to visit her dentist who lived in Waterford.

PS *Venus*, PS *Undine*, SS *Kestrel*

These small steamers were used as ferry-boats at Waterford. The *Venus* came to the Suir in 1829 where she remained until her career came to a sudden end in 1839—her engine fell through her bottom!

TSMV *Officer*

This motor launch is stationed at Waterford. In summer she runs on short cruises on the river and often goes as far as Duncannon, the village where James II and William III embarked when leaving Ireland, at different times, in 1690

9: CORK HARBOUR

Cork Harbour has been a port of call for transatlantic liners for over a hundred years. It is also the birthplace of in-shore steamship services in Ireland. The latter began in 1815 and continued, without a break, until 1925, thereby providing the longest-lived local steamship service in the whole of Ireland. After the close-down, excursions continued to be run by the ocean liner tenders and other small craft stationed in the harbour. The tenders have generally been based on Cobh, the port where Queen Victoria landed in 1849 and which was known as Queenstown from 1849 to 1922.

In the early days the in-shore steamers were the property of individual owners. The change to company ownership came in the early 1840s when the Clyde shipbuilders Tod & McGregor sent some paddle steamers to Cobh and these ultimately formed the nucleus of the Citizens' River Steamers Co. This company lasted from 1844 to 1890 and in its lifetime owned a total of thirteen ships. In 1850 the Cork, Blackrock & Passage Railway became interested in shipping, an interest which finally gave them the distinction of owning the largest, and longest surviving, railway steamer fleet in Ireland. The BCPR steamers in their later days were painted green and were known as the 'Green Boats'. Their advertisements were usually headed by the symbol |ee
|ooks
|ovely
. The River Company's steamers usually went up the Lee to Cork whereas the railway vessels normally worked from Passage where passengers boarded the train for Cork. The River steamers provided five or six sailings on week-days between Cork and Cobh, several of which were extended to Aghada. The railway, on the other hand, provided a fixed interval service with sailings from Passage at twenty minutes past each hour, immediately after the arrival of the connecting trains which had left Albert Quay Station (Cork) on the hour. The steamers were due at Cobh twenty-five minutes after sailing from Passage, having called at Monkstown Pier, Haulbowline and Glenbrook Baths on the way. Some of the sailings were extended to Crosshaven and Aghada, where the railway installed a 'station master'

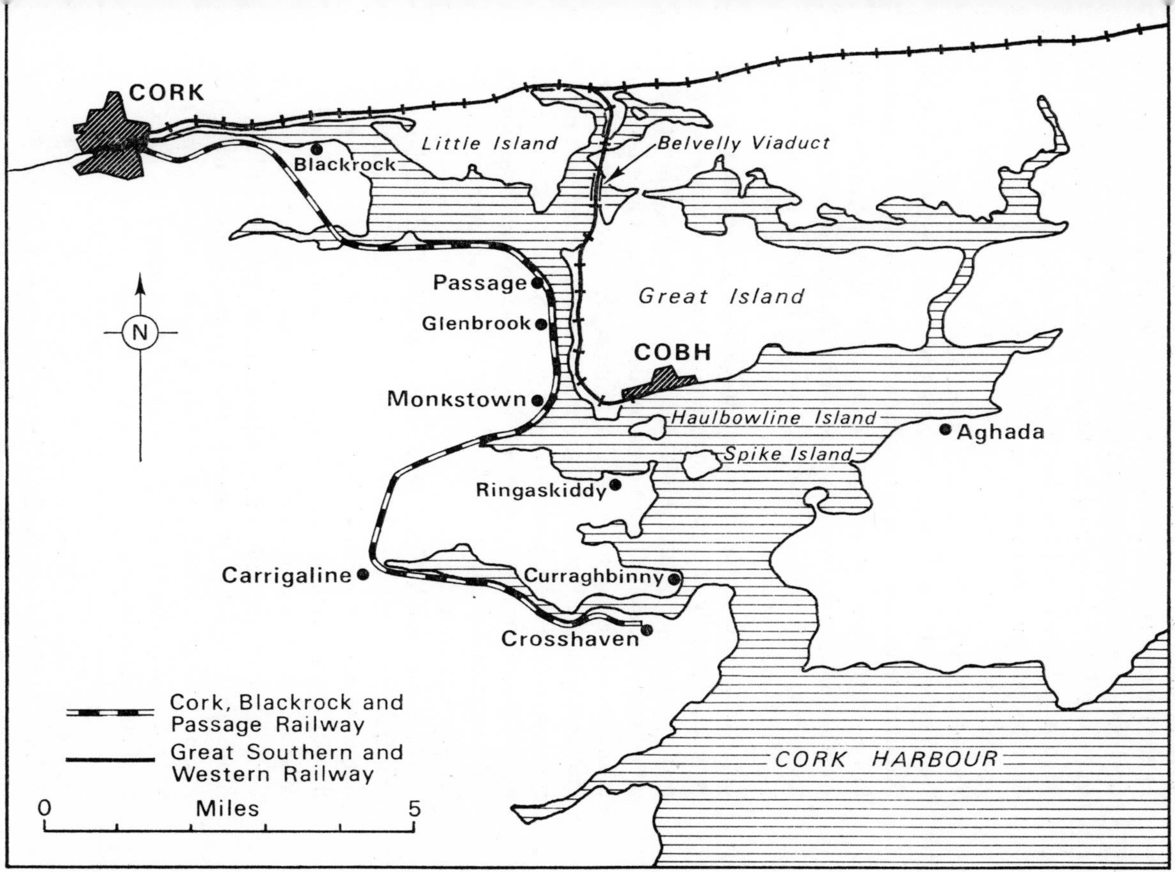

Cork Harbour

to look after its interests. Combined rail and steamer tickets from Cork to Cobh cost 1s 4d first and 8d third whereas the same journey by the River Company's boats cost 1s and 8d. These were the normal fares but, on the occasions when the two companies were enjoying a real good 'hate', fares would be reduced to 2d and time-tables would be so arranged that rival steamers were due at Cobh, Haulbowline and the other stopping places at the same time. The first to arrive at a pier generally collected the lion's share of the traffic so each captain did all he could to ensure his vessel was not second.

In 1890 the River Co went into liquidation and its vessels, which by that time were in a run-down condition, were acquired by the railway. In 1902 part of the extension of the CBPR from Passage to Crosshaven was completed and the railway moved its 'packet station' to Monkstown Pier. By this time, however, a decline in traffic had already set in. This led to a reduction in the number of sailings and an increase in the overall journey time from Cork to Cobh to fifty minutes. In bad weather, especially in fog, the crossing at times took hours. On one particular summer Sunday in 1893 the *Monkstown* and another steamer set off from Crosshaven with over 700 day-trippers on board. Fog set in and the vessels had to lie off Curraghbinny for several hours. They ultimately reached Passage at 2.40 am and the connecting train got its passengers to Cork as dawn was breaking on Monday morning. The excursionists were not so miserable as they should have been, for the kind-hearted residents at Curraghbinny had rowed out to feed the hungry with tea and buns.

When the British Naval Base was located in Cork Harbour the Admiralty ran ferries between Cobh, Spike Island and the other establishments in the harbour. The British War Office also maintained a fleet of small steamers two of which, the *General McHardy* and the *Wyndham*, remained at Cobh after the British had handed over the harbour forts to the Irish in July 1938. In recent years the civilian inter-island service had been maintained by large diesel launches owned by Marine Transport Services Ltd. The liner tenders, which at one time were privately owned, are now owned and managed by the Cork Harbour Commissioners.

PS *City of Cork*, PS *Waterloo*

The *City of Cork* was the first steamer to be built in Ireland. She was launched at Andrew & Michael Hennesey's Boat Yard, Passage, on Saturday 10 June 1815 and, later in the same year, began to ply between Cobh and Cork. In 1837 she was rebuilt after which she continued in service until about 1850. She had a wooden hull 86ft long and a single mast. She was powered by a Bolton & Watt 12hp engine which gave her a speed of 6½ knots. As she became older she became so decrepit that it is said she was once stopped by a shoal of jelly fish. In her prime a club atmosphere prevailed on board, the latest London papers were provided in her saloon and sea-water baths were available for her passengers.

The *Waterloo* was built at Passage in 1816. She was of about the same size as her consort. Her engine was built by James Atkinson at the Hives Iron Works in Cork and was probably the first marine engine to be built in Ireland. It was certainly the first marine engine in that country to be rebuilt, for a second cylinder was added after a few years. The career of this vessel as a passenger carrier ended in 1850 when she was converted to a lighter. Her hull is reputed to have been broken up in 1865.

PS *Princess Charlotte*, PS *Lee*

The *Princess Charlotte* was built on the Clyde in 1814 and came to Cork about 1820. Little is known concerning her stay at Cork except that on one occasion an illicit poteen still was found in action in her engine room.

The *Lee* was built in London in 1825 and arrived at Cork in the early 1830s. Like the *City of Cork* she too had salt-water baths on board. She remained for only ten years in Ireland and foundered off Newquay, Cornwall, on her way back to England in 1840.

PS *Air*, PS *Eagle*

These vessels were the first of the many tugs to be stationed on Cork Harbour. The *Air* was built on the Clyde in 1825 and was acquired by the St George SP Co in 1831, who used her for towing and excursion work. In the mid-1830s she often ran to Youghal and made the occasional weekend trip to Glengariffe. She was sold to Bristol owners in 1840. The *Eagle* arrived in 1838. She was the first iron steamer to be registered at Cork, where she remained until scrapped in 1851.

PS *Queen*, PS *Maid of Erin*, PS *Prince*, PS *Princess*, PS *Royal Alice*, PS *Malabar*

The first four steamers were originally owned by Tod & McGregor who sent them to Cork over the years 1838–43. In 1844 the vessels formed the nucleus of the Citizens' River Steamers Co fleet. The *Queen* and *Maid of Erin* arrived in 1838. After a few years they went to Waterford, but it was not long before they were back on the Lee. In 1850 the *Queen* was chartered to the CBPR to initiate the railway's first steamer service. The *Princess* and *Prince* arrived in 1841 and 1844 respectively. Both had figureheads, that on the *Prince* was a man on a horse and the *Princess* carried the head and shoulders of a lady.

The *Royal Alice* was also a Tod & McGregor steamer. She was acquired by the River Co in 1847 and remained at Cork until 1862. She was sloop-rigged with one mast and did not have a figurehead. The *Malabar* was stationed at Cork in the spring of 1844.

PS *Prince Arthur*, PS *Prince of Wales*

These vessels were acquired by the Citizens' River Steamers Co in 1861. The *Prince Arthur* had arrived at Cork ten years previously and had spent her time working as a privately owned passenger steamer in the harbour. The *Prince of Wales* was built at Glasgow in 1858 for Dublin shipowners, who immediately sent her to Cork. She was the first in-shore steamer at Cork to have paddles with feathering floats.

PS *Citizen*, PS *Lee*, SS *Erin*, PS *Lily*, PS *City of Cork*, PS *Erin*

These vessels were the property of the Citizens' River Steamers Co. The *Citizen* and *Lee* were sister ships. They were built on the Clyde in 1861 and spent all their working lives at Cork. The *Erin* was a small screw steamer which was used mainly for cargo. She was sold to the Malcolmsons of Waterford in 1862 who used her on the Suir and on the Shannon.

The *Lily* was the smallest steamer owned by the company. She was built at Cork in 1861 for the River Blackwater but never seems to have left the Lee, until her sale to Holywood owners in 1871. In the North she set up a record of twenty minutes for the run from Belfast to Holywood (see Vol 1). She was a double-ended vessel with a bow rudder designed to help her negotiate the bends on the Blackwater.

In 1866 the company took delivery of the *City of Cork* from G. Robinson & Co, the Cork shipbuilders. She was the first in-shore steamer on the Lee to have a steel hull. She is reputed to have completed the journey from Cork to Cobh in forty minutes.

The PS *Erin* was the last steamer acquired by the company. She was built as the *Rosneath* for the Greenock & Helensburgh SB Co. Four years later she was purchased by foreign owners, who changed her name to *Rosolio*. In 1872 she was acquired by the River Co who changed her name to *Erin*. On the liquidation of the company in 1890 she, and her consorts *Citizen*, *City of Cork* and *Lee* were purchased by the CBPR for

£800. The *Erin* and *City of Cork* were scrapped almost immediately, the *Citizen* was cut up in 1891 and the *Lee* in 1893.

PS *Albert*, PS *Fairy*, PS *Queenstown*, PS *Victoria*

The CBPR used chartered vessels from the beginning of its steamer services in 1850 until it got the necessary parliamentary authority in its Act of 1881 to have steamers of its own. In 1855 the *Queenstown* became a private yacht but the other three were retained on charter until the railway purchased them in the early 1880s. The *Fairy* spent part of her 'middle career' on the Blackwater.

PS *Albert*, PS *Glenbrook*, PS *Monkstown*

In the early 1880s the CBPR fleet was augmented by the arrival of these vessels. The *Glenbrook* was built at Poplar in 1877 and arrived at Cork four years later. The *Albert* and *Monkstown* were built by McIlwaine & Lewis of Belfast. The *Albert*, when built, had the engine belonging to the *Albert* of 1854 which had been traded in as part payment for the new vessel. In 1891 a compound diagonal engine built by M. Paul & Co of Dumbarton was fitted as a replacement for the original, simple, oscillating engine. The *Glenbrook* was scrapped in 1903, the *Monkstown* was sold in April 1910 and the *Albert* remained at Cobh until the close down of the railway steamer service in 1925. She was towed to England and scrapped in 1927.

TSS *Rostellan*, TSS *Queenstown*

These small vessels were the only screw steamers built for the railway. They normally worked cargo to the quays at Cork whereas the other steamers ran to and from Passage. Both vessels were built by McIlwaine & McCall of Belfast in the early 1890s and remained at Cork until the close down of the railway steamer service. The *Queenstown* was then sold to Lydney (Glos) owners with whom she remained until the 1939–45 war; the *Rostellan* stayed in Ireland and was scrapped in the late 1930s.

PS *Audrey*, PS *Mabel*

These vessels came to Cork in 1909 and 1910 respectively. After a short time they were chartered by the CBPR who used the *Audrey* on the Aghada run on weekdays and on excursion work on Sundays. At the end of the charter she went to Dublin and finally returned to England in 1914. The *Mabel* returned to England in 1918.

PS *Empress*, PS *Hibernia*

The *Empress* was built in 1893 for the Goole & Hull SP Co. During the 1914–18 war she was acquired by the Tay SB Co who sold her to the CBPR in 1918. She remained with her new owners for about four years and was then sold for scrap. She was unique among Irish in-shore paddle steamers in having a triple-expansion engine.

The *Hibernia* was chartered by the CBPR in October 1922. She plied between Cobh and the quays at Cork until the railway line between Monkstown Pier and Cork was re-opened after the Civil War. She returned to Plymouth in April 1923.

PS *Arran Castle*, PS *Daisy*, PS *Mosquito*, PS *Smoker*, PS *Commissioner*

These vessels were employed at Cork in the early 1860s. The *Arran Castle* was used as a tender for the Inman Line whose vessels called at Cork on their way to New York.

The *Daisy* was owned by the Cork SS Co, who used her mainly as a tug. In 1866 she was acquired by Cardiff owners but was sold back to Cork in 1881. She was broken up in 1888. In the early 1860s she was employed for a time on the Blackwater and, in the days before the opening of the railway between Cork and Youghal, she frequently plied between these two places.

The *Mosquito* was built locally to be a liner tender in 1864. After a few years she was sold to foreign owners. The *Smoker* and *Commissioner* were built at Cork as tenders for the Cork Harbour Commissioners in 1862.

PS *America*, PS *Ireland*, PS *Flying Fish*, TSS *Morsecock*, SS *Lyonesse*

Until the 1890s the tugs at Cork also acted as tenders to the ocean liners when they called to embark passengers and collect mail. The first steamers to be used exclusively as tenders were the Clyde Shipping Co's paddle steamers *America* and *Ireland*, which were stationed at Cobh from 1891 to 1928. The *Ireland* was then sold to Belgian owners and the *America* was acquired by the Anchor Line, who changed her name to *Seamore*. Under her new name she acted as a tender at Derry until the outbreak of the 1939–45 war (see Vol 1). The Clyde Shipping Co's tug *Flying Fish* was also stationed at Cork where she was often pressed into acting as a passenger tender.

The *Morsecock* was built in 1877 as the Admiralty salvage vessel *Stormcock*. In 1922 she was acquired by Mr Samuel Palmer who changed her name to *Morsecock*. She remained at Cobh until the 1950s, employed as an ocean tug and working on the occasional excursion to Ballycotton.

In the 1920s the liners of the Anchor, Cunard and White Star Lines were generally looked after by the *America* and *Ireland*, whilst the *Morsecock* acted as tender to the vessels of the United States Lines.

The salvage tug *Lyonesse* was at Cork over the years 1917 to 1928. She is reputed to have made occasional excursion trips on Sunday afternoons.

PS *Duke of Devonshire*

This vessel spent most of her working career on the south coast of England. She came to Cork in 1934, where she was employed on local excursion work until her return to England in July 1936. She then became a member of the Cosens's fleet and her name was changed to *Consul*. In 1968 she was sent to Woolston, on the river Itchen, for breaking up. At the time she was over seventy years old and was the senior paddle steamer on the south coast of England. A full account of the career of this vessel was published in the May 1969 issue of *Ships Monthly*

TSS *An Saorstat*, TSS *Failte*, TSS *Blarney*, TSS *Shandon*, TSS *Killarney*

These former Mersey ferries were used as tenders at Cork between 1927 and 1962. The *An Saorstat* and *Failte* were originally the Wallasey Corporation ferries *Rose* and *Lily*. They were purchased by Mr Samuel Palmer in 1927, who gave them Irish names and used them for tender and excursion work at Cobh until their sale to the British & Irish Steel Corporation in 1941. The *Failte* was wrecked in 1943 but the *An Saorstat* survived until 1951.

The *Blarney* and *Shandon* also came from Wallasey. The former was built as the *Iris* in 1906 and was given the title *Royal* in 1919 for the part she played in the Zeebrugge raid in April 1918. In 1932 she was sold to Messrs S. R. & R. F. Palmer who used her first at Dublin and then transferred her to Cork in May 1937. The *Shandon* was originally the *John Joyce*. She too spent a few years at Dublin before going to Cork in May 1939. Both vessels were acquired by the Cork Harbour Commissioners in 1946 who gave them local names. The rest of their working lives was spent at Cork.

The *Killarney* was originally named *Francis Storey*. In her early days she worked between Liverpool and Seacombe and later was put on the New Brighton run. During the 1939–45 war she was requisitioned as an Admiralty net carrier but survived to return to ferry work after the Armistice. In 1951 she was acquired by the Cork Harbour Commissioners who renamed her *Killarney*. She was broken up in 1962.

TSMV *Blarna*, TSMV *Cill Airne*

These diesel-engined tenders were built by the Liffey Dockyard in Dublin and arrived at Cork in September 1961 and April 1962 respectively. The traffic for which they were ordered failed to materialise and the *Blarna* was sold to Bermuda for £150,000 in July 1965; she has subsequently been renamed *Canima*. The *Cill Airne* is still in service in Cork Harbour.

Marine Transport Services Ltd

The small craft of Marine Transport Services Ltd are now a familier sight at Cobh. The company was formed in the 1930s by Mr Daniel Fitzpatrick, who has been its managing director for many years. The company's fleet includes coasters, lighters and small, passenger-carrying vessels. All the last mentioned are diesel-operated and have one-man control, ie the steering and engines are both controlled from the wheelhouse.

Marine Transport Services' largest passenger-carrying vessel is the *David F*. She was completed in 1962 and is certified to carry 330 passengers. The other passenger-carrying vessels of the company are the *William J*, *Billet*, *Geata Ban*, *Ingot*, *John L*, *Marianne*, *Thomas O'S*, and *190*; the dimensions of the larger vessels are given in the Fleet List.

10: INLAND NAVIGATIONS

The Boyne

THE Boyne was navigable, at one time, for barge traffic from the tideway at Oldbridge, near Drogheda, to Navan. In 1905 a steam passenger launch, named *Ros-na-Righ* started making three round trips weekly between Oldbridge and Navan. Circular tour tickets were issued at 4s which enabled tourists to go by river to Navan and to return to Drogheda by train, the fare included conveyance by jaunting car between Drogheda and Oldbridge. The service closed down a few years before the 1914–18 war. Today the twenty locks, which made the river navigable for commercial traffic, are in a state of decay and the river is passable only by canoe.

Lough Corrib

Lough Corrib is the second largest lake in Ireland. Its northern shore is within a few miles of Lough Mask, to which it is connected by an underground river. In the early 1850s a canal, four miles in length, was dug between the two lakes but it was abandoned in 1853 when it was found the water seaped through the porous limestone so rapidly that it was impossible to fill it. The path dug for the canal can still be seen near Cong today.

There was little shipping on Lough Corrib until 1852. Early in that year the dredging of the outlet to the sea had been completed and in August a lock (130ft × 20ft) was opened to enable small steamers to get from the Corrib to Galway Bay. Little sea-bourne traffic penetrated to the lough but the lock and canal did enable the Corrib steamers to get to the dry docks in the port of Galway for their annual surveys and so dispensed with the expense of maintaining dry-dock facilities on the lough. Steamer services reached their peak in 1906 and 1907 when three vessels plied on the lough. After this a decline set in and all passenger services stopped during the 1914–18 war. In recent years the only public transport on the lough have been motor launches making half-day trips from Galway and other tourist resorts on the lake. Among the vessels so employed is the *Maid of Coleraine* which arrived from the

Bann in 1866 (see Vol 1, p 178). There have never been any steamships on Lough Mask.

PS *O'Connell*, PS *Enterprise*, PS *Father Daly*, PS *Lioness*

These four vessels worked on the Corrib in the 1850s. Sir William Wild in his book *Lough Corrib* claims the *O'Connell* was the first steamer on the lough. She was a small coaster which was stationed at Galway; illustrations of her appear in the *Illustrated London News* for 8 June 1850. The *Father Daly* is said to have been the first steamer to carry passengers, and the *Lioness* ran on the first regular passenger service on the lough, which opened between Galway and Maam on 19 July 1860.

PS *Eglinton*

This vessel was owned originally by the Lough Corrib SN Co but in her latter days she was registered as the property of Lord Ardilaun. She was built for the Corrib and made her maiden voyage on 7 July 1862. For the next thirty-six years she plied regularly at least three times a week between the Wood Quay at Galway and Cong, with a call at Kilbeg en route. In summer a daily service was usually maintained. The fares charged ranged between 3s and 4s for a cabin passage and from 1s 6d to 2s deck.

SS *St Patrick*, SS *Cliodhna*

The *St Patrick* was built locally and replaced the *Eglinton* on the Galway–Cong run in 1898. She remained on the lough until the 1914–18 war. On the arrival of the Shannon Development Co's *Fairy Queen* on the lough in 1906 a fare war broke out between the newcomer and the *St Patrick*. This reached a climax when one could get from Galway to Cong for 6d. The *Cliodhna* traded for several years between Galway and Maam in the early days of the twentieth century.

SS *Fairy Queen*, SS *Countess Cadogan*

The first named of these steamers worked on the Corrib from August 1906 until replaced by the *Countess Cadogan* in September 1913. Both steamers came from the Shannon.

The Shannon

The Shannon is the longest river in the British Isles. It rises in Cuilcagh Mountain in County Cavan and enters the sea at Loop Head in County

Battle Bridge –
Pastunna

"over 100 miles"

21

payingyourbill

Online payment

You can pay quickly, easily and s
any debit or credit card at www.v

Direct Debit

Take the hassle out of paying your bi
with a Direct Debit. Choose when you
and 22nd of the month. Simply visit **w**

Internet and telephone banking

To pay by home or telephone banking
20-74-09 and account number 805 4
your customer number found on your

Payment card

You can pay with our payment card at
To get a payment card visit **www.veoli**

Clare. In its 224 mile journey it broadens out to form lakes, the largest of which are Lough Allen, Lough Ree and Lough Derg. All the lakes are windswept and can be exceedingly dangerous, as the water can get rough very quickly and on Lough Derg there is the additional hazard of rapidly developing fogs. The lakes and every reach of the river have taken their toll of shipwreck and disaster. In December 1907 the Grand Canal cargo steamer *Portumna* and her tow of eight barges were marooned for several days on Lough Derg and fifty years earlier, on the same lough, the passenger steamer *Duchess of Argyle* was holed when she hit a rock during a fog. Fortunately in both these cases there was no loss of life due to the competent seamanship of those in charge, for the Shannon watermen have always been good seamen, who know and respect their river.

In the latter part of the nineteenth century the non-tidal part of the river was navigable from Lough Allen to Limerick, a distance of 150 miles. Today, however, the requirements of the hydro-electric power station at Ardnacrusha, near Limerick, have so reduced the level of the water in the upper reaches that navigation ends at Battle Bridge, some six miles north of Carrick-on-Shannon.

The creation of an inland navigation on the Shannon was one of the objects of an Act passed by the Irish Parliament in 1715. In the course of the next hundred years the river was made passable after a fashion. Some of the works of this early navigation are still in existence, such as the narrow canal at Magazine Road, Athlone. The navigation in use today was built by the Shannon Commissioners in the period 1840–50. The Commissioners were established in 1835 to supervise the navigation of the entire river which had previously been the responsibility of three different bodies. The duties of the Shannon Commissioners were taken over by the Board of Public Works in 1846, since which time the maintenance of the navigation on the river has been a direct government responsibility.

The Commissioners rebuilt the navigation from Battle Bridge to Lough Derg, but they did little to improve either the river between Battle Bridge and Lough Allen, or the canal between Killaloe and Limerick. The result is that today there is a magnificent stretch of water some 115 miles in length between Battle Bridge and Killaloe with five locks; those north of Lough Ree are 120ft × 30ft, and the two between Lough Ree and Lough Derg are even larger (155ft × 40ft). Unfortunately the narrow locks (105ft × 19ft) between Killaloe and Limerick prevent sea-going vessels from getting up the river. No attempt was made to remove this bottleneck when the Limerick Canal was reconstructed at the time of the building of the Ardnacrusha power station in the 1920s, for the locks of the new canal are of approximately the same size as those they replaced.

Traffic on the river reached a peak in the mid-1840s when 105,000 tons of merchandise and 20,000 passengers were carried annually. Nearly all of this was on the reach between Limerick and the Grand Canal. There was a little traffic between the Grand Canal and Athlone, but above Lough Ree it was light. Traffic to and from the Royal Canal was also meagre and that to the Erne, via the Ballinamore Canal, was virtually non-existent.

For the past hundred years the Grand Canal Co and its successors, the CIE, have been the principal carriers on the river. In the early days traffic was worked by John Grantham's Shannon SP Co, a company which was acquired in March 1829 by the Inland SN Co. The latter was itself absorbed by the City of Dublin SP Co a few months later. In the early 1840s the City of Dublin SP Co had a monopoly of the river trade. Its *Marquis Wellsley* worked between Shannon Harbour and Athlone, its *Avonmore*, *Dunally* and *Gazelle* ran between Shannon Harbour and Portumna and its *Lady Lansdowne*, *Lady Burgoyne* and *Clanricarde* plied on Lough Derg. The completion of the large locks at Meelick and Athlone in 1846 enabled the larger Lough Derg steamers to get up the river to Shannon Harbour, Athlone and places further north.

In 1857 the Midland Great Western Railway, who owned the Royal Canal, opened a steamer service of its own on the river. This action ultimately forced the City of Dublin SP Co to withdraw from the Shannon trade. In the early 1860s the railway steamers themselves were laid up and for the next thirty-five years there were no regular passenger steamers stationed on the river. Goods, however, continued to be carried; this part of the Shannon trade now became the monopoly of the Grand Canal Co, who had first put steamers of its own on the river in the mid-1840s.

In 1897 a vigorous attempt was made to revive passenger services. This was carried out by the Shannon Development Co, an organisation which received a grant of £9,500 from the Government as well as subsidies from local railways and from the counties which bordered on the river. By 1898 it had placed six steamers on the Shannon—two were regularly employed on the Athlone–Killaloe service, a journey which took about eight hours; another made a daily round trip between Athlone and Roosky; the fourth worked between Roosky and Carrick-on-Shannon; the fifth was employed on the trans-Lough Derg ferry and the sixth was in reserve. The company's 1898–9 timetable is given in Table 2. The conditions of the subsidy required the vessels to operate all year, but these were relaxed when it became obvious there was no winter traffic. Even in summer support was poor. The services were gradually curtailed until, in 1905, they were limited to the daily run between Killaloe and Banagher. In connection with these sailings the Great Southern & Western Railway issued round-trip tickets from Dublin at 13s which covered the rail journey to Banagher, the river cruise with lunch on board and the return journey from Killaloe to Dublin. The service closed down at the beginning of the 1914–18 war.

TABLE 2

Shannon River Service 1898–9

Winter		Summer				Summer		Winter	
Mon Fri	Thur	Dly	Dly			↑ Dly	Dly ↑	Tues Sat	Wed
	0930	1200		—	Carrick-on-Shannon	1800			1630
		1415		14	Roosky	1545			1400
	1130		1545		Roosky		1215		
	1330		1750	29	Lanesborough		1000		1140
	1630		1945	49	Athlone		0800		0830
0930		1000			Athlone	1630		1630	
1200		1245		72	Banagher	1320		1330	
1630		1745		108	Killaloe	0815		0830	
		↓	↓						

Trans-Lough Derg Service, daily in summer; Monday, Tuesday, Friday, Saturday in winter. Steamers connect with Athlone–Killaloe service at Williamstown.

(Distances from Carrick-on-Shannon are given in English miles)

Regular passenger services started again in June 1955 when the CIE launch *St Brendan* made her initial trip on the river. In 1956 she was joined by the *St Ciaran*. Both vessels operate in summer, when they work afternoon and evening excursions from the towns along the river and provide longer cruises for the patrons of the CIE coach tours. In the 1960s numerous small cabin cruisers were built for private hire firms and in 1961 an enterprise was started which provides six-day cruises, patrons of which live on board. This is the first occasion that proper sleeping accommodation has been provided on a commercial inland 'steamer' in Ireland. Goods traffic, however, has declined. In

1959 CIE, who had taken over the Grand Canal Co in June 1950, ceased to carry goods on the river and disposed of the 'Grand Canal Warehouses', which had been a prominent feature on the quays on the Shannon for over a hundred years.

PS *Marquis Wellsley*

The first steamer on the Shannon was John Grantham's *Marquis Wellsley*. She was a double-hulled vessel with a paddle wheel between her hulls. Her registered tonnage was about 100 tons and her 12hp engine gave her a speed of about 3 knots. She was built by the Horsley Iron Works at Tipton, Staffs, and arrived at Lough Derg in 1825. This made her the first iron steamer to ply in Ireland, and the second lake steamer in the country; the first lake steamer went into service on Lough Neagh four years earlier. On the formation of the Inland SN Co in 1829 she was transferred to the new company who put her on the Athlone–Shannon Harbour run, a trip she performed twice a week in a time of about eight hours. She remained on the Shannon for over thirty years and was last reported as fit for duty, but laid up, in 1858.

PS *Lady Lansdowne*, PS *Clanricarde*

The *Lady Lansdowne* was one of the largest river steamers to work in Ireland, and was the first iron vessel to be built by John Laird (now Cammell, Laird) of Birkenhead. She had a 90hp engine with two wrought iron cylinders 38in × 42in. Her career on the Shannon began in the winter of 1833–4, when she was put together at Killaloe, having been taken there in sections by canal as her size prevented her from going through the small locks on the Limerick–Killaloe part of the river. She spent nearly all her working life making a daily round trip with passengers and goods between Killaloe and Portumna. After the completion of the large locks at Meelick and Athlone she occasionally went up stream and made her first visit to Athlone in June 1849. She certainly gave her owners good value for money, for she continued in service until the mid-1850s, after which she was laid up at Killaloe where her hull still lies some three feet below the surface of the lake. A photograph of part of her 'remains' was published in a paper on Charles Wye Williams which was written by J. Foster Petree and published in Vol 39 of the *Transactions of the Newcomen Society*.

In the early 1840s the City of Dublin SP Co carried out trials on the use of turf fuel on board the *Lady Lansdowne*. In these it was found that whereas she required 24 tons of coal a week at a cost of £18 she could be run on 55 tons of turf at about half the price. The outcome of the trials was that the company converted some of its other steamers to turf fuel, an action which reduced its coal consumption from 3,100 tons in 1839 to 720 tons in 1843; in the latter year 7,000 tons of turf were consumed.

The *Clanricarde* was built in 1829 and spent the greater part of her time as a tug on Lough Derg. From time to time she acted as relief steamer on the Killaloe–Portumna passenger service.

PS *Avonmore*, PS *Gazelle*, PS *Dunally*

These three vessels were originally employed on the Portumna–Shannon Harbour reach at a time when the locks on this part of the river were too small to take the large Lough Derg steamers.

The *Avonmore* was a stern-wheeler. When she went into service in 1835 she generally sailed from Shannon Harbour every morning for Portumna, where her passengers transferred to the Lough Derg steamer. On her return journey she would often be crowded with passengers en route from Limerick to Shannon Harbour, where they joined the Grand Canal fly boats to continue their journey to Dublin. In her latter days she was often used on the Athlone–Killaloe run. The *Gazelle* had a double hull and a stern paddle wheel which was flanked by her two rudders. In Dr James Johnson's *Tour of Ireland* (published 1848) there is a somewhat jaundiced account of a trip in this vessel which progressed 'at a slow rate along a dull canal and through flat meadows'. The *Dunally* had a double hull and it seems probable that she, too, was a stern-wheeler.

Nonsuch

This peculiar horse-drawn canal boat worked for several years between Limerick and Killaloe. She had a sectionalised hull 80ft long, with a 'fixed' amidships section to which a bow and stern were attached by hinges. On entering a lock the bow and stern were raised thereby enabling the vessel to get into the 60ft pond; in addition raising the bow acted as a brake, for the 'square front' of the amidships portion offered so much resistance to the water that the vessel could enter a lock at 9mph and yet be pulled up before the 'blunt front end' reached the inner lock gates. Charles Wye Williams, the designer of the boat, claimed the 80ft hull made the water resistance less than that of a conventional 60ft canal boat. A short paper on this peculiar vessel was read before the Institution of Civil Engineers on 3 March 1840.

PS *Lady Burgoyne*, PS *Wye*

This vessel arrived in the early 1840s, when she was put to run along with the *Lady Lansdowne* on Lough Derg. After the completion of the Shannon improvements in 1846 she extended her run to Athlone, and in the mid-fifties was scheduled to make three round trips a week between Athlone and Killaloe. She was ultimately driven off the river in the late 1850s by the railway steamers which are reputed to have carried local passengers for nothing!

Thom's Directory for 1848 lists the *Wye* as one of the City of Dublin SP Co's steamers employed on the Shannon.

PS *Duchess of Argyle*, PS *Artizan*, SS *Lord Lorton*, PS *Midland*

In 1858 the Midland Great Western Railway advertised a through rail and steamer service from Dublin (Broadstone) and Limerick. Passengers left Broadstone at 7.15 am and got to Athlone about four hours later. Here they boarded the steamer for Killaloe, where they joined a horse bus which was due in Limerick at 6.45 pm. The fares for the 145 mile journey from Dublin were 12s 6d first and 6s third and deck. This compared favourably with 23s 9d first and 10s 9d third charged by the Great Southern & Western Railway for the 129 mile journey from Dublin (Kingsbridge) and Limerick, but rail passengers left Kingsbridge at 7 am and arrived at Limerick at 1.10 pm.

The Shannon part of the route was operated by the *Duchess of Argyle* and the *Artizan*. These vessels were acquired by the MGWR in 1857. They got from the Clyde to Limerick under their own steam. Here they were cut into sections, which were floated to Athlone, where they were put together again. Both steamers were transferred to the GSWR when the MGWR gave up its lease of the Grand Canal in June 1860. Two years later passenger services were suspended and the vessels were left to rot at Killaloe.

The *Duchess of Argyle* was built in 1848 as a yacht, but shortly afterwards became a commercial passenger steamer and was the first member of the Campbell fleet on the Clyde. Her new owners removed her after boiler and funnel, thereby making her the prototype of many subsequent Clyde steamers, viz a single funnel forward of her paddles. She was always a fast ship and is reported to have returned a time of 1hr 34min for the twenty-four miles from Portumna to Killaloe. The *Artizan* was built at Rutherglen for service on the Clyde at Glasgow in 1856. She made her maiden voyage on the Shannon on 17 August 1857.

The *Midland* and *Lord Lorton* were the first steamers owned by the railway. The former was advertised to ply between Athlone and Lough Derg in the early summer of 1857. The *Lord Lorton* was built in 1855 but was sold to the Waterford SS Co a few years later. She sometimes carried passengers and as late as 1880 the MGWR authorised the issue of combined rail and steamer tickets from the South of Ireland to Ballyhaunis (Co Mayo) via the *Lord Lorton*.

PS *Shannon*, SS *Athlone*, SS *Brian Boru*, SS *Dublin*, SS *Limerick*

The *Shannon* was owned by the Grand Canal Co. She came to the river in 1846 and was normally employed in carrying goods and towing lighters to and from the Grand Canal at Shannon Harbour. When the railway steamers were withdrawn from the Athlone–Killaloe run in the early 1860s the Grand Canal Co used this vessel on a somewhat intermittent passenger/cargo service on the same route which continued, on and off, until her sale in 1868. Accommodation on board was reputed to be 'very rough', nevertheless, she was advertised as carrying a stewardess to wait on female passengers. The fares charged were 6s cabin and 4s deck.

The other steamers were employed in the cargo trade over the years 1865–1900. All four were, at times, 'pressed' into taking picnic parties and Sunday School outings for trips on the river.

SS *Lady of the Lake*

This steamer was owned by the Waterford & Inland Navigation Co, an organisation which was closely associated with the Waterford & Limerick Railway. She was stationed on Lough Derg from 1883 until about 1910. She was used mainly for cargo but at times was advertised to work 'shilling' Sunday afternoon cruises from Killaloe.

SS *Fairy Queen*

The Shannon Development Co reopened the passenger service on the Shannon with this vessel on Sunday 18 June 1897. She was four years old at the time, having previously been employed on pleasure trips on the Forth and Clyde Canal. In the summer of 1906 she went to Lough Corrib, where she remained until the end of 1913. After this she returned to Scotland where she remained until the early 1920s. An illustrated article on the *Fairy Queen* was published in Vol 57 (1893) of *Engineering*.

SS *Countess Cadogan*, SS *Lady Betty Balfour*

These two steamers were built for the Shannon Development Co by Bow McLachlan & Co of Paisley in 1897. The *Countess Cadogan* replaced the *Fairy Queen* on Lough Corrib and made her maiden commercial voyage on that lake on Sunday 17 May 1914. After the suspension of the Lough Corrib service she was acquired by N. Cook of Aberdeen, with whom she remained until the mid-1930s. In 1905 the *Lady Betty Balfour* left the Shannon for Bantry Bay. A year later she went to Warrenpoint, where she was stationed until she joined the fleet of N. Cook at Aberdeen during the 1914–18 war.

SS *Countess of Mayo*

This steamer had a varied career. In her first season she carried the Duke and Duchess of York (later King George V and Queen Mary) from Killaloe to Banagher, where they joined a special train to take them to the north. An illustrated account of the journey is given in the *Illustrated London News* for 11 September 1898, and the Royal patronage was commemorated by naming the steamer passage between Killaloe and Banagher the *Duke of York* route. In 1908 the *Countess of Mayo* went to Warrenpoint, where she was engaged in local cruising on Carlingford Lough. Six years later she was acquired by David MacBrayne who used her on the Kinloch–Ballahulish run, after which she went to Invergordon. She ended her days as the Tyne ferry *Walker*.

SS *Olga*, SS *Shannon Queen*

These vessels came to the Shannon in 1897 and 1898 respectively. The *Olga* was the smallest steamer owned by the company and was usually employed on the cross-Lough Derg service between Scariff and Dromineer. She was three years old when she arrived in Ireland and was lost in 1909 when being towed back to England. The *Shannon Queen* was built as the *Manchester* in 1892, for cruising on the Manchester Ship Canal. Trips between Runcorn and Manchester in the rain do not seem to have been a great financial success for, within a few years, she was sold to the Shannon Development Co, who renamed her *Shannon Queen*. In her early days on the river she usually worked above Athlone but was moved to the *Duke of York* route in 1906. She was the last vessel to run between Banagher and Killaloe and was on this run when the service was suspended just before the 1914–18 war.

Cruising on the Shannon can at times be very cold as there is little shelter from the prevailing winds. Even in midsummer some of the passengers have to go into the cabin to keep warm but *fresh air fiends* stick it out on deck. In the days of the Shannon Development Co these 'hearties' used to keep themselves warm by hugging the funnel.

TSMV *St Brendan*, TSMV *St Ciaran*

In June 1955 the *St Brendan* made her first trip on the river. In the next year she was joined by the larger *St Ciaran*. Both vessels are owned by the CIE and crossed the Irish Sea under their own power in the spring of 1955 and 1956 respectively. The *St Brendan* was built as the *L'Ombre* for working on the Seine during the Paris exhibition of 1937. She then moved to the Thames where she became the *Cardinal Wolsey*. The *St Ciaran* was formerly the *Wroxham Belle*. She was built at Rowhedge in Essex for service on the Norfolk Broads. Both vessels have steel hulls, twin screws, and large observation saloons forward. They ply regularly on all parts of the river between Killaloe and Lanesborough and make occasional trips further north. The friendly service and spotless condition of both vessels are a credit to their crews.

SSMV *St James*, SSMV *St Brigid*, SSMV *St Patrick*, SSMV *Linquenda*

In 1945 the CIE acquired the large steel barges *St James*, *St Patrick* and *St Brigid*. The latter two came from the Avon, where they had been known as the *Avon King* and *Avon Queen* respectively. All three vessels were fitted with Bollinder engines which gave them a service speed of 11 knots. When CIE retired from the Shannon cargo trade the *St Brigid* was acquired by a private owner who converted her to a houseboat and the other two vessels were laid up. In 1961 the *St Patrick* was purchased by Irish Botels Ltd who fitted her out at Shannon Harbour as a cruising yacht with accommodation for twelve passengers in single and two-berth cabins. In 1962, the same company, who in the meantime had changed its name to Irish Floatels Ltd, obtained the *St James* and fitted her out in a similar manner. In January 1964 the company's third vessel, the *Linquenda*, arrived on the Shannon. She had been a Rhine barge and had to be brought from the Continent to Limerick as deck cargo, as it was considered to be unsafe to take her round the south-west of Ireland in winter. From Limerick she went to Athlone under her own power. Later in the same year she joined her two consorts in operating six-day cruises; on these passengers pay an all-inclusive fare which covers living on board and the cost of shore excursions. The accommodation is good, the service friendly, and the staff is efficient.

MV *Jolly Roger*, MV *Hilda*

The *Jolly Roger* was owned by the Portumna Pleasure Boat Co. She worked on the river for a short time in the late 1920s. In the autumn of 1964 the Ormonde Hotel at Nenagh took delivery of the *Hilda* from Holland. She is a modern canal cruising launch with central heating and a transparent roof. She is used for local trips on Lough Derg.

Grand and Royal Canals

Passenger services by horse-drawn fly boats operated on the Grand and Royal canals in the first half of the nineteenth century. The former ran between Dublin, Shannon Harbour and Athy, and those on the Royal Canal between Dublin and Longford. Full descriptions of the passenger traffic on the canals is given in Delany's book *The Canals of the South of Ireland* and in Rolt's *Green and Silver*.

ACKNOWLEDGEMENTS

No book has ever been put together without the ready cooperation of others. In particular the author would like to thank the librarians and their staffs at the City and Linen Hall Libraries, Belfast; Bristol City Museum; British Museum Newspaper Library, Colindale; British Transport Archives, Paddington; Maritime Institute of Ireland, Dun Laoghaire; Mitchell Library, Glasgow; National Library of Ireland, Dublin; National Maritime Museum, Greenwich; Waterford Municipal Library and the City and University Libraries, Southampton. He also records his appreciation of the cooperation received from the following—British Rail Shipping Services; British & Irish SP Co; Coast Lines; Head Line; Marine Transport Services; Newry Port & Harbour Trust and the Shannon Car Ferry Ltd.

The assistance of Mr R. W. Berkeley in obtaining photographs and steamship plans is again acknowledged with thanks as is the help received from Messrs T. J. Edgington, B. Moody, G. Morrison, W. McGrath, H. M. Rea and N. S. Robins in finding suitable photographs. The maps were drawn by Mr A. S. Burn of the Geography Department, Southampton University.

The author places on record his appreciation of the way in which Dr P. J. Flanagan and Messrs Grahame Farr, G. E. Langmuir, T. B. O'Loughlin, A. W. H. Pearsall and A. B. Swan so willingly gave him the benefit of their extensive knowledge of shipping and transport. Finally he thanks Mesdames M. R. Banks, B. Johnston, B. M. Garrett and D. M. Marshallsay, Dr J. de Courcy Ireland, Rev Bro W. J. Dargan, and Messrs A. S. E. Browning, J. J. Carroll, R. S. Christiansen, P. W. Elkins, B. J. Foley, D. Fryer, C. D. Glynn, R. P. Hendry, K. Mackenzie, Kevin Murray, J. C. McNeill, P. O'Rorke, P. Thompson, A. P. Underhay, and Commander L. Ahern, INS, for assistance given either in the collection of material or preparation of the manuscript.

BIBLIOGRAPHY

BOOKS	Reference used in Fleet Lists
Anderson, E. B. *Sailing Ships of Ireland*, Dublin, 1951	A1
Barrie, D. S. *Dundalk, Newry and Greenore Railway*, Lingfield, 1957	DB1
Barry, W. J. *History of the Port of Cork Steam Navigation*, Cork, 1916	—
Bonsor, N. R. P. *North Atlantic Seaway*, Prescot, 1955	—
Burtt, F. *Cross-channel and Coastal Paddle Steamers*, 1937	B1
Steamers of the Thames and Medway, 1949	B2
Chandler, G. *Liverpool Shipping*, 1960	C1
Clegg, W. P., and Styring, J. S. *Steamers of British Railways*, Prescot, 1962	CS1
British Nationalised Shipping, Newton Abbot, 1969	CS2
Delany, V. T. H., and Delany, D. R. *Canals of the South of Ireland*, Newton Abbot, 1965	—
Duckworth, C. L. D., and Langmuir, G. E. *Clyde and Other Coastal Steamers*, Glasgow, 1939	DL1
Clyde River and Other Steamers, 2nd ed, Glasgow, 1946	DL2
Railway and Other Steamers, 2nd ed, Prescot, 1968	DL3
West Coast Steamers, 2nd ed, Prescot, 1966	DL4
West Highland Steamers, 3rd ed, Prescot, 1967	DL5
Farr, G. *West Country Passenger Steamers*, 2nd ed, Prescot, 1967	F1
Flanagan, P. *Transport in Ireland, 1880–1910*, Dublin, 1969	F2
Fletcher, R. A. *Steamships*, 1910	F3
Grimshaw, G. *British Pleasure Steamers*, 1945	G1
Kennedy, J. *History of Steam Navigation*, Liverpool, 1903	K
Kennedy, N. W. *Records of Early British Steamers*, Liverpool, 1933	—
Lindsay, W. S. *History of Merchant Shipping*, 1876	—
McNeill, D. B. *Coastal Passenger Steamers and Inland Navigations in the North of Ireland*, Belfast, 1967	N1
Coastal Passenger Steamers and Inland Navigations in the South of Ireland, Belfast, 1967	N2
Irish Passenger Steamship Services, Vol 1, Newton Abbot, 1969	N3

McQueen, A. *Clyde River Steamers of the Last Fifty Years*, Glasgow, 1923 —
Echoes of Old Clyde Paddle Wheels, Glasgow, 1924 —
Marmion, A. *Maritime Ports of Ireland*, 1855 —
Paterson, A. J. S. *The Golden Years of Clyde Paddle Steamers*, Newton Abbot, 1959 —
Reader, E. R. *History of the City of Cork SP Co (1936) Ltd*, privately published, 1951 R1
The B. and I. Story, privately published, 1951 —
Rolt, L. T. C. *Green and Silver*, 1949 —
Spratt, H. P. *Transatlantic Paddle Steamers*, 2nd ed, Glasgow, 1967 —
Stretton, C. E. *Chester & Holyhead Railway*, Leeds, 1901 —
Thornley, F. C. *Steamers of North Wales*, 2nd ed, Prescot, 1962 T1
Thornton, E. C. B. *South Coast Pleasure Steamers*, 2nd ed, Prescot, 1969 T2
Vale, E. *Ships of the Narrow Seas*, London, 1937 —
Williamson, J. *Clyde Passenger Steamers from 1812 to 1901*, Glasgow, 1904 —

BRITISH PARLIAMENTARY PAPERS

1822 (417) VI Fifth Report of the Select Committee on the roads from London to Holyhead; (Appx 1).

1830 (647) XIV Twenty-second Report of the Commissioners of Inquiry into the collection and management of the Revenue—Post Office.

1831/32 (716) XVII Report from the Select Committee on the Postal Communications with Ireland.

1839 (273) XLVII Report on Steam Vessel Accidents.

1845 (349) XLVII A return of the names and details of all steam vessels registered in the ports of the United Kingdom.

1849 (339) LI Captain Denham's report on passenger accommodation in steamers between Ireland and Liverpool.

1851 (196) LII Return of the registered steam vessels in the United Kingdom on 1 January 1851.

1857 (196) XXXIX Report on the Commission appointed by the Lord Commissioners of the Admiralty to enquire into the expediency of altering the present system of lighting established for steam and sailing vessels.

1857/58 (488) LII Return of the whole of the steam vessels in the United Kingdom on 1 January 1858.

NEWSPAPERS

Belfast Newsletter; Carlisle Journal; Cork Constitution; Cork Examiner; Drogheda Argus; Drogheda Conservative; Drogheda Independent; Drogheda Journal; Dundalk Democrat; Freeman's Journal; Galway Express; Galway Mercury; Galway Pilot; Galway Vindicator; Irish Independent; Irish Times; Kerry Weekly; Limerick Chronicle; Limerick Reporter; Munster News; Newry Commercial Telegraph; Newry Reporter; Saunder's Newsletter; Skibbereen Eagle; Tralee Mercury; Waterford Chronicle; Waterford Mirror; Waterford News; Westmeath Independent; Wexford Conservative; Wexford Independent

PERIODICAL PUBLICATIONS

Bradshaw's Railway Guide; Dublin Almanac; Engineer; Engineering; Falconer's Railway Guide (Dublin); *Illustrated London News; Lloyd's Register of Shipping; Marine News; Mariners Mirror; Mercantile Navy List; Nautical Magazine; Navy List; Red Guide* (Dublin); *Rupert Jones List; Sea Breezes; Shipping Handbook* (Dublin); *Shipping World; Ships Monthly; Thom's Directory* (Dublin); *Wyer's Guide* (Dublin)

FLEET LISTS

Key

THE name of each vessel generally appears once only, under the heading of the route on which it was employed for the longest time. Vessels which changed their names on moving from one route to another have an entry under each name.

Col 1 Date built.

Col 2 Name and type of propulsion: PS paddle steamer; SS single-screw steamer; TSS twin-screw steamer; TrSS triple-screw steamer; SSMV single-screw motor vessel; TSMV twin-screw motor vessel; QSMV quadruple-screw motor vessel; SS* auxiliary screw steamer.

Col 3 Hull material, I iron; S steel; W wood.

Col 4 Length to nearest foot.*

Col 5 Breadth to nearest foot.*

Col 6 Type of engine: S single-expansion steam; C compound; T triple-expansion; Q quadruple expansion; R steam turbine; D diesel.

Col 7 Place of building.

Col 8 Date broken up; *in service 1970

Col 9 Books in which illustrations of the vessel may be found, the reference key is given in the bibliography. The location of models easily accessible to the public is also given in this column.

α Belfast Transport Museum
β Glasgow Art Gallery (Kelvingrove)
γ Liverpool City Museum
δ London, Science Museum (South Kensington)
ε London, Transport Museum (Clapham Common).

* If not known registered tonnage is given in brackets.

Chapter 1

Government Mail Steamers

1	2	3	4	5	6	7	8	9
1823	*Aladdin/Jasper*, PS	W	126	21	S	Falmouth	1848	
1847	*Banshee*, PS	I	189	27	S	Rotherhithe	1864	
1847	*Caradoc*, PS	I	191	26	S	Blackwall	1870	
1823	*Cinderella/Cuckoo*, PS	W	120	20	S	London	1840c	
1827	*Dragon/Zephyr*, PS	W	120	21	S	Harwich	1848	
1826	*Escape/Doterel*, PS	W	120	21	S	Harwich	1848	
1845	*Fire Queen*, PS	I	163	20	S	—	1883	
1831	*Flamer*, PS	W	155	22	S	Rotherhithe	1850	
1822	*George*, PS	W	—	—	S	Liverpool	—	
1834	*Gulnare/Gleaner*, PS	W	120	23	S	Chatham	—	
1824	*Harlequin/Sprightly*, PS	W	119	20	S	London	1848	
1819	*Ivanhoe/Boxer*, PS	W	102	18	S	Greenock	1846	
1821	*Lightning/Royal Sovereign/ Monkey*, PS	W	102	20	S	Rotherhithe	1841	
1847	*Llewellyn/St Patrick*, PS	W	240	27	S	Blackwall	1895	
1821	*Meteor*, PS	W	(200	T)	S	Rotherhithe	1830	
1847	*St Columba*, PS	W	190	27	S	Birkenhead	—	
1819	*Talbot*, PS	W	93	18	S	Port Glasgow	1833	

1	2	3	4	5	6	7	8	9
1821	*Tartar*, PS	W	—	—	S	—	—	
1845	*Trident*, PS	I	161	31	S	Blackwall	1869	
1848	*Vivid*, PS	W	150	22	S	Chatham	1894	
1822	*Vixen*, PS	W	115	19	S	Deptford	—	
1826	*Watersprite*, PS	W	107	17	S	Harwich	—	
1826	*Wizard/Otter*, PS	W	120	20	S	Harwich	1891	

City of Dublin SP Co

1	2	3	4	5	6	7	8	9
1860	*Connaught*, PS	I	338	35	S	Birkenhead	1898	A1, δ
1897	*Connaught*, TSS	S	360	42	T	Birkenhead	1917	
1849	*Eblana*, PS	I	210	27	S	Glasgow	1884	
1885	*Ireland*, PS	S	366	38	S	Birkenhead	1900	A1, B1
1860	*Leinster*, PS	I	343	35	S	London	1897	A1, B1, F3
1896	*Leinster*, TSS	S	360	42	T	Birkenhead	1918	
1860	*Munster*, PS	I	337	35	S	Birkenhead	1898	A1
1897	*Munster*, TSS	S	360	42	T	Birkenhead	1924	
1851	*Prince Arthur*, PS	I	199	27	S	Blackwall	1893	B1, DL4, T1
1860	*Ulster*, PS	I	337	35	S	Birkenhead	1897	γ
1896	*Ulster*, TSS	S	360	42	T	Birkenhead	1924	K

Railway Steamers (Holyhead–Dublin/Dun Laoghaire)

1	2	3	4	5	6	7	8	9
1860	*Admiral Moorsom*, PS	I	220	30	S	Govan	1885	

1	2	3	4	5	6	7	8	9
1863	*Alexandra*, PS	I	227	28	S	Birkenhead	1902	
1888	*Anglesey*, TSS	S	302	33	T	Belfast	1911	
1847	*Anglia*, PS	I	190	26	S	London	1910c	
1900	*Anglia*, TSS	S	329	39	T	Dumbarton	1915	DL3
1919	*Anglia*, TSS	S	381	45	R	Dumbarton	1935	
1884	*Banshee*, PS	I	310	34	C	Birkenhead	1909	A1, B1
1848	*Cambria*, PS	I	245	27	S	Birkenhead	1883	B1
1897	*Cambria/Arvonia*, TSS	S	329	39	T	Dumbarton	1925	
1920	*Cambria*, TSS	S	381	45	R	Dumbarton	1949	DL3
1949	*Cambria*, TSMV	S	397	56	D	Belfast	*	
1965	*Dover*, TSS	S	369	57	R	Tyneside	*	
1869	*Duchess of Sutherland*, PS	I	251	30	S	Hebburn	1908	
1868	*Duke of Sutherland*, PS	I	244	30	S	Hebburn	1887	
1848	*Hibernia*, PS	I	193	26	S	Liverpool	1897	
1900	*Hibernia*, TSS	S	329	39	T	Dumbarton	1915	
1920	*Hibernia*, TSS	S	381	45	R	Dumbarton	1949	CS1, CS2
1949	*Hibernia*, TSMV	S	396	56	D	Belfast	*	CS1, CS2
1965	*Holyhead Ferry I*, TSS	S	369	57	R	Hebburn	*	CS2, DL3

1	2	3	4	5	6	7	8	9
1885	*Irene*, TSS	S	301	33	C	Belfast	1906	
1880	*Lily*, PS	S	300	33	S	Birkenhead	1905	γ
1952	*Normannia*, TSS	S	309	49	R	Dumbarton	*	CS2
1883	*North Wall*, TSS	S	300	33	C	Port Glasgow	1905	
1887	*Olga*, TSS	S	302	33	T	Birkenhead	1908	
1933	*Princess Maud*, TSS	S	330	51	R	Dumbarton	*	CS1, CS2
1845	*Queen*, PS	W	158	23	S	Dumbarton	—	
1876	*Rose*, PS	I	292	32	S	Birkenhead	1896	δ
1848	*Scotia*, PS	I	194	27	S	London	1865c	
1902	*Scotia/Menevia*, TSS	S	330	39	R	Dumbarton	1928	DL3, *a*
1921	*Scotia*, TSS	S	381	45	R	Dumbarton	1940	ε
1845	*Sea Nymph*, PS	I	206	29	S	Greenock	1880	
1876	*Shamrock*, PS	I	292	32	S	Birkenhead	1898	
1905	*Slieve Bawn*, TSS	S	300	39	T	Belfast	1935	
1908	*Slieve Bloom*, TSS	S	300	37	T	Barrow	1918	
1921	*Slieve Donard*, TSS	S	300	39	T	Barrow	1954	CS1, CS2
1908	*Slieve Gallion*, TSS	S	300	37	T	Barrow	1937	
1904	*Slievemore*, TSS	S	300	37	T	Belfast	1932	
1902	*Snowdon*, TSS	S	300	37	T	Birkenhead	1936	
1900	*South Stack*, TSS	S	300	36	T	Birkenhead	1931	

1	2	3	4	5	6	7	8	9
1864	*Stanley*, PS	I	239	29	S	Greenock	1890	
1853	*Telegraph*, PS	I	244	28	S	Govan	1884	
1880	*Violet*, PS	S	300	33	S	Birkenhead	1903 A	1, DL3, δ

Railway Steamers (Holyhead–Greenore)

1	2	3	4	5	6	7	8	9
1897	*Connemara*, TSS	S	272	35	T	Dumbarton	1916	DB1, DL3
1868	*Countess of Erne*, PS	I	241	29	S	Dublin	1935	
1919	*Curraghmore/Duke of Abercorn*, TSS	S	307	40	R	Dumbarton	1935	DB1, N3
1874	*Earl Spencer*, PS	I	254	29	S	Birkenhead	1896	
1870	*Edith*, PS	I	251	30	S	Hebburn	1912	
1873	*Eleanor*, PS	I	252	30	S	Hebburn	1881	DB1, V1
1881	*Eleanor*, PS	S	254	30	C	Birkenhead	1902	
1898	*Galtee More*, TSS	S	276	35	T	Dumbarton	1926	DB1, DL3
1912	*Greenore*, TrSS	S	306	41	R	Birkenhead	1926	DB1, *a*
1877	*Isabella*, PS	S	254	30	S	Birkenhead	1898	
1908	*Rathmore/Lorraine*, TSS	S	300	40	T	Barrow	1932	DL3
1895	*Rosstrevor*, TSS	S	272	35	T	Dumbarton	1926	

1	2	3	4	5	6	7	8	9
1878	*Adela*, SS	I	200	32	C	Port Glasgow	1917	
1845	*Albert*, PS	I	147	23	S	Liverpool	1887	
1836	*Athlone*, PS	W	145	23	S	Liverpool	1855c	
1829	*Ballinasloe*, PS	I	138	24	S	Liverpool	1860c	
1820	*Belfast*, PS	W	115	20	S	Belfast	1835c	
1884	*Belfast*, SS	I	192	24	C	W. Hartlepool	1928	
1826	*Birmingham*, PS	W	141	25	S	Liverpool	1860c	
1892	*Blackrock*, SS	S	240	32	T	Barrow	1922c	
1815	*Britannia*, PS	W	93	16	S	Port Glasgow	1829	
1825	*Britannia*, PS	I	135	24	S	Liverpool	1829	
1896	*Carlow/Lady Carlow*, SS	S	260	34	T	Port Glasgow	1925	
1876	*Cavan*, PS	I	250	27	C	Birkenhead	1896	
1824	*City of Dublin*, PS	W	(200	T)	S	Liverpool	1840c	
1824	*City of Londonderry*, PS	W	(250	T)	S	Liverpool	—	
1825	*Commerce*, PS	W	129	21	S	Liverpool	1859	
1899	*Cork*, SS	S	260	34	T	Port Glasgow	1918	
1896	*Cumbria*, SS	S	198	30	T	Troon	1925	
1855	*Despatch*, SS	I	217	25	S	S. Shields	—	
1846	*Diamond*, SS*	I	130	20	S	Liverpool	1875c	

1	2	3	4	5	6	7	8	9
1846	*Dublin*, SS*	I	146	19	S	Hull	—	
1866	*Dublin*, SS	I	174	28	S	Dublin	1890	
1837	*Duchess of Kent*, PS	W	155	23	S	Liverpool	—	
1837	*Duke of Cambridge*, PS	W	158	23	S	Glasgow	—	
1892	*Eblana*, SS	S	213	32	C	Ardrossan	1923	γ
1846	*Emerald*, SS*	I	129	20	S	Liverpool	1880c	
1874	*Express*, SS	I	191	24	C	W. Hartlepool	1911	
1891	*Galway*, PS	S	263	27	C	Port Glasgow	1915	γ
1886	*Hare*, SS	S	216	60	T	Whiteinch	1918	DL1
1825	*Hibernia*, PS	W	133	23	S	Liverpool	1849	
1844	*Iron Duke*, PS	I	178	27	S	Liverpool	—	γ
1897	*Kerry/Lady Kerry*, SS	S	260	34	T	Port Glasgow	1924	
1867	*Kildare*, PS	I	262	27	S	Birkenhead	1895	
1903	*Kilkenny*, SS	S	270	36	T	Port Glasgow	1926	
1918	*Killiney/Lady Killiney/Ardmore*, SS	S	255	36	T	Dundee	1940	
1906	*Lady Connaught/Longford*, TSS, ex-*Heroic*	S	320	41	Q	Belfast	1952	
	Lady Killiney, SS, see *Killiney*							

1	2	3	4	5	6	7	8	9
1911	*Lady Leinster/Lady Connaught*, TSS, ex-*Patriotic*	S	325	42	T	Belfast	1956	
1924	*Lady Limerick/ Lairdscastle*, SS	S	277	38	T	Ardrossan	1945	
1923	*Lady Louth/ Lairdsburn*, SS	S	277	38	T	Ardrossan	1953	DL1
1906	*Lady Munster/ Louth*, SS, ex-*Graphic*	S	320	41	Q	Belfast	1951	DL1
1826	*Leeds*, PS	W	141	25	S	Liverpool	1852	
1937	*Leinster/Ulster Prince*, TSMV	S	353	50	D	Belfast	*	DL1
1948	*Leinster*, TSMV	S	367	50	D	Belfast	*	
1968	*Leinster*, TSMV	S	387	59	D	Passage West	*	
1874	*Leitrim*, PS	I	249	27	C	Birkenhead	1899	
1824	*Liffey*, PS	W	133	23	S	Liverpool	1845c	
1837	*Liverpool*, PS	W	(500	T)	S	Liverpool	—	
1846	*Liverpool*, SS*	I	116	19	S	—	—	
1870	*Longford*, PS	I	250	27	S	Birkenhead	1896	γ
1894	*Louth/Lady Louth/ Bandon/Lady Galway*, SS	S	261	34	T	Port Glasgow	1938	DL1
1869	*Magnet*, SS	I	195	32	C	Waterford	1895c	
1852	*Mail*, SS	I	150	20	S	—	—	
1826	*Manchester*, PS		(220 T)		S	Liverpool	1829	

1	2	3	4	5	6	7	8	9
1880	*Mayo*, PS	I	263	27	C	Birkenhead	1903	
1884	*Meath*, PS	I	263	27	C	Birkenhead	1906	A1, B1
1824	*Mersey*, PS	W	144	21	S	Liverpool	1860c	
1825	*Mona*, PS	I	125	20	S	Liverpool	—	
1832	*Mona*, PS	W	98	17	S	Port Glasgow	—	
1821	*Mountaineer*, PS	W	(200	T)	S	Greenock	1829	
1868	*Mullingar*, PS	I	261	27	C	Dublin	1896	
1938	*Munster*, TSMV	S	353	50	D	Belfast	1940	
1948	*Munster*, TSMV	S	367	50	D	Belfast	*	
1968	*Munster*, TSMV	S	362	58	D	Hamburg	*	
1827	*Nottingham*, PS	W	140	25	S	Liverpool	—	γ
1845	*Pearl*, SS*	I	116	20	S	—	—	
1839	*Prince*, PS	W	165	24	S	Liverpool	—	
1839	*Princess*, PS	W	165	24	S	Liverpool	—	
1837	*Queen Victoria*, PS	W	155	23	S	Liverpool	1853	
1845	*Roscommon*, PS	W	165	22	S	—	—	
1838	*Royal Adelaide*, PS	I	171	24	S	Paisley	—	S1
1837	*Royal William*, PS	W	176	26	S	Liverpool	1888	K, δ
1824	*Shamrock*, PS	W	(220	T)	S	Liverpool		
1832	*St Columb*, PS	W	121	18	S	Port Glasgow	—	
1851	*St Kiaran*, PS	W	116	19	S	—	—	
1827	*Sheffield*, PS	W	(230	T)	S	Liverpool	1828	

1	2	3	4	5	6	7	8	9
1854	*Standard*, SS	I	174	25	S	London	1887	
1860	*Star*, SS	I	160	21	S	Port Glasgow	1887	
1851	*Times*, SS	I	159	21	S	Govan	1905c	
1860	*Torch*, SS	I	160	21	S	Port Glasgow	1872	
1824	*Town of Liverpool* PS	W	—	—	S	Liverpool	1827	
1848	*Trafalgar*, PS	I	189	29	S	Glasgow	1875	
1819	Waterloo, PS	W	100	17	S	Greenock	1840	
1846	*Waterwitch*, SS*	I	120	20	S	Dumbarton	—	
1895	*Wicklow/Lady Wicklow*, SS	S	260	34	T	Port Glasgow	1949	
1846	*Windsor*, PS	I	246	28	S	Liverpool	1875c	

Government Mail Steamers

1	2	3	4	5	6	7	8	9
1824	*Comet/Lucifer*, PS	W	125	23	S	Liverpool	1842	
1826	*Dolphin/Shearwater*, PS	W	145	26	S	Harwich	1848	
1826	*Etna*, PS	W	127	23	S	Liverpool	1840c	
1840	*Medina*, PS	I	171	33	S	Pembroke	1863	
1838	*Medusa*, PS	I	171	33	S	Pembroke	1870c	
1838	*Merlin*, PS	I	171	33	S	Pembroke	1863	
1834	*Richmond/Redwing*, PS	W	144	15	S	Glasgow	1849	
1826	*Thetis/Avon*, PS	W	146	26	S	Harwich	1840c	
1826	*Urgent*, PS	W	170	26	S	Liverpool	1849	

Chapter 3

Dublin–Barrow

1	2	3	4	5	6	7	8	9
1855	*Glasgow*, SS ex-*Garland*	I	187	23	C	Kelvinhaugh	1891	
1864	*Liverpool*, SS	I	199	26	S	Glasgow	1918c	

Dublin–Bristol

1831	*Albion*, PS	W	151	25	S	Bristol	1837	
1862	*Apollo*, PS	I	234	26	S	Greenock	1885	F1, R1
1871	*Argo*, SS	I	231	31	C	Govan	1908	F1
1855	*Calypso*, SS	I	190	27	S	Dumbarton	1886	
1865	*Calypso*, SS	I	182	25	S	Glasgow	1890	F1
1827	*City of Bristol*, PS	W	144	23	S	Bristol	1840	δ
1822	*Duke of Lancaster*, PS	W	103	17	S	Liverpool	1845	
1858	*Flora*, PS	I	216	26	S	Greenock	1864	
1822	*George IV*, PS	W	110	20	S	Bristol	1839	
1853	*Juno*, PS	I	163	20	S	Bristol	1863	
1847	*Juverna*, PS	I	191	30	S	Bristol	1876	F1
1830	*Killarney*, PS	W	147	25	S	Bristol	1838	
1835	*Osprey*, PS	W	148	23	S	Bristol	1864	
1822	*Palmerston*, PS	W	105	20	S	Bristol	1844	
1837	*Phoenix*, PS	W	132	18	S	Bristol	1859	

1	2	3	4	5	6	7	8	9
1842	*Rose*, PS	W	153	23	S	Bristol	1864	
1865	*Rosetta/Defence*, PS	I	220	26	S	Cubitt Town	1880	
1839	*Shamrock*, PS	W	152	23	S	Bristol	1863	
1835	*Star*, PS	W	125	20	S	Bristol	1860c	

Dublin–Cumberland Coast

1847	*Ariel*, PS	I	173	23	S	Port Glasgow	1873	β
1845	*Ben-My-Chree*, PS	I	165	—	S	Glasgow	—	
1874	*Caledonian*, SS	I	201	26	C	Govan	1908	
1865	*Countess of Eglinton*, SS	I	166	24	S	Whiteinch	1871	
1826	*Cumberland*, PS	W	(200	T)	S	Holyhead	1851c	
1834	*Earl of Lonsdale*, PS	W	125	20	S	Whitehaven	1858c	
1866	*Kittiwake*, SS	I	160	22	S	Glasgow	1882	
1873	*Midland*, SS	I	200	26	C	Renfrew	1891	
1831	*Mona's Isle*, PS	W	116	19	S	Port Glasgow	1851	B
1834	*Newcastle*, PS	W	145	24	S	Birkenhead	—	
1871	*North British*, SS	I	201	26	C	Whiteinch	1879	
1842	*Prince of Wales*, PS	I	160	25	S	Glasgow	1870c	
1843	*Princess Alice*, PS	I	165	23	S	Glasgow	—	
1844	*Queen*, PS	I	158	23	S	Liverpool	—	
1826	*St Andrew*, PS	W	(100	T)	S	Dumbarton	—	

1	2	3	4	5	6	7	8	9
1856	*Silloth*, SS	I	155	21	S	Port Glasgow	1922	
1825	*Solway*, PS	W	(200	T)	S	Liverpool	1841	
1870	*South Western*, SS	I	191	26	C	Port Glasgow	1904	
1864	*Waverley*, PS	I	216	26	—	Newcastle	1913	
1865	*Waverley*, PS	I	222	27	C	Glasgow	1873	
1848	*Whitehaven*, PS	I	181	24	S	—	1870c	
1854	*William McCormick*, PS	I	205	28	S	Kelvinhaugh	1869	
1893	*Yarrow/Assaroe*, SS	S	230	32	T	Glasgow	1947	

Dublin–Glasgow

1835	*Arab*, PS	W	130	22	S	Glasgow	1855c	
1834	*City of Carlisle*, PS	W	131	21	S	Liverpool	—	
1874	*Duchess of Marlborough*, SS	I	172	23	C	Barrow	1901	
1873	*Duke of Argyll*, PS	I	250	29	S	Port Glasgow	1905	DL1
1892	*Duke of Fife/Sparrow*, SS	S	244	32	T	Troon	1940c	
1906	*Duke of Montrose/Tiger/Lairdsforest/Lady Louth*, SS	S	275	37	Q	Dundee	1934	DL1
1899	*Duke of Rothesay/Puma*/Lairdsford, SS	S	265	35	T	Dundee	1934	

1	2	3	4	5	6	7	8	9
1870	*Duke of Leinster*, PS	I	250	29	S	Port Glasgow	1911	
1835	*Eagle*, PS	W	164	25	S	Greenock	—	
1864	*Earl of Carlisle*, PS	I	243	26	S	Greenock	1883	
1866	*Earl of Dublin/ Duke of Edinburgh*, PS	I	262	28	S	Port Glasgow	1870	
1826	*Erin*, PS	W	132	22	S	Greenock	1851	
1912	*Ermine*, SS	S	300	40	T	Govan	1916	
1885	*General Gordon/ Duke of Gordon/ Wren*, SS	S	230	31	T	Glasgow	1920	
1858	*Havelock*, PS	I	223	26	S	Govan	1865c	
1851	*Herald*, PS	I	200	24	S	Port Glasgow	1865c	
1952	*Irish Coast*, TSMV	S	340	52	D	Belfast	*	C1
1854	*Irishman*, SS	I	170	21	S	Paisley	1900	
1861	*Lancefield*, SS	I	145	23	S	Govan	1886	
1862	*Lord Clyde*, PS	I	243	26	S	Greenock	—	
1863	*Lord Gough*, PS	I	243	26	S	Greenock	1893	
1898	*Magpie/Lairdsgrove*, SS	S	265	34	T	Glasgow	1948	DL1
1865	*Marquis of Abercorn*, PS	I	260	30	S	Kirkaldy	1869	
1835	*Mercury*, PS	W	137	20	S	Port Glasgow	1850c	
1828	*Scotia*, PS	W	(170	T)	S	Greenock	—	

1	2	3	4	5	6	7	8	9
1957	*Scottish Coast,* TSMV	S	343	53	D	Belfast	*	
1865	*Thistle,* SS	I	198	25	S	Glasgow	1905c	
1846	*Viceroy,* PS	I	—	—	S	Govan	1850	

CHAPTER 4

Drogheda–Liverpool

1	2	3	4	5	6	7	8	9
1846	*Brian Boroimhe*, PS	I	180	27	S	Port Glasgow	1879	
1862	*Colleen Bawn*, PS	I	221	28	C	Glasgow	1901	A1, B1
1903	*Colleen Bawn*, TSS	S	260	36	T	Barrow	1931	α
1829	*Fair Trader*, PS	W	134	23	S	Greenock	—	
1844	*Faugh-a-ballagh*, PS	I	178	26	S	Greenock	1876	
1835	*Grand Ueile*, PS	W	148	24	S	Greenock	1847	
1833	*Green Isle*, PS	W	137	—	S	Greenock	—	
1834	*Irishman*, PS	W	144	23	S	Greenock	—	
1895	*Iverna*, PS	S	255	30	T	Glasgow	1912	DL1, DL3
1895	*Kathleen Mavourneen*, PS	S	260	31	C	Seacombe	1903	F3, B1
1849	*Leinster Lass*, PS	I	200	27	S	Port Glasgow	1885	
1871	*Lord Athlumney*, PS	I	233	28	C	Glasgow	1888	
1903	*Mellifont*, TSS	S	260	36	T	Barrow	1933	
1878	*Nora Creina*, PS	I	251	29	C	Glasgow	1912	
1845	*St Patrick*, PS	I	184	26	S	Greenock	1876	
1826	*Town of Drogheda*, PS	W	124	23	S	Greenock	1849	
1876	*Tredagh*, PS	I	241	29	C	Glasgow	1904	γ

Dundalk and Dundalk & Newry SP Cos

1	2	3	4	5	6	7	8	9
1867	*Amphion*, SS	I	151	21	S	Inverkeithing	1895c	
1877	*Bessbrook*, SS	I	182	27	C	Glasgow	1928	
1827	*Corsair*, PS	W	120	20	S	Port Glasgow	—	
1844	*Dundalk* PS	I	171	25	S	Port Glasgow	—	
1899	*Dundalk*, TSS	S	236	32	T	Glasgow	1918	
1855	*Earl of Erne*, PS	I	219	32	S	Port Glasgow	1926	DL1
1835	*Emerald Isle*, PS	I	135	21	S	Liverpool	—	
1862	*Emerald Isle*, PS	I	236	28	S	Govan	1898	
1856	*Enterprise*, PS	I	222	28	S	Newcastle	1899	
1838	*Finn MacCoull*, PS	W	141	22	S	Dumbarton	1848	
1828	*Glasgow*, PS	W	146	23	S	Greenock	1855c	
1856	*Independence*, PS	I	202	25	S	Glasgow	—	
1892	*Iveagh*, SS	S	190	29	T	Glasgow	1930	
1866	*Newry*, SS, ex-*Earl of Belfast*	I	177	24	S	Govan	1911	
1847	*Pride of Erin*, PS	I	194	26	S	Port Glasgow	1883	

Newry–Great Britain, pre-1870

1833	*Antelope*, PS	W	139	19	S	Whiteinch	—	
1855	*Despatch*, SS	I	190	25	S	—	—	
1837	*Devonshire*, PS	W	157	23	S	Glasgow	—	B1

1	2	3	4	5	6	7	8	9
1851	*Eagle*, SS	I	165	25	S	—	—	
1826	*Eclipse*, PS	W	108	18	S	Dumbarton	1835	
1869	*Elaine*, SS	I	194	24	S	Belfast	1899	
1860	*Fairy Queen*, PS	I	175	20	S	Dundee	—	
1826	*Fingal*, PS	W	133	22	S	Greenock	1851c	
1863	*Garland*, PS	I	229	25	S	Greenock	1881	
1826	*George IV*, PS	W	(150 T)		S	Liverpool	—	
1823	*Henry Bell*, PS	W	(150 T)		S	Liverpool	1840c	
1844	*Iron Prince*, PS	I	120	17	S	Liverpool	1860c	
1826	*Londonderry*, PS	W	110	18	S	Dumbarton	1840c	
1856	*Mystery*, SS	I	143	19	S	—	1868	
1835	*Pearl*, PS	W	140	17	S	Blackwall	1862	
1836	*Rover*, SS	W	137	21	S	Glasgow	1852	
1837	*Victoria*, PS	W	114	21	S	Belfast	—	

CHAPTER 5

Rosslare–Fishguard

1	2	3	4	5	6	7	8	9
1961	*Caledonian Princess*, TSS	S	353	57	R	Dumbarton	*	CS1, CS2
1956	*Duke of Rothesay*, TSS	S	364	55	R	Dumbarton	*	CS1, CS2
1908	*St Andrew/ Fishguard*, TrSS	S	351	41	R	Clydebank	1933	
1932	*St Andrew*, TSS	S	327	47	R	Birkenhead	1967	CS1, CS2
1906	*St David/Rosslare*, TrSS	S	351	41	R	Clydebank	1933	
1932	*St David*, TSS	S	327	47	R	Birkenhead	1944	
1947	*St David*, TSS	S	300	48	R	Birkenhead	*	CS2
1906	*St George*, TrSS	S	352	41	R	Birkenhead	1929	
1906	*St Patrick*, TrSS	S	351	41	R	Clydebank	1929	DL3, F3
1930	*St Patrick*, TSS	S	281	41	R	Kelvinhaugh	1941	
1947	*St Patrick*, TSS	S	300	48	R	Birkenhead	*	CS1

Rosslare–Le Havre

1967	*Dragon*, TSMV	S	442	72	D	Nantes	*	
1968	*Leopard*, TSMV	S	442	72	D	Nantes	*	

Waterford–Bristol/Liverpool

1844	*Camilla*, PS	I	175	23	S	London	1863c	
1829	*City of Waterford*, PS	W	148	25	S	Bristol	1833	

1	2	3	4	5	6	7	8	9
1873	*Clio*, SS	I	230	28	C	Kingshorn	1914	
1836	*Clonmel*, PS	I	155	21	S	Birkenhead	1841	
1904	*Clodagh/ Coningbeg*, SS	S	271	36	T	Troon	1917	
1879	*Comeragh*, SS	I	230	30	C	Glasgow	1906	
1886	*Dunbrody/Arklow*, SS	I	245	32	T	Glasgow	1931	
1828	*Gipsy*, PS	W	139	23	S	Liverpool	1845	
1859	*Gipsy*, SS	I	206	30	S	Waterford	1878	F1
1895	*Kincora*, SS	S	230	32	T	Newcastle	1901	
1868	*Lara*, SS	I	238	32	C	Waterford	1908	
1849	*Mars*, SS	I	185	25	S	Waterford	1862	
1834	*Mermaid*, PS	W	150	24	S	Birkenhead	1845	
1861	*Nora*, SS	I	178	26	S	Cork	1880	
1826	*Nora Creina*, PS	W	138	22	S	Birkenhead	1846	
1852	*Ondine*, SS	I	195	22	S	—	1865c	
1878	*Reginald*, SS	I	240	32	C	Glasgow	1914	DL1
1825	*St Patrick*, PS	W	130	20	S	Liverpool	1831	
1832	*St Patrick*, PS	W	149	25	S	Liverpool	1838	
1833	*Water Witch*, PS	W	151	24	S	Birkenhead	1833	
1833	*William Penn*, PS	W	160	25	S	Liverpool	1856	
1860	*Zephyr*, SS	I	210	28	S	Waterford	1889	

Waterford–New Milford/Rosslare

1	2	3	4	5	6	7	8	9
1850	*City of Paris*, SS	I	164	22	S	Greenwich	1875	
1850	*Courier*, PS	I	179	27	S	Glasgow	1870c	
1825	*Crocodile/Adder*, PS	W	131	20	S	Harwich	1848	
1902	*Great Southern*, TSS	S	276	36	T	Birkenhead	1934	
1867	*Great Western*, PS	I	220	25	S	Renfrew	1905	B1, DL5
1902	*Great Western/ GWR 20*, TSS	S	276	36	T	Birkenhead	1933	DL3
1933	*Great Western*, TSS	S	283	40	T	Birkenhead	1967	CS1, CS2
1858	*Griffin*, SS	I	155	20	S	Inch Green	1900	
1874	*Limerick*, PS	I	252	29	C	Renfrew	1902	
1851	*Malakhoff*, PS	I	194	25	S	Millwall	1884	F1
1873	*Milford*, PS	I	251	29	C	Renfrew	1901	
1880	*Pembroke*, PS/TSS	S	254	31	C/T	Birkenhead	1925	
1829	*Prospero*, ex-*Belfast*, PS	W	129	20	S	Port Glasgow	1864	
1827	*Sibyl*, PS	W	111	20	S	Liverpool	1848	
1867	*South of Ireland*, PS	I	220	26	S	Renfrew	1883	
1841	*Troubadour*, PS	I	173	24	S	Liverpool	—	
1864	*Vulture*, PS	I	243	26	C	Whiteinch	1886	

1	2	3	4	5	6	7	8	9
1874	*Waterford*, PS	I	251	29	C	Renfrew	1905	B1, F1, DL3
1912	*Waterford*, TSS	S	275	38	Q	Newcastle	1945c	

Steamers Sailing from Wexford

1822	*Abbey*, PS	W	76	17	S	Liverpool	1839	
1848	*Ayrshire Lass*, PS	I	88	19	S			
1862	*Briton*, PS	I	176	24	S	Glasgow	1892	F1
—	*Clanalpin*	—	—	—	—	—	—	
1860	*Colonist*, SS	I	154	23	S	—	—	
1889	*Eden Vale*, SS	S	180	27	T	Ayr	1923	
1854	*Ellan Vannin*, PS	I	172	20	S	Birkenhead	—	
1845	*Fire Fly*, PS	I	164	22	S	Glasgow	1867	
1826	*Harriett*, PS	W	90	15	S	Liverpool	—	
1874	*Henry Allen*, TSS	I	128	21	S	Bristol	1885	
1826	*Kingstown*, PS	W	(70 T)		S	Chester	—	
1877	*Loch Nell*, SS	I	90	21	C	Paisley	1915c	
1826	*Marquiss Wellesley*, PS	W	123	19	S	Dublin	1837	
1854	*Mars*, PS	I	180	19	S	—	1863	
1892	*Menapia*, SS	S	212	28	T	Sunderland	1917	
1855	*Montagu*, SS	I	190	25	S	Newcastle	1891	
1826	*Ormrod*, PS	W	79	17	S	Chester	1865c	

1	2	3	4	5	6	7	8	9
1850	*Oscar*, SS	I	156	23	S	Dumbarton	1882	
1854	*Pharos*, PS	W	182	25	S	Glasgow	—	
1837	*Town of Wexford*, PS	W	152	20	S	Wexford	1853c	
1867	*Voltaic*, SS	I	209	27	C	Greenock	1912c	

Chapter 6

Cork and St George SP Co

1	2	3	4	5	6	7	8	9
1878	*Agate*, SS	I	120	20	C	Rutherglen	—	
1846	*Ajax*, PS	I	206	27	S	Liverpool	1854	
1850	*Albatross/Cymba*, SS	I	224	29	S	Glasgow	1894	
1909	*Ardmore*, SS	S	260	36	T	Dundee	1917	
1921	*Ardmore/Lady Longford/ Lairdshill*, SS	S	274	38	T	Ardrossan	1957	
1910	*Bandon*, SS	S	266	37	T	Wallsend	1917	
1876	*Belle*, SS	I	235	31	C	Greenock	1886	R1
1856	*Bitterne*, SS	I	213	30	S	Cork	1878	
1846	*Blarney*, SS	I	134	19	S	Cork	1875	
1889	*Blarney*, SS	I	257	33	T	Hull	1926	
1853	*Cormorant*, SS	I	260	36	S	Cork	1894	
1855	*Dodo*, SS	I	255	36	S	Cork	1904	
1878	*Dotterel*, SS	I	265	32	C	Liverpool	1905	
1826	*Earl of Roden*, PS	W	(200 T)		S	Liverpool	1843	
1822	*Emerald Isle*, PS	W	146	23	S	Liverpool	—	
1832	*Express*, PS	W	135	21	S	Liverpool	1844	
1854	*Falcon*, SS	I	211	28	C	Cork	1890	
1848	*Gannet*, SS	I	159	24	S	Cork	—	

1	2	3	4	5	6	7	8	9
1888	*Glanmire*, SS	I	242	33	T	Dundee	1912c	
1893	*Glengariff*, SS	S	264	35	T	Newcastle	1924	
1837	*Grand Turk*, PS	W	135	30	S	Greenock	—	
1860	*Halcyon*, SS	I	212	29	S	Cork	1872	
1828	*Herald*, PS	W	146	22	S	Chester	—	R1
1835	*Hercules*, PS	W	148	25	S	Liverpool	—	
1823	*Hibernia*, PS	W	141	24	S	Liverpool	—	
1860	*Ibis*, SS	I	254	31	S	Cork	1865	R1
1866	*Ida*, SS	I	211	28	S	Newcastle	1871	
1903	*Inniscarra*, SS	S	281	38	T	Newcastle	1918	
1826	*Innisfail*, PS	W	129	25	S	Liverpool	—	
1896	*Inisfallen*, SS	S	272	36	T	Newcastle	1918	γ
1930	*Innisfallen*, TSMV	S	321	46	D	Belfast	1940	
1948	*Innisfallen*, TSMV	S	327	50	D	Dumbarton	1968*	
1968	*Innisfallen*, TSMV	S	386	59	D	Rendsberg	*	
1836	*Juno*, PS	W	160	23	S	Greenock	—	
1868	*Juno*, PS	I	262	30	S	Glasgow	1901	F1
1835	*Jupiter*, PS	W	158	25	S	Greenock	1850c	
1895	*Kenmare*, SS	S	264	35	T	Newcastle	1918	
1921	*Kenmare*, SS	S	274	38	T	Ardrossan	1956	
1891	*Killarney*, SS	I	257	33	T	Dundee	1917c	

1	2	3	4	5	6	7	8	9
1919	*Killarney*, SS, ex-*Moorfowl*	S	265	36	T	Glasgow	1937	
1893	*Killarney*, TSS, ex-*Classic*	S	311	38	T	Belfast	1930	
1825	*Lee*, PS	W	131	22	S	Chester	1851	
1880	*Lee*, SS	I	263	36	C	Renfrew	1917	R1
1905	*Lissmore*, SS	S	260	36	T	Dundee	1917	
1898	*Logic*, TSS	S	311	38	T	Belfast	1936	*a*
1825	*Lord Blayney*, PS	W	(200	T)	S	Liverpool	1833	
1828	*Magdalena*, PS	W	(150	T)	S	Liverpool	—	
1914	*Maple*, SS	S	261	36	T	Troon	1952	DL1, *β*
1847	*Minerva*, PS	I	219	25	S	Liverpool	1854	
1865	*Minna*, SS	I	239	30	C	Glasgow	1889	
1843	*Nimrod*, PS	I	177	25	S	Liverpool	1860	
1836	*Ocean*, PS	W	154	22	S	Liverpool	1862	
1855	*Osprey*, SS	I	214	30	S	Cork	1866	
1850	*Pelican*, SS	I	206	28	S	Cork	1895	
1845	*Preussischer Adler*, PS	I	185	28	S	Liverpool	1884	R1
1844	*Sabrina*, PS	I	152	25	S	Liverpool	1880	
1824	*St David*, PS	W	120	17	S	Liverpool	—	
1883	*St Finbar*, SS	I	246	34	C	Glasgow	1912	

1	2	3	4	5	6	7	8	9
1822	*St George*, PS	W	134	22	S	Liverpool	1830	
1832	*St George*, SP	W	135	20	S	Liverpool	—	
1822	*St Patrick*, PS	W	130	22	S	Liverpool	—	
1825	*Severn*, PS	W	131	22	S	Liverpool	1848	
1864	*Shandon*, SS	I	250	28	C	Newcastle	—	R1
1837	*Sirius*, PS	W	208	26	S	Leith	1847	K, $\beta\gamma\delta$
1843	*South Western*, PS	I	143	18	S	Blackwall	1865c	
1825	*Superb*, PS	W	135	29	S	Rotherhithe	1835	
1838	*Tiger*, PS	W	156	26	S	Hull	1855c	
1871	*Upupa*, SS	I	231	28	C	Newcastle	1903	
1843	*Vanguard*, PS	I	183	26	S	Port Glasgow	1868	
1832	*Victory*, PS	W	154	24	S	Liverpool	1853	
1874	*Viking*, SS	I	140	20	C	Dumbarton	1889	
1837	*Vulture*, PS	W	(340 T)		S	Birkenhead	—	
1831	*William IV*, PS	W	115	21	S	Deptford	1848	
1823	*William Huskisson*, PS	W	(250 T)		S	Greenock	—	
1872	*Xema*, SS	I	267	35	C	Newcastle	1914	

CHAPTER 7

Antrim Iron Ore Co

1	2	3	4	5	6	7	8	9
1903	*Glendun*, SS	S	226	33	T	Derry	1935	
1906	*Glenravel*, SS	S	232	34	T	Troon	1915	
1905	*Glentaise*, SS	S	218	33	T	Leith	1944	

Belfast–London

1839	*Aurora*, PS	W	153	23	S	Belfast	1861	
1825	*Erin*, PS	W	(400	T)	S	Liverpool	1833	
1855	*Excelsior*, SS	I	175	23	S	Newcastle	—	
1853	*Malvina*, SS	I	227	25	S	—	—	
1855	*Ossian*, SS	I	213	26	S	Glasgow	—	
1855	*Temora*, SS	I	215	26	S	Glasgow	—	

Clyde Shipping Co

1881	*Aranmore*, SS	I	220	30	C	Renfrew	1918	
1890	*Aranmore*, SS	I	242	35	T	Dundee	1916	
1906	*Aranmore*, SS	S	246	35	T	Dundee	1916	
1861	*Arklow*, SS	I	222	28	S	Kelvinhaugh	1880	
	Arklow, see *Dunbrody*							
1880	*Ballycotton*, SS	I	225	30	C	Renfrew	1899	
1911	*Ballycotton*, SS	S	253	36	T	Dundee	1945c	
1936	*Beachy*, SS	S	273	38	T	Kelvinhaugh	1941	
1883	*Cloch*, SS	I	216	29	C	Glasgow	1926	

1	2	3	4	5	6	7	8	9
	Coningbeg, see *Clodagh*							
1874	*Copeland*, SS	I	225	19	C	Glasgow	1888	
1894	*Copeland*, SS	I	247	34	T	Dundee	1917	
1923	*Copeland*, SS	S	270	37	T	Dundee	1963	
1876	*Corsewell*, SS	I	230	31	C	Greenock	1876	
1869	*Cumbrae*, SS	I	207	27	S	Renfrew	1880	
1882	*Cumbrae*, SS	I	230	32	C	Glasgow	1895	
1892	*Dungeness*, SS	I	246	34	T	Dundee	1935	
1878	*Dunmore*, SS	I	231	33	C	Glasgow	1882	
1869	*Eddystone*, SS	I	191	26	C	Port Glasgow	1882	
1886	*Eddystone*, SS	S	233	33	T	Dundee	1930	
1927	*Eddystone*, SS	S	271	37	T	Glasgow	1960	
1878	*Fastnet*, SS	S	145	24	C	Glasgow	1910	
1895	*Fastnet*, SS	S	245	35	T	Dundee	1918	
1914	*Fastnet*, SS	S	175	28	T	Paisley	1956	
1927	*Fastnet*, SS	S	250	37	T	Dundee	1958	
1914	*Formby*, SS	S	270	36	T	Dundee	1917	DL1
1896	*Garmoyle*, SS	S	250	34	T	Dundee	1917	
1917	*Goodwin*, SS	S	270	37	T	Dundee	1955	DL1
1885	*Inishtrahull*, SS	S	231	33	T	Glasgow	1894	
1856	*Killarney*, SS	I	171	22	S	Greenock	1884	

1	2	3	4	5	6	7	8	9
1865	*Kinsale*, SS	I	191	25	S	Renfrew	1872	
1895	*Lizard*, SS	S	247	34	T	Dundee	1959	
1917	*Longships*, SS	S	270	37	T	Dundee	1939	
1861	*Pladda*, SS	I	182	25	S	Port Glasgow	1890	
1889	*Pladda*, SS	I	243	34	T	Dundee	1945	
1907	*Pladda*, SS	S	252	36	T	Greenock	1949	
1876	*Portland*, SS	I	230	31	C	Greenock	1935	
1887	*Portland*, SS	I	241	34	T	Dundee	1907	
1877	*Rathlin*, SS	I	230	31	C	Port Glasgow	1922	
1905	*Rathlin*, SS	S	252	35	T	Glasgow	1951	DL1
1936	*Rathlin/Glengariff*, SS	S	272	38	T	Kelvinhaugh	1964	
1870	*Rio Formosa*, SS	I	120	20	C	Liverpool	1897	
1878	*Rockabill*, SS	I	136	21	C	Glasgow	1884	
1931	*Rockabill*, SS	S	272	37	T	Glasgow	1963	
1864	*Saltee*, SS	I	182	25	S	Port Glasgow	1925c	
1885	*Saltees*, SS	S	186	28	C	Glasgow	1906	
1899	*Saltees*, SS	S	250	35	T	Dundee	1930c	
1865	*Sanda*, SS	I	191	25	S	Renfrew	1887	
1892	*Sanda*, SS	I	243	34	T	Dundee	1920c	
1911	*Sanda*, SS	S	250	35	T	Dundee	1920c	

1	2	3	4	5	6	7	8	9
1903	*Sheerness*, SS	S	250	35	T	Dundee	1927	
1881	*Skellings*, SS	I	160	26	C	Belfast	1884	
1921	*Skerries*, SS	S	270	36	T	Dundee	1949	
1871	*Skerryvore*, SS	I	220	28	C	Renfrew	1918	
1882	*Skerryvore*, SS	I	226	31	C	Belfast	1916	
1898	*Skerryvore*, SS	S	250	34	T	Dundee	1960	
1871	*Toward*, SS	I	220	29	C	Port Glasgow	1916	
1883	*Toward/Teviot*, SS	I	230	32	C	Glasgow	1929	DL1
1899	*Toward*, SS	S	250	35	T	Dundee	1915	DL1
1923	*Toward*, SS	S	270	37	T	Linthouse	1943	
1860	*Tuskar*, SS	I	171	24	S	Port Glasgow	1885	
1863	*Tuskar*, SS	I	182	25	S	Port Glasgow	1891	
1890	*Tuskar*, SS	I	243	34	T	Dundee	1917	
1920	*Tuskar*, SS	S	270	36	T	Dundee	1944	
1962	*Tuskar*, SSMV	S	295	45	D	Glasgow	*	
1890	*Valentia*, SS	S	156	25	T	Dundee	1922	
1856	*Vivandière*, SS	I	151	21	S	Renfrew	—	
1911	*Warner*, SS	S	253	36	T	Dundee	1917	DL1
1869	*Wicklow*, SS	I	221	29	S	Port Glasgow	1931	
1882	*Wicklow*, SS	I	225	31	C	Greenock	1885	

Belfast–Bristol

1	2	3	4	5	6	7	8	9
1911	*Afton*, SS	S	242	34	T	Port Glasgow	1917	DL1
1869	*Ailsa*, SS	I	214	17	S	Glasgow	1880	
1907	*Annan*, SS	S	242	33	T	Troon	1958	DL1
1859	*Antona*, SS	I	163	23	S	Glasgow	1862	
1863	*Antona*, SS	I	190	27	S	Glasgow	1878	
1877	*Avon*, SS	I	220	29	T	Port Glasgow	1903	
1924	*Beauly*, SS	S	242	34	T	Troon	1903	
1848	*Brigand*, SS	I	139	22	S	Glasgow	1858	
1924	*Brora*, SS	S	242	34	T	Troon	1959	DL1
1864	*Clutha*, SS	I	190	27	S	Glasgow	1894	
1857	*Corsair*, SS	I	150	22	S	Glasgow	1876	
1894	*Ettrick*, SS	S	230	32	T	Glasgow	1924	
1903	*Findhorn*, SS	S	242	33	T	Troon	1956	
1889	*Humber*, SS	S	230	32	T	Port Glasgow	1892	
1857	*Jura*, SS	I	178	22	S	Glasgow	1879	
1886	*Medway*, SS	S	225	32	C	Glasgow	1963	
1863	*Princess Alexandra*, SS	I	213	28	S	Port Glasgow	1915	
1874	*Severn*, SS	I	211	28	C	Glasgow	1907	

1	2	3	4	5	6	7	8	9
1881	Solway, SS	I	220	30	C	Glasgow	1936	
	Teviot, see *Toward* (1883)							
1892	*Tweed*, SS	S	230	32	T	Glasgow	1918	
	Dublin–London							
1865	*Avoca*, SS	I	228	31	S	Cork	1890	
1948	*Caledonian Coast*, TSMV	S	227	40	D	Aberdeen	*	
1846	*Citizen*, SS*	I	146	19	S	Hull	1875c	
1836	*City of Limerick*, PS	W	143	22	S	Liverpool	—	
1869	*Countess of Dublin*, SS	I	220	28	S	Dublin	1894	
1842	*Duke of Cornwall*, PS	W	170	26	S	Liverpool	—	
1850	*Foyle*, SS	I	196	26	S	—	—	
1947	*Hibernian Coast*, TSMV	S	227	40	D	Aberdeen	*	
1916	*Lady Cloé*, SS	S	260	38	T	Middlesbrough	1945	
1853	*Lady Eglinton*, SS	I	228	28	S	Glasgow	1888	
1911	*Lady Gwendoline*, SS	S	300	40	T	Port Glasgow	1956	
1891	*Lady Hudson-Kinahan*, SS	S	274	34	T	Troon	1945	
1888	*Lady Martin*, SS	S	270	34	T	Belfast	1934	

1	2	3	4	5	6	7	8	9
1878	*Lady Olive*, SS	I	250	30	C	Glasgow	1922c	
1897	*Lady Roberts*, SS	S	275	35	T	Troon	1935	K1
1915	*Lady Wimborne*, SS	S	260	38	T	Port Glasgow	1955	
1865	*Lady Wodehouse*, SS	I	225	29	S	Dublin	1897	
1894	*Lady Wolseley*, SS	S	275	35	T	Barrow	1915	K1
1852	*Nile*, SS	I	164	25	S	—	1854	
1846	*Ranger*, SS*	I	118	20	S	London	1870c	
1845	*Rose*, SS*	I	119	20	S	—	—	
1832	*Royal Tar*, PS	W	154	27	S	Aberdeen	—	
1845	*Senator*, SS*	I	—	—	S	—	1848	
1845	*Shamrock*, SS*	I	129	20	S	—	1860c	
1826	*Shannon*, PS	W	153	27	S	London	—	
1814	*Thames*, PS	W	80	16	S	Port Glasgow	1835	A1, B1
1826	*Thames*, PS	W	(400	T)	S	London	1841	
1845	*Tribune*, SS*	I	123	20	S	Hull	1847	
1827	*William Fawcett*, PS	W	75	15	S	Liverpool	1840c	δ

Galway–Liverpool

1853	*Tubal Cain*, SS*	I	152	23	S	Paisley	1862	β
1855	*Vigilant*, SS	I	179	22	S	S. Shields	1890c	

Limerick–Glasgow/Liverpool/London

1	2	3	4	5	6	7	8	9
1883	*Ardnamult*, SS	I	226	33	C	N. Shields		
1854	*Brandon*, SS	I	216	27	C	Glasgow	—	
1883	*Creaden*, SS	I	166	25	C	S. Shields	—	
1874	*Earnholm*, SS	I	175	24	T	Glasgow	1916c	
1850	*European*, SS	I	196	25	S	Govan	1900c	
1856	*Express*, SS	I	199	25	S	Glasgow	—	
1871	*Fairholm*, SS	I	120	20	S	Glasgow	1874	
1852	*Holyrood*, SS	I	192	27	S	Govan	1882	
1855	*Mangerton*, SS	I	203	25	C	—	—	
1847	*Secret*, SS	I	133	22	S	—	—	
1855	*Victory*, SS	I	210	27	S	—	—	

Waterford–London

1847	*Dublin*, SS*	I	146	19	S	Hull	1875	
1830c	*Margaret*, PS	W	—	—	S	—	—	

Head Line
(All vessels 1877–1939; passenger/cargo steamers post-1945)

1919	*Ballygally Head*, SS	S	400	43	T	Belfast	1959	
1884	*Bengore Head*, SS	I	324	37	C	Glasgow	1917	
1922	*Bengore Head*, SS	S	310	45	T	W. Hartlepool	1941	

1	2	3	4	5	6	7	8	9
1877	*Bickley*, SS	I	176	28	C	Sunderland	1884	
1881	*Black Head*, SS	I	249	31	C	Belfast	1912	
1912	*Black Head*, SS	S	279	40	T	W. Hartlepool	1917	
1894	*Bray Head*, SS	S	330	42	T	Newcastle	1917	
1901	*Carrigan Head*, SS	S	371	46	T	Belfast	1934	
1958	*Carrigan Head*, SS	S	459	62	R	Belfast	*	
1918	*Dunaff Head*, SS	S	390	51	T	Belfast	1941	
1889	*Dunmore Head*, SS	S	302	40	T	Belfast	1917	
1879	*Fair Head*, SS	I	232	32	C	Belfast	1935	
1917	*Fanad Head*, SS	S	390	52	T	Belfast	1939	
1913	*Garron Head*, SS	S	283	40	T	W. Hartlepool	1917	
1883	*Glen Head*, SS	I	257	35	C	S. Shields	1934	
1897	*Glenarm Head*, SS	S	360	46	T	Belfast	1918	
1884	*Horn Head*, SS	I	322	37	C	Belfast	1894	
1906	*Howth Head*, SS	S	380	48	T	Belfast	1917	
1886	*Inishowen Head*, SS	S	342	40	C	Belfast	1917	
1965	*Inishowen Head*, SSMV	S	495	64	D	Sunderland	*	
1919	*Kenbane Head*, SS	S	400	52	T	Belfast	1940	
1902	*Lord Antrim*, SS	S	375	47	T	Belfast	1934	
1900	*Lord Downshire*, SS	S	406	49	T	Belfast	1929	

1	2	3	4	5	6	7	8	9
1902	*Lord Londonderry*, SS	S	427	53	Q	Flensburg	1934	
1892	*Malin Head*, SS	S	346	43	T	Belfast	1910	
1918	*Melmore Head*, SS	S	390	52	T	Belfast	1942	
1913	*Orlock Head*, SS	S	283	40	T	W. Hartlepool	1916	
1921	*Orlock Head*, SS	S	283	40	T	W. Hartlepool	1940	
1891	*Ramore Head*, SS	S	402	45	T	Belfast	1924	
1899	*Rathlin Head*, TSS	S	470	53	T	Belfast	1929	
1953	*Rathlin Head*, SS	S	430	59	R	Belfast	*	
1952	*Roonagh Head*, SS	S	455	60	R	Belfast	*	
1883	*Teelin Head*, SS	S	275	35	C	Belfast	1918	
1894	*Torr Head*, TSS	S	453	50	T	Belfast	1917	
1923	*Torr Head*, SS	S	400	52	T	Belfast		
1961	*Torr Head*, SSMV	S	455	62	D	Sunderland	*	
1880	*White Head*, SS	I	250	31	C	Belfast	1917	

Atlantic SN Co

1	2	3	4	5	6	7	No of round voyages
1852	*Adelaide*, SS	I	288	38	S	—	2
1857	*Adriatic*, PS	W	352	50	S	New York	5
1863	*Anglia*, PS	I	365	40	S	Hull	1
1852	*Argo*, SS	I	254	39	S	—	1†

1	2	3	4	5	6	7	No of round voyages
1852	*Brazil*, SS	I	254	39	S	—	1
1857	*Circassian*, SS	I	242	39	S	—	8
1861	*Columbia*, PS	I	365	40	S	Hull	4
1860	*Connaught*, PS	I	360	40	S	Newcastle	2†
1853	*Golden Fleece*, SS	I	254	39	S	—	1
1861	*Hibernia*, PS	I	360	40	S	Newcastle	4
1848	*Indian Empire*, PS	W	245	40	S	New York	2
1852	*Jason*, SS		263	39	S	—	2
1854	*Pacific*, PS	I	255	32	S	Millwall	3,δ
1851	*Parana*, PS	W	305	42	S	Newcastle	3
1858	*Prince Albert*, SS	I	286	38	S	—	14
1855	*Propeller*, SS	I	184	27	S	—	1†

† Foundered en route

Chapter 8

Bantry Bay

1	2	3	4	5	6	7	8	9
1884	*Countess of Bantry*, SS	I	92	17	C	Belfast	1935	
1906	*Lady Elsie*, SS	S	87	19	C	Greenock	1936	F3, N2
1901	*Princess Beara*, SS	S	115	21	C	Greenock	1948	N2

Blackwater

1	2	3	4	5	6	7	8	9
1840c	*Countess*, PS	W	—	—	S	—	—	
1860	*Daisy*, PS	W	70	14	S	N. Shields	1888	
1885	*Dartmouth Castle*, PS	S	100	13		Hayle	1913	F3, N2
1882	*Ness Queen*, PS	I	102	14	S	Cobham Island	1905	
1892	*Sibyl*, SS	W	60	9	C	Cowes	—	
1839	*Star*, PS	W	74	14	S	—	—	

Carlingford Lough

1	2	3	4	5	6	7	8	9
1866	*Dodder*, PS	I	148	17	S	Dublin	1880	
1896	*Greenore/ Cloghmore*, PS	S	122	22	C	S. Shields	1925	F3, N1
1869	*Mersey*, PS	I	106	20	S	Seacombe	1897	
1898	*Pilot*, SS	S	114	18	C	Port Glasgow	—	
1850c	*Pioneer*, SS	—	—	—	S	—	—	
1896	*Pioneer*, TSS	I	60	14	C	Newry		
1910	*St George*, TSMV	W	56	11	D	Conway	1950c	

Clear Island

1	2	3	4	5	6	7	8	9
1930	*Dun an Oir*, SSMV	W	31	9	D	Baltimore	1960c	
1960	*Naomh Ciaran*, TSMV	W	—	—	D	Arklow	*	

Dublin Bay

1	2	3	4	5	6	7	8	9
1875	*Alderney*, SS	I	175	25	C	Newcastle	—	
1864	*Anna Liffey*, PS	—	—	—	—	Dublin	—	
1830	*Arran Castle*, PS	W	104	15	S	Port Glasgow	1855c	
1815	*Caledonia*, PS	W	96	15	S	Port Glasgow	—	
1940c	*Clear Water*, TSMV	—	—	—	D	—	—	
1892	*Cynthia*, PS	I	153	21	C	S. Shields	1933	B2, G1
1861	*Dublin*, PS	—	—	—	S	—	—	
1888	*Duke of Abercorn*, TSS, ex-*Britannia*	S	120	19	C	Grangemouth	1915	
1863	*Erins King*, PS, ex-*Heather Belle*	I	160	21	S	Liverpool	1900	N2
1827	*Glasgow*, PS	W			S	Port Glasgow	—	
1815	*Hibernia*, PS	W	77	24	S	Greenock	—	
1867	*Integrity*, PS	W	86	18	S	N. Shields	—	
1835	*Isle of Bute*, PS	W	110	15	S	Port Glasgow	—	S, W1
1861	*Kingstown*, PS	I	151	20	S	Whiteinch	1885c	

1	2	3	4	5	6	7	8	9
1905	*Knight Errant*, SS	S	96	22	T	Liverpool	1935	
1888	*Knight of the Cross*, TSS	S	120	24	T	Dundee	1925	
1893	*Knight Templar*, SS	S	95	20	T	Govan	1929	
1840c	*Larsen*, TSMV	—	—	—	D	—	—	
1835	*Loch Goil*, PS	W	—	—	S	Glasgow	—	
1861	*Royal Charlie*, PS	I	71	15	S	—	—	
1875	*Storm*, SS, ex-*Rose*	I	180	26	C	Goole	—	
1848	*Tara*, TSMV, ex-*Poole Belle*	W	68	20	D	Poole	*	
1942	*Western Lady II*, TSMV	W	112	18	D	London	—	
1867	*Wonder*, PS	I	95	18	S	Newcastle	—	

Galway Bay

1899	*Cathair-na-Gaillimhe*, TSS, ex-*Lancashire*	S	151	41	T	Kinghorn	1948	
1872	*Citie of the Tribes*, PS	I	100	19	S	S. Shields	1912	F3
1912	*Dun Aengus*, SS	S	121	24	C	Dublin	1959	
1893	*Duras*, SS	I	96	18	C	S. Shields	1916	F3, N2
1930	*Galway Bay*, TSS, ex-*Calshot*	S	147	33	T	Southampton	*	
1951	*Nabro*, SSMV	W	61	16	D	Arklow	*	

1	2	3	4	5	6	7	8	9
1957	*Naomh Eanna*, SSMV	S	137	27	D	Dublin	*	N2
1952	*Ros Breasil*, SSMV	W	48	15	D	Killybegs	*	

Shannon Estuary

1	2	3	4	5	6	7	8	9
1844	*Cardiff Castle*, PS	I	170	19	S	Greenock	—	
1827	*Clarence*, PS	W	92	16	S	Dumbarton	1840c	
1833	*Dover Castle*, PS	W	112	15	S	Shoreham	—	
1866	*Elwy*, PS	I	210	25	S	Rutherglen	—	
1861	*Erin*, SS	I	119	15	S	Port Glasgow	1890	
1841	*Erin-go-bragh*, PS	I	126	22	S	Liverpool	1862	
1881	*Flying Huntsman*, PS	I	122	20	S	S. Shields	1912	N2
1834	*Garryowen*, PS	I	125	22	S	Birkenhead	1870c	
1857	*Kelpie*, PS	I	191	18	S	Glasgow	1862	
1852	*Koh-i-Norr*, PS	I	146	11	S	Glasgow	1855	
1864	*Mermaid*, PS, ex-*Largs*	I	161	19	S	Glasgow	1903	F3, N2
1863	*Rosa*, PS	I	130	19	S	Waterford	1893	
1892	*Shannon*, PS	I	160	21	C	Belfast	1918c	F3, N2
1968	*Shannon Heather*, QSMV	S	148	45	D	Dartmouth	*	
1891	*The Mermaid*, PS	I	160	20	S	London	1927	G1

Suir and Barrow

1	2	3	4	5	6	7	8	9
1837	*Duncannon*, PS	I	115	19	S	Birkenhead	1855c	
1867	*Ida*, PS	I	149	19	S	Waterford	1909	N2
1857	*Kestrel*, SS	I	64	12	S	Deptford	1914	
1947	*Officer*, TSMV	W	64	15	D	Shepperton	*	
1840c	*Repealer*, PS	—	—	—	S	—	—	
1837	*Shamrock*, PS	I	130	17	S	—	1868	
1840	*Taff*, PS	I	94	16	S	Bristol	1851	
1861	*Tintern*, PS	I	127	19	S	Waterford	1898	
1847	*Undine*, PS	I	90	9	S	London	1864	
1866	*Vandaleur*, PS	I	147	19	S	Waterford	1907	
1827	*Venus*, PS	W	—	—	S	—	1839	

1	2	3	4	5	6	7	8	9
1854	*Albert*, PS	I	133	15	S	West Ham	1881	
1881	*Albert*, PS	I	141	16	S	Belfast	1927	F3, N2
1897	*Audrey*, PS	S	126	21	C	Wallsend	1929	T2
1861	*Citizen*, PS	I	160	18	S	Port Glasgow	1891	
1815	*City of Cork*, PS	W	86	13	S	Passage	1850c	
1866	*City of Cork*, PS	S	151	17	S	Cork	1890	
1896	*Duke of Devonshire*, PS	S	175	20	C	London	1968	F1, T2
1893	*Empress*, PS	S	140	17	T	Whiteinch	1922	
1866	*Erin*, PS, ex-*Rosolio*/*Rosneath*	I	149	16	S	Port Glasgow	1890	N2
1853	*Fairy*, PS	I	96	13	S	West Ham	1890c	
1877	*Glenbrook*, PS	I	136	16	S	Poplar	1903	
1904	*Hibernia*, PS	S	105	26	C	Dartmouth	1928	
1825	*Lee*, PS	W	101	16	S	London	1840	
1861	*Lee*, PS	I	160	18	S	Port Glasgow	1893	
1861	*Lily*, PS	I	120	15	S	Cork	1880c	
1891	*Mabel*, PS	S	106	16	S	Newcastle	1918	
1838	*Maid of Erin*, PS	I	104	16	S	Glasgow	—	
1840c	*Malabar*, PS	W	—	—	S	—	—	
1882	*Monkstown*, PS	I	145	16	S	Belfast	—	

1	2	3	4	5	6	7	8	9
1843	*Prince*, PS	I	130	17	S	Glasgow	1862	
1851	*Prince Arthur*, PS	I	155	16	S	Glasgow	—	
1858	*Prince of Wales*, PS	I	150	17	S	Glasgow	—	
1841	*Princess*, PS	I	133	18	S	Glasgow	1856	
1814	*Princess Charlotte*, PS	W	65	10	S	Greenock	1850	
1838	*Queen*, PS	I	91	13	S	Glasgow	1862c	
1851	*Queenstown*, PS	I	113	15	S	West Ham	—	
1892	*Queenstown*, TSS	S	92	16	C	Belfast	1940c	
1891	*Rostellan*, TSS	S	95	16	C	Belfast	1935c	
1847	*Royal Alice*, PS, ex-*Princess Alice*	I	145	18	S	Glasgow	—	
1852	*Victoria*, PS	I	134	15	S	West Ham	1855	
1816	*Waterloo*, PS	I	88	13	S	Cork	1865	

Tenders, including passenger-carrying tugs

1825	*Air*, PS	W	95	17	S	Port Glasgow	1862	
1891	*America/Seamore*, PS	I	132	23	S	S. Shields	1946	F3
1900	*An Saorstat*, TSS, ex-*Rose*	S	157	42	T	Liverpool	1951	
1860	*Arran Castle*, PS	W	101	16	S	Glasgow	—	
1961	*Blarna*, TSMV	S	151	41	D	Dublin	*	
1906	*Blarney*, TSS, ex-*Royal Iris*	S	152	41	T	Hebburn	1961	DL4, γ

1	2	3	4	5	6	7	8	9
1962	*Cill Airne*, TSMV	S	152	41	D	Dublin	*	N2
1862	*Commissioner*, PS	I	108	18	S	Cork	1914c	
1962	*David F*, SSMV	S	71	21	D	Zwolle	*	N2
1836	*Eagle*, PS	I	102	18	S	Perth	1851	
1901	*Failte*, TSS, ex-*Lily*	S	157	42	T	Liverpool	1943	
1886	*Flying Fish*, PS	I	122	20	S	S. Shields	—	F3
1928	*General McHardy*, SS	S	82	17	T	Dartmouth	1970	
1959	*Ingot*, SSMV	S	65	18	D	Zwolle	*	
1891	*Ireland*, PS	I	132	23	S	S. Shields		
1934	*John Adams*, SSMV	S	85	18	D	Thame, Yorks	*	
1954	*John L*, SSMV	S	62	15	D	—	*	
1922	*Killarney*, TSS, ex-*Francis Storey*	S	150	40	T	Troon	1962	DL4
1889	*Lyonesse*, SS	I	170	25	T	Hayle	1928	F1
1877	*Morsecock*, TSS	S	156	25	C	Birkenhead	1953	
1864	*Mosquito*, PS	I	101	18	S	Cork	—	
1910	*Shandon*, TSS, ex-*John Joyce*	S	152	39	T	Birkenhead	1962	
1862	*Smoker*, PS	I	94	19	S	Cork	—	
1945c	*William J*, SSMV	S	81	18	D	Belgium	*	
1903	*Wyndham*, SS	S	85	18	T	Falmouth	1968	

CHAPTER 10

Boyne

1	2	3	4	5	6	7	8	9
1900c	*Ros-na-Righ*, SS	W	—	—	—	—	—	F3, N2

Lough Corrib

1900c	*Cliodhna*, SS	—	—	—	—	—	—	
1862	*Eglinton*, PS	I	116	16	S	Liverpool	1904	
1850c	*Enterprise*, PS	—	—	—	S	—	—	
1850c	*Father Daly*, PS	—	(40 T)		S	—	—	
1860	*Lioness*, PS	W	82	16	S	S. Shields	—	
1962	*Maid of Coleraine*, SSMV	W	53	15	D	—	—	
1850c	*O'Connell*, PS	—	—	—	—	—	—	
1898	*St Patrick*, SS	—	(40 T)		S	Galway	—	

River Shannon

1856	*Artizan*, PS	I	113	12	S	Rutherglen	1865c	
1863	*Athlone*, SS	I	72	13	S	Drogheda	1916c	
1835	*Avonmore*, PS	I	(100	T)	S	Liverpool	—	
1850c	*Brian Boru*, SS		90	14	S	—	—	
1829	*Clanricarde*, PS	W	(130	T)	S	Liverpool	1850c	
1897	*Countess Cadogan*, SS	S	70	14	C	Paisley	1932	F3, N2

1	2	3	4	5	6	7	8	9
1897	*Countess of Mayo*, SS	S	70	14	C	Rutherglen	1939c	F3
1862	*Dublin*, SS	I	72	13	S	Drogheda	1910c	
1848	*Duchess of Argyle*, PS	I	151	15	S	Dumbarton	1865c	
1829	*Dunally*, PS	—	—	—	S	Birkenhead	—	
1893	*Fairy Queen*, SS	S	63	14	C	Irvine	1935	
1832	*Gazelle*, PS	I	—	—	S	Greenock	—	
1964	*Hilda*, SSMV	—	—	—	D	—	—	
1920c	*Jolly Roger*, SS	W	—	—	D	—	—	
1897	*Lady Betty Balfour*, SS	S	70	14	C	Paisley	1922	
1842	*Lady Burgoyne*, PS	I	—	—	S	—	1860c	
1833	*Lady Lansdowne*, PS	I	135	17	S	Birkenhead	1860c	
1880	*Lady of the Lake*, SS	I	67	13	S	Drogheda	1910c	
1862	*Limerick*, SS	I	72	13	S	Drogheda	—	
1960c	*Linquenda*, SSMV	S	85	16	D	Holland	*	
1855	*Lord Lorton*, SS	I	67	14	S	Greenwich	1880c	
1824	*Marquis Wellsley*, PS	I	(120 T)		S	Tipton	1860c	
1855c	*Midland*, PS	—	—	—	S	—	—	
1837	*Nonsuch* (horse drawn)	I	80	7	—	—	1846	

1	2	3	4	5	6	7	8	9
1894	*Olga*, SS	S	50	12	S	Canning Town	1909	
1937	*St Brendan*, TSMV, ex-*Cardinal Woolsey*	S	68	14	D	—	*	
1931	*St Brigid*, SS, ex-*Avon Queen*	S	85	15	D	Brimscombe	*	
1936	*St Ciaran*, TSMV, ex-*Wroxham Belle*	S	77	16	D	Rowhedge	*	N2
1939	*St James*, SS	S	73	15	D	Dublin	*	N2
1935	*St Patrick*, SS, ex-*Avon King*	S	86	16	D	Bristol	*	N2
1846	*Shannon*, PS	W	72	15	S	—	1881	
1892	*Shannon Queen*, SS	S	54	10	C	Bristol	1914c	
1840c	*Wye*, PS	—	—	—	S	—	—	

GENERAL INDEX

For individual vessels see Steamships Index

STEAMSHIPS INDEX

Bold figures indicate pages in the Fleet List